OPENING UP

OPENING UP

Speaking Out in the Church

Edited by

Julian Filochowski and **Peter Stanford**

DARTON · LONGMAN + TODD

First published in 2005 by
Darton, Longman and Todd Ltd
1 Spencer Court
140–142 Wandsworth High Street
London SW18 4JJ

The right of the contributors to be identified as the Authors
of this work has been asserted in accordance with the
Copyright, Designs and Patents Act 1998.

ISBN 0–232–52624–9

A catalogue record for this book is available from the British Library.

Designed and produced by Sandie Boccacci
Phototypeset in 10/12pt Times New Roman
Printed and bound in Great Britain by CPI Bath

To mark the 60th birthday of Martin Pendergast

Contents

Introduction

'Too much theology', Enda McDonagh reminds us, 'lacks the human warmth of friendship.' Appropriately for a largely Catholic occasion, *Opening Up* is not a monochrome or tidy gathering. There is no common experience, temperament, register or angle of vision. But each voice, in its individual and sometimes contrary way, is a reflection on love, truth and justice in the Catholic Church spoken in honour of a friend.

That friend is Martin Pendergast, who, in the words of one of the contributors, has 'given most of his life to cherishing those who are on the margins, whether of society or the Church'. Martin's characteristic instinct is to safeguard the dignity of the human person, friend or stranger, wherever it is threatened, whether by poverty, by abuse, by humiliation or by denial of their human rights.

Martin was born in Melksham, Wiltshire, on 22 August 1945, but spent his childhood in Plumstead, south London. He joined the Carmelite order shortly after leaving school and went on to study in Dublin and Rome. After ordination he took an MA at Bristol University, where his research led to increasing involvement with progressive Catholic movements. Withdrawing from his religious community Martin worked with overseas students in London before becoming a full-time social worker, specialising in child care and, later, in HIV/AIDS work. In 1987 Martin co-founded Catholic AIDS Link, a registered charity providing support for people living with or affected by HIV/AIDS; more recently he was appointed executive secretary of Catholics for AIDS Prevention and Support (CAPS), the charity formed to succeed Catholic AIDS Link, and he was a catalyst in the founding of 'Positively Catholic' - a support group for Catholics living with HIV. In her essay, the religious sister Eva Heymann recalls her work with Martin and a brave sprinkling of other Catholics in the 1980s, trying to bring something of Christ's compassion, love and healing to people living with AIDS. It was lonely, painful work. 'Where was the Church?' Eva found herself asking.

In 1976 Martin had chaired the first public conference in the UK on 'The Catholic Church and Homosexuality'. This marked the beginning of his career as an occasional irritant to some Catholic groups. It was also at this event that Martin met Julian Filochowski, later to become director of CAFOD, the Church's official overseas aid and development agency. The private Mass held in London on 9 June 2001 to celebrate

Martin and Julian's 25 years of 'friendship and commitment in the pursuit of justice' attracted unwelcome media attention and drew a scurrilous reaction from some Catholics, but the remarkable warmth and breadth of the support they received showed how dramatically attitudes have changed in the years since their first meeting.

Martin was a founder member of the Lesbian and Gay Christian Movement (LGCM) and of its RC Caucus. He assisted at the birth of 'Called to be One' – a national pastoral network for Catholic parents of lesbian and gay people. For the last 5 years he has been the liturgy co-ordinator of what has come to be known as 'the Soho Mass', a popular twice-monthly mass held in Central London for lesbian and gay Catholics, their families and friends.

Martin has a very active ecumenical gene. Over the years he has been a board or committee member of a host of Christian initiatives. He is currently Chair of Christians for Human Rights (CHR), a coalition of groups and individuals working to promote the 1998 Human Rights Act. In 2000 he was appointed a member of the government's independent advisory group on teenage pregnancy, holding a particular remit, together with Canon Jane Fraser, to create links with Britain's faith communities.

Martin's story – one of constancy in faith with unexpected twists in where his Catholicism has taken him – is a not-so-unusual trajectory for an English Catholic of the second half of the twentieth century. While its structures and attitudes and activities may have often failed to reflect the love and justice which should characterise the people of God and Body of Christ, Martin nevertheless describes the Catholic Church as 'a sign of the Spirit still moving, breathing, fluttering across the face of the earth'. In spite of some lively disputes with its authorities over the years Martin has said that 'Catholicism is as much part of my being now as it was when I was serving Mass in St Patrick's, Plumstead, in the late 1950s.'

Tensions and paradoxes run through the essays and poems in *Opening Up*: between faithfulness and intellectual restlessness, between obedience and rebellion, between longing and resignation. They remind us of the perpetual tension in Catholicism between its security, wealth and power and its purpose to serve the poor and the broken-hearted, to bring God's love to the forgotten people of the world. As Timothy Radcliffe writes: 'It is the dynamic relationship between the centre and the edges that kneads the dough of our eucharistic bread.'

Julian Filochowski uses a particularly evocative phrase in describing the Church as 'a global people united in sacrament and solidarity striving to follow the Lord in this broken and divided world'. The Jesuit writer John Allan Loftus points out in his essay that '*We* are Church. Together. We are multi-hued, we are female as well as male, we are gay and straight, we are all sinners and all would-be saints. And we must learn again to listen to each other.' Martin is good at speaking out, and he knows how to listen. And he knows that there is more to friendship than conversation. When he's needed, he shows up, and he does what he can to help. His assiduousness might occasionally wind us up, but his magnificent cooking always winds us down. The journey to truth is by way of love and friendship, as Cardinal Walter Kasper is quoted here as saying. Truth is sometimes hard to grasp when it is written down or announced from a pulpit, but we see it come alive in the lives of our friends.

And so, Martin, with thanks and admiration, to mark your sixtieth birthday on 22 August 2005, we offer you this collection of essays, reflections and poems: *Opening Up: Speaking Out in the Church*.

Note on the Contributors

James Alison, priest and theologian, is the author of *Knowing Jesus*, *The Joy of Being Wrong*, *Faith Beyond Resentment: Fragments Catholic and Gay*, and *On Being Liked*. He lives in London, but travels and teaches extensively in continental Europe, the US and Latin America.

Julie Clague lectures in the School of Divinity at the University of Glasgow and works mainly in the areas of Catholic moral theology, social teaching, bioethics and gender issues. She co-edits the journals *Feminist Theology* and *Political Theology*.

Jim Cotter is an ordained Anglican based in north-west Wales. He is a founder member of the Lesbian and Gay Christian Movement, a contributor to the old *Gay News* and author of *Good Fruits*, *Quiverful*, and *Pleasure, Pain and Passion*, which explored more general issues of sexuality and spirituality.

Julian Filochowski was director of CAFOD, the Catholic Agency for Overseas Development, from 1982 to 2003.

Valerie Flessati works freelance for Pax Christi and other organisations. She lectures on peace and justice courses at the Missionary Institute, London.

Jane Fraser is an Anglican priest and a qualified social worker. She worked with Brook Advisory Centres for 30 years. She is a Faith Advisor to the Teenage Pregnancy Unit's Independent Advisory Group. She is also Chair of The Centre for the Study of Christianity and Sexuality (CSCS).

Jon D. Fuller MD is a Jesuit and Associate Professor of Medicine at Boston University School of Medicine. He is also a staff member at the Center for HIV/AIDS Care and Research at Boston Medical Center.

Conor Gearty is Rausing Director at the Centre for the Study of Human Rights and Professor of Human Rights Law at the London School of Economics.

Jeannine Gramick is a Sister of Loretto who has been engaged in lesbian/gay ministry since 1971. In 1999, the Vatican's Congregation for the Doctrine of the Faith prohibited her from any pastoral work with lesbian or gay persons. She is currently involved in a ministry of education and advocacy on behalf of gay and lesbian persons.

Alan Griffiths taught liturgy at Wonersh Seminary before taking up parish ministry in Ringwood, Hampshire. He is the author of *Celebrating the Christian Year* and *A Basic Catholic Dictionary*.

Eva Heymann is a member of the Society of the Holy Child Jesus, a Catholic religious order, founded in 1846. Her professional life was in teaching and later in psychiatric social work and family therapy.

Mark D. Jordan, 52, is Asa Griggs Candler Professor of Religion in Emory University. His books include *The Invention of Sodomy in Christian Theology, The Silence of Sodom: Homosexuality in Modern Catholicism, The Ethics of Sex, Telling Truths in Church, Blessing Same-Sex Unions*, and *Rewritten Theology: Aquinas After His Readers*.

Robert Kaggwa was born in Uganda and is a member of the Society of Missionaries of Africa. He was the first Cardinal Hume Visiting Fellow at the Margaret Beaufort Institute in Cambridge. He was recently appointed Chaplain at Roehampton University in London.

James F. Keenan is a Jesuit and Professor of Theological Ethics at Boston College, Chestnut Hill, Massachusetts. Among his recent works are *Moral Wisdom: Lessons and Texts from the Catholic Tradition* and *The Works of Mercy: The Heart of Catholicism*.

Kevin Kelly is parish priest at the shared Catholic/Anglican Church of St Basil & All Saints, Hough Green, Widnes. He is also Emeritus Senior Research Fellow in Moral Theology at Liverpool Hope University.

Bruce Kent is vice-president of Pax Christi and CND. He spent 29 years as a Catholic priest before retiring in 1987 to continue his work in the peace movement.

John Allan Loftus SJ is a licensed psychologist in private practice and the Director of the Jesuit Urban Center in Boston, Massachusetts. He is the former President of Regis College in the University of Toronto, and former Executive Director of Southdown, Canada's large treatment facility for clergy and religious.

Enda McDonagh is Emeritus Professor of Moral Theology at the Pontifical University of Maynooth, Ireland.

Wilfrid McGreal, 65, is a Carmelite priest and Prior of Faversham in Kent. He is a well-known broadcaster on the BBC and author of *Guilt and Healing*, *Praying in the Carmelite Spirit* and *At the Fountain of Elijah: The Carmelite Tradition*.

Diarmuid O'Murchu MSC, a priest and social psychologist, belongs to the Sacred Heart Missionary congregation. His written works include *Quantum Theology*, *Evolutionary Faith*, and most recently, *Catching Up with Jesus*.

Aidan O'Neill, 44, is an Edinburgh lawyer and a member of the Matrix Chambers, London. He practises as a QC in both Scotland and England, specialising in constitutional and human rights law.

Timothy Radcliffe was Master of the Dominicans from 1992 to 2001.

Ann Smith has been involved with HIV/AIDS for more than 20 years and has pioneered innovative education and training work, particularly with church communities and organisations in Africa, Asia, Latin America and Europe. She has been a programme adviser and consultant to Catholic agencies worldwide. She has spoken and written extensively on the pandemic and in 2002 co-authored *The Reality of HIV/AIDS* with Enda McDonagh.

Jon Sobrino is a Jesuit priest and theologian and founder of the Romero Pastoral Centre at the Jesuits' Central American University in San Salvador. His many published works include *Christology at the Crossroads*, *Jesus the Liberator*, *The Principle of Mercy*, and *Companions of Jesus*. He was joint editor, with Ignacio Ellacuría, of *Mysterium Liberationis: Fundamental Concepts of Liberation Theology*.

PART ONE

THE BIG PICTURE

Chapter One

Kneading the Dough of the Eucharist

Timothy Radcliffe OP

I wish to open this timely book by sharing a few thoughts about the Church and social marginality. The Church lives a certain tension in her relationship with those on the margins.

On the one hand the Church is a community, or a network of communities. This implies that it is a community which has a centre, which grants us a sense of belonging. As with any community, there are those who belong and those who do not. Often, especially in the West, this has placed it at the centre of society, identified with those in power. Officially or not, the Church is often part of the Establishment.

And yet Christ sought out as the first members of his Church those who were on the edge: prostitutes, tax collectors, lepers and sinners. And so within the Church there is, or should be, a dynamic relationship between the centre and the edges. Paradoxically those at its centre should be those whom society considers to be marginalised. It is this dynamic relationship of centre and margins that, I believe, kneads the dough of our eucharistic bread.

This is a theme that also helps us to understand something special about Martin Pendergast, to whom this book is dedicated. One cannot imagine a more solid and, in some ways, traditional Catholic than Martin. There is something rock-like about Martin's faith. Without wanting to embarrass him, it is the obvious centre and thread of continuity of his life.

Yet Martin has given most of his life to cherishing those who are on the margins, whether of society or the Church. I first met Martin nearly twenty years ago, in connection with care for people living with AIDS. He was there almost before any other Catholic in this country. He has consistently been concerned for anyone suffering from any form of marginalisation, whether because of poverty or sexual orientation or whatever.

This tension, being a committed member of the Church and yet always reaching out to the margins, is necessarily painful. Some people live that pain just as frustration. It can be a draining and debilitating experience, of endless compromise, of just managing to hang in there by a thread. This has not been my impression of Martin. No doubt there is often pain and frustration, and yet I have the impression that he lives this tension above all fruitfully and with hope. The tension between the centre and the margins is part of the dynamism of the life of the Church, and always has been so. The pain may be that of renewal and rebirth rather than of just sterile hurt.

Centre and edges

I would like to concentrate on how the Church relates to social marginalisation rather than marginalisation within the Church, which is another vast topic. My hope is that by exploring how the Church lives within this tension between the centre and the edges, we will understand a little better the witness that Martin offers us.

Having bravely settled on this theme, I am alarmed at how ill equipped I am to write about the margins of society. In terms of every indicator, I come from plumb in the centre. My work as a chaplain at Imperial College, London, in the 1970s was almost the only time I have glimpsed what it might be like to be on the margins: I got involved with the students in a soup kitchen in a central London park. Once we had distributed mugs of delicious soup, it was the tradition for the students to sit with everyone for half an hour and share the food together. Once another charity arrived with its competing – and notoriously disgusting – soup. When I turned it down, the distributor gave me a dressing down: in my poverty I must not be too proud to accept help. This won me considerable street cred.

As Master of the Dominican Order, I went to the marginalised places of our world. I spent a fair bit of time in war zones, such as Rwanda, Burundi, the Congo and Iraq. I met lepers at centres in Asia and Africa and visited innumerable AIDS clinics as well as the poor and violent barrios of Latin America. But I was always only a visitor. I went to support my brethren and sisters who worked in these places. I have never lived in the margins.

There was always the risk of slipping into a sort of tourism of compassion. Maybe the subtitle for this essay should be, to use the words of the Cistercian monk Thomas Merton, 'The Conjectures of a Guilty Bystander'.

It would be presumptuous of me to try to articulate the wisdom and spirituality of the marginalised. They must speak and we must listen. All that I can do is to reflect a little on the different forms of marginalisation that we encounter and how they relate to the Last Supper.

The first question that this Guilty Bystander would ask is this: if we are looking at marginalisation, then it is marginalisation in relationship to what? Zygmunt Bauman, a social scientist at the universities of Warsaw and Leeds, has argued that our society is in the process of a deep transformation. We are moving out of a previous form of capitalism that is typified by Ford cars. In fact it is usually called Fordism.

This was founded on the production in industrial centres of heavy goods, cars and steel and ships and so on. The labourers came to places like London and Manchester to seek work and the products they made were exported around the world. And this implied a strong mutual commitment of capital and labour. They fought great battles, but like a grumpy married couple, they remained wedded to each other. The workers needed wages and the factories needed a trained and stable workforce.

When Henry Ford doubled the wages of his workers it was not because he wished them to be wealthy, but because he had to keep them from his competitors. So in this society it was clearer where were the margins. The marginalised were those who clustered around these industrial centres: the unemployed, or those with no fixed contract or no expertise to give them security. They were encamped around the walls of the city. There was a geography of centres: industrial centres, central economies, central cities and central countries. Military and economic empires defined periphery and centre.

Liquid modernity

Now, however, we are entering a new world, which Bauman calls 'Liquid Modernity'. And the things that zing around the World Wide Web are not so much heavy objects but signs and symbols, information, logos and brand names. These exchanges build up our global village.

Of course, you can argue that millions of people are marginalised here too. The vast majority of Africans do not have access to the Internet. Some 65 per cent of all human beings have never used a telephone, and 40 per cent do not have electricity. One might say there are marginalised people who sit on the edges of our global village just as they did around the great industrial cities of our ancestors. Yet in a sense everyone does belong now. There are the bonds of the drug trade, the sale of arms, of money laundering, the criminal mafias, prostitution, the diamond trade and the sale of body parts. No one escapes these networks. Africa may be largely excluded from the networks of investment and legitimate trade, but the civil wars in places like the Congo and Angola tie the continent in with the sale of arms, diamonds and minerals. Colombia may be marginal to many forms of legitimate economic trade, and yet, like Afghanistan, it is at the centre of the drug trade.

The powerful people in this new world of Liquid Modernity are not those who are settled at the centre and who draw people to their factories to seek work. They are the nomads who can wander around the world at will. The old pact between capital and labour is broken. The rich are those who can quickly disengage and move on. Power is mobility.

So instead of contracts for life, one has short-term contracts, rolling contracts or no contracts at all. Bauman writes: 'Brief encounters replace lasting engagements. One does not plant a citrus tree to squeeze a lemon.'[1]

I remember crossing the border from the USA into Mexico to visit our Dominican community in Mexicali. There are hundreds of *maquiladoras*, factories where workers have virtually no rights at all, producing for American multinationals. If there is any fuss with labour, then the multinationals will just get up and go.

Bauman continues:

> People who move and act faster, who come nearest to the momentariness of movement, are now the people who rule. And it is the people who cannot move as quickly, and more conspicuously yet the category of people who cannot at will leave their place at all, who are ruled. Domination consists in one's own capacity to escape, to disengage, to 'be elsewhere', and the right to decide the speed with which all that is done – while simultaneously stripping the people on the dominated side of their ability to arrest or constrain their moves or to slow them down.[2]

Many multinationals now do not bother to own solid things like factories. They do not wish to be tied down. For Nike, it is enough to own the brand name. Others can get on with the time-consuming business of building sweatshops and employing people. Owning the idea and the name is enough if one wishes to be unencumbered. The nomad travels light.

Of course there are centres. New York, London and Tokyo are all centres. September 11 was a symbolic attack on the centres of American economic and military power. But the nomad, with cellphone and laptop, can be anywhere. And so governments must cooperate in the mobility of capital, knocking down the barriers and allowing free access. The true centres today are not of place or nation but in the information networks. Scott Lash and John Urry, sociologists from Lancaster University, wrote that we have moved 'from place to flow, from space to stream, from organized hierarchies to disorganization'.[3] Social structures have been replaced by information structures. The poor today are not so much the dispossessed as the disconnected.

So marginalisation is complex. The metaphor is spatial, and the poor and powerless do suffer from exclusion from various spaces and places. But there are all sorts of other marginalisations. They are marginalised from networks of information and communication, disconnected. They are marginalised in the sense that governments resist their movement. They must stay put while the nomads move on. They are marginalised from decision-making process, from power. They are marginalised from the identity of the rich and powerful.

Ending exclusion

So how can we as a church respond to these complex and overlapping exclusions? How can we be a sign of the Kingdom in which all of humanity will belong?

The first form of marginalisation from which the poor suffer is exclusion from the networks of information. To be at the centre is not spatial; it is to have access to knowledge. The rich own information rather than solid things like buildings. Just take one example – crop seeds. Many of the poor of our planet depend upon the fertility of the land. They struggle to live on the annual miracle of planting and harvesting. The rich, by contrast, do not need to take ownership of their land. It is enough to own the fertility of the seeds, as their intellectual property.

About ten major companies are buying germ plasm. According to Jeremy Rifkin, President of the Foundation on Economic Trends in Washington, they 'then slightly modify the seeds or strip out individual genetic traits, or recombine new genes into the seeds and secure patent protection over their "inventions". The goal is to control, in the form of intellectual property, the entire seed stock of the planet.'[4]

As a church, we may react on two fronts. First of all there is the struggle to prevent the rich from taking possession of the fertility of the planet. It is not theirs or anyone's to own. There is the struggle of advocacy by bodies like CAFOD to resist this scandalous stealing of what is humanity's common possession. There are also the thousands of ways in which the programmes of these agencies try to open the gates into the networks of information for the poor.

The rich are the gatekeepers. We must go around opening the gates, springing the locks, handing over the passwords. We go around merrily opening the doors into the cellars where the best wines are locked away. In Brazil there have been some amazing results from teaching basic computer skills to people from the poorest barrios of São Paolo. Once they have access to the net, they do astonishing things.

Think of the state of Chiapas in Mexico. There, the guerrillas used the World Wide Web brilliantly in their resistance to the government. For some mysterious reason, as I discovered during my visit to Mexico, the government is convinced that the Dominicans are behind it all. I was followed by secret police for three weeks and interrogated by government ministers at length.

As a church, we also offer this information society something else – wisdom, which may ultimately be far more subversive. Seventy years ago T. S. Eliot wrote: 'Where is the wisdom we have lost in knowledge?/ And where is the knowledge that we have lost in information?'[5]

Eucharistic wisdom

Faced with these multiple marginalisations, the Church offers a eucharistic wisdom. This is a way of seeing and being that is in fundamental opposition to the exclusions of our society. The World Wide Web is the heart of the information society. We can use it, if we have the imagination, to spread something quite different, which is the wisdom of the Gospel and of the marginalised. We can see the nature of this wisdom by looking at how the Eucharist responds to various forms of marginalisation.

The poor are marginalised from the centres of power. It is well established that most of the international institutions that are supposed to be at the service of overcoming poverty and building a fairer world, such as the World Trade Organisation, the World Bank and the International Monetary Fund, are not run democratically. They are at the service of the interests of the rich nations. Structural adjustment loans often have the effect of opening up poor economies to exploitation by the rich. Noam Chomsky has argued that the United States is primarily interested in the United Nations only in so far as it can serve its own goal of global dominance. What can our eucharistic wisdom offer in response? What does it say about power?

The Last Supper was celebrated in the face of the clash of two sorts of power. There was the brutal power of the military and religious authorities who were coming to arrest Jesus and kill him. And there was the power of Jesus, which was that of signs. The whole gospel of John is structured around his signs, from the wedding at Cana to the raising of Lazarus. This is a different sort of power. It is not magical. Jesus is no more a first-century Gandalf than St Peter is Frodo. Jesus' power lay in the meaning of what he did. His signs spoke God's word, which creates and re-creates. It is a semiotic and sacramental power, which is the speaking of a word of truth.

As the soldiers draw near to arrest Jesus, the synoptic gospels tell us that he performed a sign, taking bread, breaking it and sharing it, saying, 'This is my body, given for you.' In St John's gospel, the clash of these two forms of power comes to a climax in the meeting of Jesus and Pilate.

Pilate says to Jesus, 'Do you not know that I have the power to crucify you?' But Jesus relies on this different sort of power. He says to Pilate, 'I have come into the world to bear witness to the truth. Everyone who is of the truth hears my voice.' Pilate replies, 'What is truth?' and notoriously does not stay for an answer. He does not need to. He has soldiers.

Easter is the vindication of the power of the man of signs over the dumb and brutal powers of this world. 'The light shines in the darkness, and the darkness has not overcome it.' Our eucharistic wisdom is that the power of meaning and of truth is ultimately stronger than any brute force. Faced with his murder, Jesus performed a sign and said, 'Do this in remembrance of me.' We do this not just in celebrating our great sign, which is the Eucharist, but in all signs that speak of meaning and truth rather than brutality. We live under an ever darker shadow of violence: September 11, the war in Iraq, the bombs in Madrid and London, the violence in the Middle East. In the face of this brutality, which over-whelmed Jesus and put him on a cross, we ultimately may make signs which speak of peace and justice. It is our faith that these are ultimately more powerful than any brute force.

One tiny example: some American Dominicans decided to commemorate the first anniversary of 9/11, by holding a month-long fast of just water. There were brethren, sisters and a lay Dominican, Sheila Provender, who, at the time of writing, is still in Baghdad as a sign of solidarity with the Iraqi people. Some others joined just for a short time. It is a good way to lose weight.

Another way

As the threat of war developed, that became another focus. We all had T-shirts that said, 'There must be another way'. We camped in Union Square, just north of Ground Zero, and spoke to hundreds of people every day who came to question us and read our pamphlets. Many Jews and Muslims joined us for prayers three times a day. The symbolic meaning of fasting was immediately understood, even by the young, except by the young man who came to eat his hamburger and French fries – sorry, Freedom fries – with us every day (they smelt ever more delicious). This symbolic act spoke. And every day there were TV cameras and journalists to transmit it.

Admittedly it does not seem to have had much effect. There are no records of President Bush phoning Prime Minister Blair to consider cancelling the war because the Dominicans were fasting. But it is through such a care for the meaning of what we say and do that we open windows for God's transforming grace in the world. It is through attentiveness to significance, and not brute force, that we share in God's speaking a word that brings the Kingdom, that says 'Let human beings flourish' and we will.

God works through small signs, the smaller the better. God reduced Gideon's army down from 30,000 people to 300 before letting him thrash the Midianites. Jesus cured only a few sick people. God needs just a tiny window for transforming grace to break through into our world, otherwise we might misunderstand the nature of his power. In *The Merchant of Venice* Portia says, 'How far that little candle throws his beams! / So shines a good deed in a naughty world.' Whatever we do to the least of Christ's brothers and sisters, we do to him. What signs can we make that speak the Kingdom now?

Let me share with you something which touched me. Recently I was visiting an AIDS hospice in Phnom Penh, run by an American priest, Jim. I had never seen such emaciated figures. Some of them would get back enough strength to go back to their families for a little while. Most came there to die. I watched one utterly skeletal figure of a young man, having his hair washed and cut, with a look of utter peace on his face.

It would be easy to wonder what difference all this will make to the course of history. A few people live a little longer and then die in dignity? It is a tiny speaking of God's word of truth and grace, which brings the Kingdom closer.

Love what is invisible

So there is marginalisation from centres of information and of power. A third marginalisation is by cutting people out from our identity. We excise them from any awareness of who we are as human beings. The early European explorers described much of the planet as *terra nullius*, unoccupied land. There was no one there that they could see. Raimond Gaiti, an Australian philosopher, wrote: 'A Spanish song often quoted by Simone Weil, says, "If you want to become invisible, there is no surer way than to become poor." Weil goes on to say, "Love sees what is invisible."'[6]

Black people are often invisible to white people, the poor to the rich, women to men. Or they are noticed only as objects rather than subjects. They have identities that are given to them, rather than ones that they share in shaping. Archbishop Rowan Williams wrote: 'Only certain people have the right to construct an identity for themselves; others have their roles scripted for them.'[7] The poor have only walk-on parts in the stories of the rich, and no ad-libbing is allowed.

Faced with this marginalisation, the Last Supper has a wisdom. It is offered 'for you and for all'. It is the sacrament of the unity of all humanity. None of us will know fully who we are until the Kingdom. In his Las Casas lecture in December 2003 in Blackfriars, Oxford, Terry Eagleton said that global identity is an oxymoron, like Alabama haute cuisine. It cannot be articulated now. We can make signs that speak of it and thus help it come to be. What are the signs that may speak of our present incompleteness?

The priority is to ensure that the marginalised make their own signs, unscripted and unexpected. It is not for us to put words into their mouths. But we too can do something. As a young student Raimond Gaiti used to work in a psychiatric hospital and he describes the effect on him of the visits of a nun.

> One day a nun came to the ward. In her middle years, only her vivacity made an impression on me until she talked to the patients. Then everything in her demeanour towards them – the way she spoke to them, her facial expressions, and the inflexions of her body – contrasted with and showed up the behaviour of those noble psychiatrists. She showed that they were, despite their best efforts, condescending, as I too had been. She thereby revealed that even such patients were, as the psychiatrists and I had sincerely and generously professed, the equals of those who wanted to help them; but she also revealed that in our hearts we did not believe this.[8]

She made the humanity of the psychiatric patients visible. Her behaviour was revelatory.

Worldwide family

When the war in Iraq was imminent, the Dominican family in the United States distributed bumper stickers saying, 'We have family in Iraq'. This referred in the first place to our Dominican sisters and brothers in Iraq, but it also was supposed to startle people into the realisation that we have Muslim brothers and sisters in Iraq. We were planning to kill our own flesh, our kith and kin.

So there is marginalisation from information networks, from power structures, from our identity. Finally, even in our liquid and nomadic world, there is still spatial exclusion. We lock people out of our space. We lock people out of our countries. There have never in human history been such vast movements of people. As with our ancestors, great tribes of people are moving west. One of the most powerful images of this were the pictures of the holding centre in Calais and the thousands of people who every day tried to get through the Channel Tunnel into England by climbing on trains. Those that were captured tried again and again.

Yet the gates are being ever more carefully guarded. In Holland and Belgium there is ever less tolerance of those who are different. Europe is in danger of initiating a vast process of exclusion.

Inside our countries there are also new areas from which the poor are excluded. Increasingly in England people live in gated communities. You must have an invitation to go inside or the security guards will not let you pass. In the United States these are called Common Interest Developments or CIDs. Jeremy Rifkin, writing at the end of the last century, reckoned that by the year 2000 there would be a quarter of a million CIDs in the States, with 48 million people living in them. There must be far more by now. They are safe havens in a world that is getting more violent. So wealth can buy one seclusion and safety from the wild people on the outside.

In the face of this marginalisation, what wisdom does the Eucharist offer? Our community is gathered around the altar in the memory of the one who was cast out. He is 'the stone which the builders rejected which has become the corner stone' (Psalm 118). As James Alison, a fellow contributor to this book, has written elsewhere: 'God is among us as one cast out.'[9]

At the centre of our worship is the One who was crucified outside the walls of the city. So the Eucharist invites us to make a home in which the dichotomy between centre and periphery is transcended. As it says in the Letter to the Hebrews, 'Therefore let us go forth to him outside the camp and bear the abuse he endured. For here we have no abiding city, but we seek the city which is to come' (13:13).

A lawyer asks Jesus who is his neighbour. The parable of the Good Samaritan turns the question on its head. Jesus concludes by asking him, 'Which one *made himself* neighbour to the man who fell among thieves?' (Luke 10:36). The parable works by shifting the focus from the centre which is Jerusalem to the periphery which is Jericho. It carries us from the holy world centred on the Temple, to the outside, the place of the unclean Samaritans. The new liturgy of holiness is enacted by the side of the road. Most fundamentally it carries us from that centre which is ourselves, asking who are our neighbours, to find ourselves centred on the man who has fallen among thieves. The parable snatches the rug of our narcissism from under our feet.

Everywhere and nowhere

When Thomas Merton became a Catholic he wrote, quoting Allan of Lille:

> Now I had entered into the everlasting movement of that gravita-
> tion which is the very life and spirit of God. God's own gravitation

towards the depths of His own infinite nature. His goodness without end. And God, that centre Who is everywhere, and whose circumference is nowhere, finding me. And He called out to me from His own immense depths.

So at the centre of Christianity is that non-place, that utopia, God whose centre is everywhere and whose circumference is nowhere. Jesus summons us beyond a universe structured by sacred centres. As he said to the Samaritan woman, 'Woman, believe me, the hour is coming when neither on this mountain nor in Jerusalem will you worship the Father ... The hour is coming, and now is, when the true worshippers will worship the Father in spirit and in truth' (John 4:21, 23). This is the paradox of Christianity: as a community, or a network of communities, it does have centres, holy places around which we gather. And yet the meaning of such centres is to point us towards the One whose centre is everywhere and whose circumference is nowhere.

Obviously this will affect how we understand what it means to celebrate the Eucharist. Our church structures – parish and dioceses – reflect an agricultural world of villages and market towns. Already the world of the Industrial Revolution strained that model. How can we understand our Christian community in the world of Liquid Modernity? How may we gather in Christian communities which do not reflect the exclusions of this modern world and which point beyond the polarities of centre and periphery? If we do not do so, then our parishes will consecrate marginalisation. Helder Camara, the Archbishop of Recife in Brazil, was often accused of being a communist because of his concern for the poor who lived in the favelas on the hills around the city. He said: 'If I do not go up the hills into their favelas to greet them as my brothers and sisters, then they will come from the hills into the cities with flags and guns.'

An image that comes to mind is that of making bread. It is a traditional metaphor for the Christian community. In the *Didache*, one of the oldest Christian documents after the New Testament, we can find it already: 'As this broken bread, once dispersed over the hills, was brought together and became one loaf, so may thy Church be brought together from the ends of the earth into thy kingdom.'[10] I must admit that I have never made bread. One of my ambitions for my sabbatical was that I would learn to do so, but time slipped by without a single loaf appearing. Like a typical modern person, instead of doing it, I watched a TV programme about it. According to Jamie Oliver, the Naked Chef, instructing his 15 apprentices, it appears to involve constantly rolling out the dough and gathering it into the centre, and rolling it out again. Bread making involves a long process of bringing the margins into the centre and then spreading the centre out into the margins.

This indeed was what the Naked Chef was doing himself, gathering in 15 unemployed people into his kitchens and teaching them how to cook and then sending them out to start their own projects. It is in this interchange of centre and margin, this kneading of the dough, that we may be a community which images Christ in whom there is neither centre nor periphery.

We knead the dough of the Eucharist through this dynamism of exchange, going out to the victims, to be one with them, and a gathering in so that they may be one with us. The typical outsider is the leper. In the Philippines we have communities of Dominicans who live and work with lepers. Many are themselves lepers.

It was profoundly moving in Manila, at a gathering of the Dominican family, to see these groups of lepers arrive to take their place in our community. They took their places in the middle of the assembly. But that is only half of the movement. Even more touching, in every sense, was the Christmas Day that I went to spend with them, being welcomed in their community, dancing and singing in their home. Such reciprocities can be complex and sensitive. In the time of apartheid, we tried to establish a relationship between a white parish in Johannesburg and a Dominican black parish in Soweto. When the parishioners from Soweto were invited to come and share the 10 a.m. Mass in Johannesburg, they accepted with delight, but they were scandalised to find that when they arrived at 2 p.m. all the white people had given up and gone home.

One moment which remains for me emblematic of the meaning of the Eucharist happened not long after I first met Martin. It was the burial of someone called Benedict, who died of AIDS. He asked me, minutes before his death, if he could be buried in Westminster Cathedral. At the time, when AIDS was hardly known, this seemed very daring but eventually it was agreed. His coffin at the centre of the most central Catholic church in England was a symbol of what the Church is called to be. He was surrounded by the ordinary people who came to that week-day Mass, as well as by people with AIDS, nurses, doctors and friends. The one who had been on the periphery, because of his illness, because of his sexual orientation, and most of all because he was now dead, was at the centre, and gathered around his body the ordinary and the excluded. The counterbalancing movement must be the presence of the Church with people who have AIDS wherever they are. We knead the bread of the Eucharist, going out and gathering in, welcoming and being welcomed, giving gifts and accepting them.

Supreme insecurity

Finally there is the insecurity of the marginalised. In this liquid fluid world, human ties are temporary. This is true at work and in the home. The average American male has 11 jobs in his working life. For everyone this implies unpredictability. For the rich nomads unpredictability can mean unexpected openings, opportunities to be exploited before one moves on. For the immobile, then it implies insecurity and vulnerability. Unpredictability dissolves the old solidarities of the working class. Trade unions lose their power and will to resist. The mutual commitment of labour evaporates. Bauman writes:

> Once the employment of labour has become short-term and precarious, having been stripped of firm (let alone guaranteed) prospects and therefore made episodic, when virtually all rules concerning the game of promotions and dismissals have been scrapped or tend to be altered well before the game is over, there is little chance for mutual loyalty and commitment to sprout and take root.[11]

The Last Supper presents us with a moment of supreme insecurity. The bonds of the community are dissolving. The disciples are about to take to their feet. In this situation Jesus gives the disciples his body once and for ever, without reserve. The Risen Lord will tell them 'Behold I am with you until the end of time' (Matthew 28:20). In a fluid world, Christianity should embody a fidelity, an unconditional commitment. Thomas Aquinas reminds us that religion comes from a word, *religio*, which means a bond. We are bound to God and to each other. Making vows, remaining faithful to those whom we love, expresses something essential about our relationship with God.

This is a fidelity to each other that we must embody within the Church. Chrys McVey, a Dominican missionary in Pakistan, wrote that the missionary does not just unpack his suitcases, he throws them away. I am often deeply impressed by brethren and sisters who have left home and gone abroad to just be with another people in a radically different culture for the rest of their lives. For St Thomas Aquinas, courage is above all endurance. It is hanging in there, when it may seem pointless. It is the courage of staying put, as a sign of God's fidelity.

We must seek to live something of that in our relationships with people who are marginalised. In the world of development, there are fads and fashions. I overheard one superior in Rome saying that 'Latin America is out and Asia is in. Liberation theology is a bit old hat now; inculturation is the new thing.' Aid agencies are looking elsewhere too. When Eastern Europe was opened up, then Africa dropped further down the priorities. When major institutional donors make grants these days, they usually wish to know what are our exit strategies. Even in development, relationships may become temporary. Priorities change, crises arise and sometimes pass; it is true that we do not wish to create dependence and our aim is to make ourselves unnecessary.

But even so, in a world crucified by poverty, in which whole continents seem at times to be trapped without exit, then fidelity is also part of our witness. We are there for the long haul. Faced with the dreadful effects of the tsunami, for how long will we remember the millions whose lives have been destroyed?

These are a few thoughts about the Last Supper and various forms of social marginalisation. I have not covered everything. Above all I am aware that I have not discussed the marginalisation of women either in society or, most scandalously, within the Church. Julie Clague will address this issue later in this section. My aim has been to look at the changing forms of marginalisation within our society.

The Last Supper is a paradoxical sign, the paradox at the heart of the Church's life. It is a sign of community, gathering in those who are cast out. It is the sign of God who is among us, 'as one cast out'. This is a tension at the heart of the Church, between forces which are centripetal and centrifugal. The balance between these forces has something of the rhythm of breathing, filling and emptying our lungs. Both are needed if we are to oxygenate our blood. Living that tension may be painful but it is fruitful. Some of us may temperamentally be more inclined to tend the hearth and gather people in, and others to go out to the forgotten. There are not many who, like Martin, are able to do both. Such people may feel torn apart sometimes, and yet bear much fruit.

Notes

1. *Liquid Modernity* (Cambridge, 2000), p. 122.
2. ibid. p. 119.
3. Scott Lash and John Urry, *Economies of Signs and Space* (London, 1994), p. 323.
4. *The Age of Access* (London, 2000), p. 66.
5. 'Choruses from "The Rock"', *The Complete Poems and Plays of T. S. Eliot* (London, 1969), p. 147.
6. *A Common Humanity: Thinking about Love and Truth and Justice* (London, 2000), p. xx.
7. *On Christian Theology* (Oxford, 2000), p. 280.
8. *A Common Humanity*, p. 18.
9. *Knowing Jesus*, (London, 1993), p. 71.
10. *Didache* 9.4, *Early Christian Writings*, trans. Maxwell Staniforth (London, 1968), p. 231.
11. *Liquid Modernity*, p. 148.

Chapter Two

Getting Real about the Option for the Poor

Jon Sobrino SJ

Translated by Clare Dixon and Francis McDonagh

We have to keep coming back to the option for the poor. The time has not come when we can let ourselves think that the last word has been said on the subject; much less that we are putting it all into practice. In this essay I want to say three things that I believe need saying.

First of all, the option for the poor is still absolutely necessary, and this not only because poverty is still a scandal, but because only by making this option real can we ensure that humankind can simply become human: so that human beings can live without being humiliated with at least a minimal self-respect, and the Church can be truly Christian, and have credibility when it speaks of God.

Secondly, poverty shows itself in a variety of ways, not only in those who live in what is called economic poverty, but in those who are isolated, despised, ignored or excluded. For instance, children who are trafficked and made victims of paedophiles, including priests, are cruelly damaged. People who are homosexual are often ostracised, and suffer discrimination simply by being what they are. They are regarded with contempt by whole communities, religions and churches, often left without any word of encouragement or pastoral support to enable them to love and live a human life to the full. And poverty is manifest (paradoxically) in non-existence: the virtual invisibility of lay people, especially women, in the Church; and most appallingly of all, in the non-existence of Africa in the real concern of wealthier parts of the world.

Thirdly, not only must we make an option to 'save the poor': we must also make a choice to 'let ourselves be saved by them'. Only through this two-way option can we move forward towards Ernst Bloch's 'utopia', so that 'the world can become a home for human beings'. Only then will it be possible 'to reverse history, subvert it and launch it in another direction' (Ignacio Ellacuría), only then will it be possible to 'humanise humanity' (Pedro Casaldáliga).

The 'depth' of the option for the poor
Ultimate reality
It would be a mistake to think that the option for the poor is something that is obvious and now accepted in our churches. But it would be an even greater mistake to think that it began in 1968, when the Catholic bishops met in Medellín, and that it was the Church that demanded it, putting it forward as a means of being human and Christian in a world of unjust poverty. (All the same, we cannot overestimate the importance of Medellín.) The most destructive aspect of this mistake would be that it completely undermines a fundamental and unchanging basis of the option for the poor, allowing it to be blown about as though it were an 'optional option' dependent on the times and seasons of history.

The option for the poor has an earlier and much higher origin: in the Old Testament it is said that 'God in his holy dwelling' is 'Father of orphans, defender of widows' (Psalm 68:5); the God of Israel's faith is beautifully described as 'the one in whom orphans find mercy' (Hosea 14:4). The Jewish people waited for centuries for the just king, and they pictured him as 'judging the poor with justice' (cf. Psalm 72:3–4). The scholar Joachim Jeremias says that 'the king's justice is not based primarily on his impartial verdict but on the protection given to the infirm, the poor, widows and orphans'. With the coming of Jesus things do not change. The good news of the Kingdom of God, which Jesus brings, is good news for the poor. Indeed Jeremias observes, 'the kingdom is *only* for the poor'.

So, long before Medellín, long before there was a Church, God and Jesus of Nazareth made the option for the poor. When we are asked now to do likewise, strictly speaking there is no other reason but that 'this is how God is'. His face is that of the ultimate reality.

Doctrine and praxis
We have just seen that the option for the poor is an ultimate demand at the level of doctrine; it is also an ultimate demand at the level of praxis. In Scripture the benchmark of right action is always linked to how we act towards the poor. Right from the start God has been asking, 'What have you done? ... Your brother's blood is crying out to me from the ground' (Genesis 4:10). '[Your father] did what is just and upright, so all went well with him. He gave judgement for the poor and needy, then all went well. Is not that what it means to know me?' Yahweh asks (Jeremiah 22:15–16). 'I am sick of burnt offerings of rams ... Cease doing evil. Learn to do good, search for justice, discipline the violent, be just to the orphan, plead for the widow' (Isaiah 1:11, 16–17). Our attitude to God

is made real in our attitude towards the poor. We can only honour the God who makes the option for the poor if we ourselves make that option. And Jesus gives us examples in several parables that leave us no room for doubt.

1. 'A Samaritan traveller who came on [the wounded man] was moved with compassion when he saw him. He went up to him and bandaged his wounds ...' (Luke 10:33–34). Every human being – orthodox Jew or Samaritan heretic – who comes across a wounded man has only two options: to pass by and ignore him, or to go up to him, look after him and take him to a safe place. This last is the option for the poor. It is made in various ways, humanitarian, developmental or structural, depending whether the wounded person is an individual or an entire people left lying by the roadside waiting to be rescued. Because of the structural nature of Third World poverty, the option for the poor in such areas has to be structural. But the important thing to stress is that we are judged according to how we respond to the poor.

   Jesus told the parable in answer to the questioner who wanted to know which is the greatest of the commandments, but the parable does not treat the Samaritan's response as based upon his wanting or needing to obey a commandment, but upon something more fundamental: the compassion and mercy he feels towards the wounded man. He is 'moved with compassion': another man's misfortune stirs him to the very depths – 'churns up his guts', as the Greek text puts it (*esplanchnisthé*). If the stirring of our entrails moves us to action to rescue someone in distress, this is the clear evidence that we have made the option for the poor.

2. 'No one can be the slave of two masters: he will either hate the first and love the second, or be attached to the first and despise the second' (Matthew 6:24). These words from the Sermon on the Mount show that we have to choose between two objective realities that are both mutually exclusive and incompatible. We cannot serve the poor and serve those who make and keep them poor, the victims and their executioners. Ultimately this does not stem from the attitude of the particular person who chooses to help: this option is not at odds with an overriding loving intention towards all people, the poor and those who make them poor – although it may well need to be expressed in a very different way. The poor and their impoverishers are mutually exclusive: in fact they coexist in a relationship of conflict. They are like the parties in a duel.

   So an option for the poor means getting involved in an objective conflict in history; it means being willing to face the consequences of the conflict, willing to bear the shock and scandal if the executioner seems to triumph over the victim. It is not conciliatory in a direct way, although we hope that it will also lead to true reconciliation; it is not a matter of being peaceable, although we hope that it will also lead to a true peace. It makes tough demands: a willingness to be constant, and the strength to bear the consequences.

3. 'Then the King will say to those on his right hand, "Come, you whom my Father has blessed ... For I was hungry and you gave me food ..."' (Matthew 25:34, 35; see the whole passage, 25:31–46). An option for the poor is a way of looking at actual events, responding to them and becoming actively involved in them; but it is also a means of becoming a human being. It is *our* rescue too, our being made whole, our salvation. In this parable of the Last Judgement, where 'all nations will be assembled', it is what leads to final salvation. Salvation of life itself, and the meaning of our present life, are decided through our option for the poor. Future condemnation and meaninglessness in the present are decided through an option that leaves the poor on one side, and that, at bottom, is always against them.

To claim that the option for the poor is salvation is to affirm that *salvation is possible*; it is to put our money on hope, on the last word of history being a blessing and not a condemnation.

An option for truth

This option for the poor is necessary, but it is difficult: difficult because of the risks we have to take for it. Loss of reputation, persecution, death – in one form or another – inexorably come to those who make the option for the poor. Beyond any nice arguments about whether liberation theology has understood it well or badly – according to the spirit of the Gospel or (as has been unjustly claimed) according to Marxist class struggle – this is the fundamental difficulty which still faces us now. Jesus of Nazareth was killed because he defended the poor. From the beginning, when on the sabbath he healed the man with the withered hand, 'The Pharisees ... began at once to plot with the Herodians against him, discussing how to destroy him' (Mark 3:6). This response is still very much with us today. But, along with these difficulties that belong to human history, there are others that stem from our nature as human beings.

One of these is the tendency to suppress the truth. 'The retribution of God from heaven is being revealed against the ungodliness and injustice of human beings who in their injustice hold back the truth' (Romans 1:18). Paul is saying here that it is not at all easy to see the truth and that, furthermore, we have an intrinsic tendency to 'hold back' this truth. To be able to recognise what is really true, to respect the truth of how things really are, is therefore a primary matter for conversion in face of the temptation to distort or suppress the truth. Paul says that covering up the truth brings negative consequences. In theological language, the wrath of God appears, so that God's self-revelation in our reality becomes unclear to us, human hearts are darkened, and God hands them over to all kinds of abominations. In the language of history, reality cries out and protests, but its most intimate truth is hidden, humanity is blinded and dehumanised. And in the end this is true for all: gentile or Jew.

From the perspective of the poor, the truth of the world can be more clearly seen for what it is. But as this reality is a sinful reality, and as sin always tries to hide itself, to be invisible, or even pass itself off as something different, being able to see the world from the perspective of the poor also requires conversion. The option for the poor is therefore above all an option for truth, a choosing to see the reality of the world as it really is.

A digression on Mark's gospel

For all that I have just said, there certainly has been progress in the churches on the option for the poor – it is taken more seriously. However, it is still very far from being taken into the mainstream, and is always at risk of being diluted or manipulated, even at the level of theory. To explain this further, let us take a look at Mark's gospel.

Today we may think that Christian faith was simple and obvious in the early communities. It wasn't. For Mark – as he shows throughout his gospel – to live out Christianity was not at all obvious, even after several decades of Christian community life. It was not easy for the religious men of Jesus' time, or even for Jesus' relatives, or for his disciples. The women understood it better, although in the end, faced with the tomb of Jesus, not even they could find words to say, and they kept silent. The gospel ends by saying that 'they were afraid' (Mark 16:8). 'Being a Christian' was not only costly but also scandalous and counter-cultural. It is widely accepted that Mark 16:9–16 was added years later, an ending that was less scandalous and more manageable within the communities.

Well, something similar can be said of the option for the poor. To live it out fully, with all its consequences, has never been easy, nor can it be said to be an obvious course to take. I do not want to offer facile parallels, but the effect of adding to 'option' the terms 'preferential', 'neither exclusive nor excluding' – quite reasonable terms, one might think – reminds us of the verses added to the end of Mark: they take away the sharpness of the original. And perhaps we could recall here what happened in Vatican II with the 'Church of the poor', a concept defended strongly by John XXIII and Cardinal Lercaro. But at the end of the first session of the Council, Lercaro said, 'Something has been lacking in the Council up to now', and he wondered, 'Where shall we find that vital impulse, that soul, shall we say that fullness of the Spirit?' And he answered himself: 'This is the time of the poor, of the millions of poor people around the world.' But in the event the Council did not take the Church of the poor seriously, and we had to wait until Medellín.

Being saved by the poor?

Finally, let us look at another stumbling block facing those thinking of making an option for the poor: this is probably the biggest obstacle, even if we don't recognise it as such. A 'Christian' option for the poor demands at the same time an option 'to be saved by the poor'. This is not easy: it challenges our self-reliance and our arrogance. But not only do we need others for our salvation, we need precisely the weak, the oppressed, the despised – and this is central to biblical faith. Some time ago I expressed this as follows:

> The Christian biblical tradition is expert in the theme of salvation and in the dynamism that creates it. *Salvation* requires a promise and, at the same time, a definite hope: a hope of fraternity, of solidarity, of table-sharing. But specific to this tradition is the premise that salvation comes from the small and the weak: a barren old woman, the tiny nation of Israel, an outcast Jew ... the small and the weak are at the centre of the dynamism of salvation. They are its bearers, not only its beneficiaries. Utopia answers to their hope, not to the hope of the powerful. It is littleness that expresses the gratuitousness of salvation, not excessive self-confidence. This tradition of the littleness that brings salvation can be found throughout Scripture, but there is more. In the Old Testament there appears the mysterious figure of the suffering servant of Yahweh, who is not only 'poor' and 'little', but also a 'victim'. And this servant is the one chosen by God to take away the sin of the world and bring salvation. To the scandal of littleness we can add the madness of the victim.[1]

As Ellacuría says, 'Only through a difficult act of faith is the author of the Servant Songs able to discover what appears to be the complete opposite of the view of history.'[2] A faith like this requires that elegance of spirit of which Pascal spoke. It does exist – not just anywhere, but in the midst of crucified peoples. Here are three examples.

From Asia: the poor, not because they are holy, but by virtue of their being powerless and rejected, are chosen for a mission: 'they are called to be the mediators of salvation for the wealthy, and the weak are called to set the strong free.'[3]

From Africa (an example from within the Church, but one that expresses the same sense strongly): 'The Church in Africa, being African, has a mission for the universal Church. The Church in Africa is the pierced heart of Christ in that torn body which is the universal Church ... through its poverty and its humility it must remind all its sister churches of the essentials of the beatitudes and announce the good news of liberation to those who have succumbed to the temptation of power, wealth and domination.'[4]

From El Salvador: 'All this blood of martyrs shed in El Salvador and thoughout Latin America, far from leading to discouragement and despair, infuses a new spirit of struggle and new hope in our people. In this way, if we are not a "new world" or a "new continent", we are, clearly and verifiably – and not necessarily for people from outside – a continent of hope. And this is an enormously important element for the future when compared with other continents which have no hope, as all they really have is fear.'[5]

Of course none of this means that we should ignore the negative dimension of the life of the poor. The crude reality is that in their world too there are ever-present human evils: child-soldiers, archaic forms of cruelty against women, cultural and religious fanaticism, cruel leaders, who are sometimes criminal and corrupt – the 'mystery of iniquity' is very much present in the world of the poor. So asking what this world can offer us, and embracing it as something necessary and beneficial, might seem to be only for the naive, people confused by the myth of the 'noble savage' – to quote a cliché. What I want to say (and very much in line with Puebla) is that just as God loves and defends the poor for the mere fact of their being poor, and not because they are good (Puebla 1142), there is also something in poverty which, by simply expressing need and unjust deprivation, has the potential for salvation. And the poor themselves, in being poor, have the potential for evangelising others (Puebla 1147). We must question ourselves seriously. It is possible to make the option to help Africa, but are we ready in all sincerity to hope for salvation from a suffering and bleeding Africa, as well as from a heroic and smiling Africa?

'Diversity' within the option for the poor

What I have called 'depth' is, in my opinion, the most important rediscovery made by Medellín and liberation theology (and these two terms serve here and in what follows as symbols). In them history uttered a word after centuries of silence. The qualitative leap to this option for the poor was taken once it was realised that *God is the God of the poor* and that *God can only be known through the poor*.

In biblical terms, there was a *kairos*, a decisive moment, and this makes me surprised at how easily people say that 'Medellín' is a thing of the past; and I find even more surprising the almost total silence about 'Medellín' in the progressive theologies of the rich world. These keep invoking Vatican II, though often in a reductionist way, invoking *only* Vatican II, even sometimes in a bourgeois version, citing it to claim, quite rightly, as we shall see, their own rights within the Church. The depth of the option for the poor thus has its roots in *God's self* and in *poverty*.

Let us look at this in more detail. The poor are those for whom survival is the most urgent task and death an ever-present possibility; those who cannot take life for granted; those who die the slow death of poverty or the sudden death of violence; those who die before their time. This is poverty seen through the lens of death. But those people are also poor who have (almost) all the powers against them: this is poverty seen through the lens of power. And there are those who cannot form an *oikos* ('household'), the fundamental nucleus of life. I use the Greek word to stress what really underlies the term 'economically poor', which is used occasionally to criticise a certain reductionism in Latin American theology. It is not just a matter of the economic dimension – it is poverty seen though the lens of want. The fact that twelve hundred million human beings live on one dollar a day, or less, is an overwhelming disaster: the *oikos*, the life-cell, becomes an impossibility.

I began in this way in order to stress the *depth* of poverty and to avoid trivialising it in the interest of some other factor. That said, it is still obvious that we need to look at the different forms in which poverty, the negation of the *oikos*, has shown itself throughout history. Aloysius Pieris, for example, gives the following description of the different forms taken by poverty in Palestine in Jesus' time. There were:

> The *socially excluded* (lepers and those with mental disabilities), those *ostracised for various religious reasons* (prostitutes and tax-collectors), those *facing cultural oppression* (women and children), those *dependent on society* (widows and orphans), those *with physical disabilities* (the deaf, the dumb, the disabled, the blind), those *suffering psychologically* (the possessed and those with epilepsy), the *spiritually humble* (simple people who feared God, repentant sinners).[6]

The same thing happens today. I think it is a great advance, especially in the Third World, that we can grasp the diversity of poverty and the specific depth of each of its expressions. Indigenous and African Americans, those concerned with issues relating to gender, to women, to care for the earth, and to different religions – each of these groups has found its voice, and this is a significant development. The hierarchy too has gradually accepted this, in Puebla and Santo Domingo, although more at the level of orthodoxy than of orthopraxis.

The way liberation theology has treated the diversity of poverty has generated debate, and I would like to make a personal comment along the lines of what Gustavo Gutiérrez has said. Gutiérrez accepts, obviously, that there have been advances in the understanding of the diversity of poor people, and he recognises that 'valuable studies have enabled us to penetrate in a particularly fruitful way into some key aspects of this complexity.'[7] Nevertheless he continues to insist – and I think he does it for reasons of principle, and not as an inflexible and self-interested defence of the origins of liberation theology – on the intuition embodied in 'Medellín'. It was then that the reality of poverty found its voice and showed its depth, and this intuition must be preserved because now, as then, 'Poverty confronts the human conscience and our way of under-standing the Christian faith with a radical, comprehensive challenge.'[8]

This does not mean that what was required then (or now) was a sort of chemically pure concept of poverty. On the other hand I do think that the general term 'poverty', with all its historical fluidity, is irreplaceable as a way of naming the negation and oppression of humanness, the situation of being in want, or being an object of contempt, and the lack of voice or name experienced by many millions of human beings. All the other 'poverties', the variants, are part of this. Each of them adds a new dimension, a nuance, a level of depth that is often unique, which gives new energy to the term 'the world of poverty', especially in its dialectical relationship with 'the world of wealth'.

But, as I have said, we have to bear in mind other manifestations of the Old Testament concept of the *anaw*, the person who is bent under the weight of life. Often they coincide with those living with *oikos* poverty, but they have their own nuance. They are *children*, the street children, the child soldiers, those coopted into prostitution and the shadowy world of paedophilia. They are the *women*, those who have to carry the burden of the home when their partner walks out, those who suffer rape and abuse, those who are effectively cheated by the sorts of jobs they can get and the pay they receive. They are the *emigrants*, the men and women who have to leave their own country, culture and religion, watch their families break up, and get treated with contempt in a foreign land. They are the *indigenous*, exploited for centuries, seduced by false promises of a better future, helplessly watching their tribe disappear. They are the millions of people living with HIV, who look on powerlessly as so many die.

And I want to mention other situations where poverty appears – some of them very ancient, others more modern – which we are only now beginning to recognise. One such is the poverty expressed in terms of *comparative damage* (a rich person is worth about eighty poor people, three Real Madrid players earn more than the budget of Greater San Salvador, which has to cover the needs of one and a half million people). We see this sort of poverty in the parable of the rich man and Lazarus. Another kind is the *anthropological poverty* that Africans are rebelling against: 'They have stolen our very being.' A third is the greater poverty of non-existence: three, four, or six million people may die, but in the public mind the Democratic Republic of Congo does not exist.

And there is a further poverty that is spreading more widely every day: the poverty of exclusion. The cruellest form of poverty at the present time is not that which exploits people, but that which excludes hundreds of millions of human beings from the sources of life and work.

Both in religions and in churches we find other forms of exclusion. Many Christian men and women, often for dubious doctrinal reasons, are ostracised and cut off from participation in the life of the Church, which causes great suffering. The result all too often is that lay people, especially lay women, have their contribution to the life of the Church greatly diminished. Often enough same-sex couples are not permitted normal participation in the liturgy, and are denied the recognition that they may be good human beings and Christians – though this varies greatly from place to place.

In relation to these groups it is important that the Church develop a solid, gospel-based theological teaching that takes account of the signs of the times and the presence of God in them, and that throws light on the option for the poor. The Church's voice must be one of welcome, not rejection; of encouragement, not rebuff. This means hard work, but there must be a predisposition in favour of those who suffer and are excluded. We have to rethink Christianity from the perspective stressed by J. B. Metz: 'Jesus did not look first at other people's sins, but at their suffering.'[9]

> Christianity very soon had serious problems with this fundamental sensitivity to the suffering of others that is inherent in its message. The unsettling question of the justice due to the innocent, which is at the very core of the biblical message, was transformed all too quickly into the issue of the salvation of sinners.[10]

Saving the poor and being saved by them

This is the option in its two-way scope: to live and give our lives to save the poor and to let them save us. Now at last we can formulate what is fundamental.

The option for the poor involves the *mercy/justice* which saves them from death; it involves *prophetic word and deed*, which save them from indignity; and it involves their being publicly and accurately named, which saves them from non-existence. And all this has to be done from a particular bias: using the *dialectic* that confronts the oppressor; showing the *partiality* that goes straight to the poor; *insertion*, so as to place oneself affectively and effectively among them; the *humility* to go down to where they are, to receive from them and to hope with them.

One last word about humility. It is obvious that none of what we have said is easy: there is an empire-building politics of imposing our will on others, but also a politics of aid and cooperation. In this latter context, the option for the poor needs to be permeated by humility: it must never become a hidden option for oneself in the very act of attempting to make an option for another, the poor person.

If we bring together all I have said about this – the bias, dialectic, partiality, insertion and humility – the theology that throws light on the option for the poor can truly be called *a theology of the cross*.

But the poor also bring salvation – not the salvation that we seek of our own accord in our lives, but that which helps us to be deeply human. Puebla makes the novel assertion that the poor evangelise us, and that they do this in two senses: they challenge the Church, calling it to conversion, and they offer it important gospel values (Puebla 1147). As we have said, the poor have power to save through the fact of being poor and through the gospel values they possess. Important elements of the salvation that is the gift of the poor to us are those that challenge us to be human. They bring us into a place of truth, demanding from us and offering to us real civilisation, real solidarity. In an extreme paradox we may say that *their* suffering makes *us* human.

It is not easy to talk about these things without becoming suspected of masochism or utopian thinking, but I would therefore like to end with some real-life examples.

In a Salvadorean refuge on All Souls' Day, the refugees could not go and place flowers on their relatives' graves. They wrote the names of their dead, most of whom had been murdered, on big flip-charts. Around them they drew flowers. Beside the names there were also black lines. 'We're Christians, aren't we? We thought that they, the enemy, ought to be on the altar as well. They are our brothers, even though they kill us.'[11]

The basic decision to live and give life, as it emerged in the aftermath of the 2001 San Salvador earthquake, showed itself in a kind of primordial holiness. There is something about disaster-victims who want to live that is spell-binding, overwhelming, humanising – something that brings salvation to the rest of us. Destitute and suffering – mainly women with their children – even in the midst of the catastrophe and the ensuing desperate daily struggle to survive, they magnificently follow and put into practice God's call to live and give life to others.[12]

In the Great Lakes region of the Democratic Republic of Congo, in endless caravans of women fleeing death, carrying little else besides their children, and in the stories of the incredible cruelty and poverty in prisons and refugee camps, here too, like a miracle, dignity, love and with it hope appear: 'The prisoners in Kigali who will today receive visits from their families, who with great effort will be able to bring them something to eat, bless and thank God. How can they not be God's favourites, and the ones from whom we have to learn gratuitousness! I received a letter from them today. Perhaps they don't realise how much we receive from them, and how they save us.'[13]

In Auschwitz prisoner rejected prisoner, but Fr Maximilian Kolbe broke this pattern. And he, a recently professed Franciscan, was able to live out something that the great intellectual tradition had failed to understand. First, he volunteered for detention, and then at a crucial moment he went one step further and asked the camp commandant to let him take the place of a married man with children who had been sentenced to death. In the death cell he strengthened the hope and prevented the despair of the other condemned prisoners.

The world of the poor is not all like that, of course. But these stories are not just pious tales. And in the everyday life of the poor they are much more plentiful than we realise. In any case what I want to stress is that in these events and actions the Church and the human race is offered a love, a self-sacrifice, a hope, a salvation, that can be found nowhere else. To grasp all this we need, it is obvious, the 'spirit of delicacy' that Pascal talked about; and it is not enough to rely on calculations and doctrines that are definitely 'the spirit of geometry' and only by good luck proper geometry, not mere charlatanry.

Three brief remarks to end with. The theologian Metz, who is not at all given to elegance of style, speaking of the victims of Auschwitz says that 'After Auschwitz we can go on praying because they prayed in Auschwitz too.'[15] Their example is no small favour to us.

Second, the question: 'What is the point of all this?' Why should we make the option for the poor, why should we work for their salvation, and why should we expect salvation from them? Years ago I wrote that the poor have 'doctrinal authority' to tell us what the ultimate truth of things is.[16] More radically, Metz talks of their moral authority: 'Moral universalism has its roots in the recognition of the *authority of those who suffer* ... the Church too is under this obedience. It cannot be codified in ecclesiological terms because the authority of those who suffer – to which we owe obedience – allows no appeal, even by the Church.'

The third point is that, whatever the most accurate definition of the salvation the poor bring us, we can certainly insist that *extra pauperes nulla salus*, 'outside the poor there is no salvation'. Of course this doesn't mean downplaying the role of the Church, but it does mean encouraging it to be the Church of the poor.

Notes

1. *Terremoto, Terrorismo, Barbarie y Utopia* (San Salvador, 2003), p. 148.
2. Ellacuría, 'El pueblo crucificado: Ensayo de soteriología histórica', *Revista Latinoamericana de Teología* 18 (1989), p. 326.
3. A. Pieris, 'Cristo más allá del dogma: Hacer cristología en el contexto de las religiones de los pobres' (I), *Revista Latinamericana de Teología* 21 (1990).
4. Engelbert Mveng, 'Iglesia y solidaridad con los pobres de Africa: Empobrecimiento antropológico' in *Identidad africana y cristiana* (Estella 1999), p. 273f. Mveng was the first Jesuit from the Cameroon. He was killed in 1995.
5. I. Ellacuría, 'Quinto centenario de América Latina: Descubrimiento o encubrimiento?', *Revista Latinoamericana de Teología* (1990).
6. Pieris, 'Cristo más allá del dogma', p. 14.
7. 'Situación y tareas de la teología de la liberación', *Revista Latinoamericana de Teología* 50 (2000), p. 111.
8. Gutiérrez, 'Situación', p. 109.
9. 'La compasión: Un programa universal del cristianismo en la época del pluralismo cultural y religioso', *Revista Latinamericana de Teología* 55 (2001), p. 27.
10. ibid. p. 28.
11. Quoted in J. Sobrino, 'Latin America: Place of sin and place of forgiveness', *Concilium* 184 (1986/2), pp. 45–56.
12. Cf. Sobrino, *Terremoto*, p. 129f.
13. Cf. ibid. p. 132.
14. Cf. Carlos Díaz, *Monseñor Oscar Romero* (Madrid, 1999), p. 243.
15. 'Facing the Jews: Christian theology after Auschwitz', *Concilium* 175 (1984/5), pp. 26–33.
16. 'The "doctrinal authority" of the people of God in Latin America', *Concilium* 180 (1984/5), pp. 54–62.

Chapter Three

Love and Justice: In God and Church, in Sexuality and Society

Enda McDonagh

Neil Astley's second major anthology of modern poetry, *Being Alive* (2004), sequel to *Staying Alive* (2002), opens with a poem by Elma Mitchell simply entitled 'This Poem' and it reads:

> This poem is dangerous; it should not be left
> Within the reach of children, or even of adults
> Who might swallow it whole, with possibly
> Undesirable side-effects. If you come across
> An unattended, unidentified poem
> In a public place, do not attempt to tackle it
> Yourself. Send it (preferably, in a sealed container)
> To the nearest centre of learning, where it will be rendered
> Harmless, by experts. Even the simplest poem
> May destroy your immunity to human emotions.
> All poems must carry a Government warning. Words
> Can seriously affect your heart.

The friend who gave me this volume as a present suggested that 'theology' might well be substituted for 'poem' as 'dangerous' to children or to adults if 'swallowed whole'. The simplest theology 'may destroy your immunity to human emotions', and 'seriously affect your heart'. Of course it too may be 'rendered harmless by experts' at 'the nearest centre of learning'.

If all this seems an over-elaborate introduction to a theological essay on 'Love and Justice' in honour of a friend, at least it helps underline the dangers any theologian faces as would-be poet or would-be expert in reflecting on the divine and human mysteries of Christian faith. The poem, the poet and the friend offer not only timely warning but loving support in facing these dangers. Too much theology lacks the human warmth of friendship, human friendship modelled on that of Jesus and his human friends, and on the love of God and neighbour, the primary characteristic of Christian life and thought. And the blessed justice-seekers of Jesus' Sermon on the Mount (a truly dangerous poem) might learn something of the searching demands of justice from the poet's search for the *mot juste*, the word that 'can seriously affect your heart'. All this applies more sharply to a moral theologian particularly in his efforts to relate love and justice across the spectrum of God, church, sexuality and society.

Liberating moral theology

The manuals of moral theology which dominated Catholic moral teaching from about AD 1600 to AD 1960 had very limited, legal perspectives on justice and sexuality and completely ignored love/friendship. With their scholastic background they might have been more mindful of their ultimate ancestor Aristotle and his discussion of friendship in the *Ethics* and of their primary Christian teacher Aquinas and his much broader virtue approach to morality and in particular his insight that charity/love was the form of all the virtues. Intended as handbooks for training confessors in the wake of the reforms of the Council of Trent, they concentrated on sins as violations of a legally formulated code of morality and gave sexual morality a very negative bias, while restricting justice issues almost entirely to issues of exchange between individuals. From 1960 and particularly after Vatican II a much broader and richer view of moral theology as a theology of Christian and human life began to address these limitations with at least some success. However, the task of such a moral theology is far from complete; and given the historical and eschatological character of Christian and human life, it never will be.

In many ways moral theology has made its most significant recent progress in areas of justice. This may be most effectively illustrated by comparing church attitudes to human rights in the late nineteenth century when it firmly rejected the current enthusiasm for them at the highest level. Indeed the Catholic Church and the late Pope John Paul II count among human rights' strongest defenders on a global scale. This does not mean that church authorities or moral theologians agree among themselves or, still less, with the wider world about particular public claims as human rights. The bitter divisions over abortion are proof enough of this and there are many other examples, some of which will surface later. More problematic and controversial still is the 'Western' tendency to translate all moral issues into 'rights language', offering a new version perhaps of the legal codes of the old manuals and with many of their reductionist consequences. While human rights are an integral part of justice discourse and so have a role in developing a morality of love/friendship, justice and sexuality, they should not exclude other approaches to a fuller moral understanding of these and other issues.

Justice and love

While justice and sex may have been restricted and distorted in the manuals of moral theology, love or charity like its companion friendship was completely ignored except for a strange and brief treatment of 'the sins against', such as scandal or cooperation in the sins of another. This undoubtedly related to the manuals' role as guides for confessors and the confession of sins, but was more deeply based on the split between moral theology and the rest of theology, particularly the study of Scripture. Vatican II's recall of moral theology to its scriptural base, which had already been initiated by various scholars, restored charity/love to the primacy that was its by New Testament right and that it had enjoyed in the seminal writings of theologians such as Augustine and Aquinas. Gerard Gillemann's *The Primacy of Charity in Moral Theology* published in the late fifties provided a crucial anticipation of the Council's ambition. At the same time inside and outside the Council, debates and documents such as John XXIII's *Pacem in Terris*, Paul VI's *Populorum Progressio* and the Council's *Gaudium et Spes* (*The Church in the Modern World*) expanded and deepened the understanding of justice in its personal and social senses. Although it did not become a primary concern of Catholic moral theologians then or later, the relation between justice and love is critical to any authentic theology of Christian living or moral theology.

Love and justice in God

In many spheres of discourse, religious and secular, academic and popular, love and justice have been sharply opposed. At the extremes of theological discourse the God of the Old Testament, Yahweh, was contrasted with the God of the New, Abba, as a God of Justice opposed to a God of Love. More careful biblical scholarship and more sophisticated theological analysis revealed the critical love dimension of Yahweh, God of Israel, and the critical justice dimension of Abba, God of Jesus Christ and of Israel.

Distinguishing but not separating or opposing justice (*sedeqah/ mispat*, Hebrew Bible) and love (*hesed/ahab*, Hebrew Bible; *agape*, New Testament) is the true message of the Hebrew and Christian Scriptures. Jesus' exchange on the greatest commandment of the Law (*mispat*), clearly referring to the inherited Law, asks 'How do you read'. His interlocutor's reply, 'Thou shalt love (*agapēseis*) the Lord your God with your whole heart and your whole soul and your neighbour as yourself', offers, as Jesus confirms, a true life-summary for the justice-seekers who are listed in the charter of discipleship, the Beatitudes of the Sermon on the Mount.

The unity of love and justice in the Godhead and in the divine creative and re-creative activity recorded in the Old and New Testaments reflects the mysterious unity and simplicity of Godself. How this unity and simplicity are combined with three distinct persons has taxed the intellectual endeavours of the greatest theological minds in the tradition from Augustine and Aquinas to the Barths and Rahners of the twentieth century. Yet the divine diversity in unity and simplicity can illuminate the meaning of both love and justice between Creator and creation and within creation itself, as well as the interrelation of love and justice internal to the divine and human spheres. Indeed it is in and through the interactions of God with human beings, history and society in the life, death and resurrection of Jesus Christ, that the tri-unity in God becomes known. These interactions in turn, from the overshadowing of Mary by the Holy Spirit at the conception of Jesus, through the distinctive roles of Father, Son and Holy Spirit at Jesus' baptism to the entire drama of Jesus' dying into the hands of the Father, his resurrection and sending of the Spirit at Pentecost, bear the indelible marks of divine Love and Justice in face of human sinfulness and lovableness. The God who so loved the world as to send his only Son to give his life a redemption for many, was in him reconciling the world with Godself. And God completed that work of justification, restoring just relations in love-reconciliation – Paul's words – by sending God's Spirit of reconciliation to call and enable Christ's disciples to be ambassadors of reconciliation in turn.

The Trinity as unity of love and justice

The mystery of the triune God surpasses all human understanding. Yet as it creates and nourishes all human existence, personal and social, it challenges that understanding to trace God's image and likeness in human person and community. The *vestigia Dei Creantis et Trinitatis* in cosmos and humanity have fascinated theologians and contemplatives for millennia. In recent times theologians such as Jürgen Moltmann have concentrated on the trinitarian shape of human community. A sharper, if less ambitious analogy, might seek to relate love and justice as analysed in human experience to the life of the Trinity as indicated in Scripture and described by some mystics.

The differentiation of Father and Son, of the First and Second Persons of the triune God, is by name and by the analogy of creation, reflected in the relationship of human father and son, the relationship of two human beings. (The gender language may be laid aside for the time being.) At the divine and human levels such differentiation involves recognition and respect ('This is my beloved Son in whom I am well pleased'; 'Into thy hands, Father, I commend my Spirit'). Such recognition of identity and otherness is the basis for justice in relationship, what the moral tradition following Aquinas called *debitum ad alterum*, what is due to the other. And it is only on the basis of such difference, recognition and respect that love and true communion or unity are possible. It is that love between divine Father and Son which constitutes the third mysterious Person of the Trinity and in its distinctiveness receives the recognition and respect in justice/equality of the first two Persons, as it completes their unity in love. Human differentiation involving recognition and respect in justice as basis for (comm)-unity in love is ultimately rooted in the tri-personal life of God, however crudely it reflects it.

In the community of disciples: the Church

Love and justice in the community of disciples operate at a number of levels. At the level of the Body of Christ, the theological and mystical substance of the community, love and justice come together as distinct yet unified, as in the Godhead itself. As we have just seen, the love which unites Father and Son and issues in the Holy Spirit respects the otherness of each divine person in the ideal of justice. So with the Church as founded in that divine reality through the mediation of Christ, each member is to hold every other in the bonds of love and the differentiation of justice.

That is the gift and call of membership of Christ's Body, of the graced sharing in the trinitarian divine life in its unity in difference, of the baptismal insertion into the communion of saints. History, however, makes clear that the communion of saints is also a communion of sinners. Love and justice are engaged in a struggle with each other and with a range of other incomplete virtues in the individual and ecclesial life of Christians. It is in this incomplete historical era that the Church seeks, in hope rather than certainty, for the fuller expression of the love and justice for which it was founded, both within its own life and structures and in the wider society. Only in the eschatological fulfilment of the Reign of God will love and justice coincide and prevail. Such fulfilment is the final stage of the human, indeed cosmic, embodiment of divine justice and love.

In the aftermath of the death of Pope John Paul II and the impact of his funeral it is clear that he contributed powerfully to love and justice in the world. His striking message on developing a 'civilisation of love' and his range of encyclicals on justice in the world as well as his travels, particularly to the poorer regions around the globe, gave eloquent testimony of this. Within the Church many Catholics were less enthusiastic about his exercise of justice in different areas, from theology to the role of women and to the treatment of gay and lesbian people. In most of this John Paul was carrying on the tradition of his immediate predecessors so it would be unfair to single out his papacy as the only or even the primary culprit. The internal structures, attitudes and activities of the institutions of the Church have failed, in varying degrees, for centuries to match the love and justice which ought always to characterise the Church as People of God and Body of Christ.

These failures have been failures in theology, in the understanding of faith-hope-love as much as in the practice of kingdom values such as justice. How the first apostolic community, the company of Jesus' friends and followers, assumed over the centuries the present, centralised juridical structures is too long and complex a story to recount here. Much of this may have been justified in particular contexts as the Christian community sought survival or faced unusual challenges of growth or decline. And the efforts at evangelical reform from time to time did not always meet with widespread acceptance. Here it is necessary to concentrate on love and justice and their understanding and practice within the Church.

The trinitarian insight of the distinction and equality of persons remains primary. Only the recognition and respect for others as equals in their otherness enables them at once to be given their due in justice and to be bonded in love and communion. The radical equality of Christians in communion rests on their baptism into Christ which then becomes through the gift of the Spirit their call and capacity to love one another as Christ has loved them. Only equality in difference permits true community and the love and justice which it embodies. The call to particular ministry in that community to guard and guide it must be fashioned after the particular model of the serving Christ and not the model of the lording gentiles. In this context baptism maintains its primacy over ordination and the People of God over its clerical and episcopal ministers, as Vatican II tried to express. The neglect of these insights has resulted in unloving and unjust treatment, even exclusion of various individuals and groups within the Church. And it has prevented many from making the contribution to faith-understanding and practice. Theology and other faith initiatives have suffered over the centuries from the absence of lay experience, skills and energy, perhaps particularly those of women, because of male clerical dominance and distrust. This has frequently been manifest in poor Christian understanding of the 'secular' worlds of civil society and sexual community/relationships.

Love and justice in sexual relationships

In the liberation of moral theology referred to earlier, the theology of marriage was moved out of the constraints of a contract in canon law to the more humane and Christian category of a community of love open to life. This allowed for a much more personal view of marriage and of sexual relationships as primarily loving rather than as primarily reproductive. This development has presented its own difficulties but it has been a powerful liberation in Catholic moral discourse just the same. No longer are sexuality and sexual relationships to be treated as either exclusively directed to reproduction or otherwise demeaning, even dirty, but as vehicles in the right circumstances of the highest Christian value, that of love. Of course the right circumstances are very important and sometimes highly disputable. In resolving the potential disputes the justice dimension of love will be a key element.

Pope John Paul II's understanding and promotion of 'a civilisation of love', including sexual love, had all the hard qualities of justice, which always involves a certain equality. That equality in sexual relations operates first of all in consent, in the equal capacity to consent – so that paedophilia is excluded, for example. But the equality required also excludes the kind of power-play and exploitation in which one party intimidates or blackmails the other. The violence of rape is not only opposed to justice but to love also. Equal or just consent is not simply a matter of the freedom of both parties but also of their maturity and commitment to each other. In biological, social as well as phenomenological terms the intimacy of bodily union betokens a mutual and continuing acceptance which one-night stands or deliberately short-term relationships do not express. Exclusivity and fidelity are part of just sexual loving.

Sexual differentiation and openness to procreation are a traditional and crucial part of sexual relationships. It has however been accepted in many traditions, including the Christian, that an infertile or childless relationship can be moral and a real marriage. The recognition of the woman's infertile period as a way of regulating procreation for Catholics from the time of Pope Pius XII has, despite the encyclical *Humanae Vitae* of Paul VI, persuaded many theologians and married couples that other means of birth regulation are acceptable and, in a further step, that sexual loving may not be irrevocably confined to just heterosexual relationships. However, such other relationships between people of the same sex would have to satisfy the same just requirements as those between people of different sexes. Equality in capacity to consent, in commitment and so in fidelity and exclusivity would be clear demands of homosexual as of heterosexual loving. In sexual relations, hetero-sexual or homosexual, as already emphasised for members of Christ's body, each partner is to hold the other in the bonds of love and the differentiation of justice.

A Christian blessing of such love and justice, without the involving the sacramental character of Christian marriage, could be appropriate to faithful disciples, if not generally accepted as yet. More urgent may be legal protection of gay citizens and partnerships from various kinds of discrimination, although this also belongs to the following and final section on love and justice in civil society and culture.

In the long journey of humanity and Christianity to a fuller under-standing and living of love and justice in sexual relations as in other areas of life, the concept and reality of friendship with God and one another will bear much revisiting. In such prayerful and reflective re-visiting, the love and justice inherent in God and manifest in Jesus will enrich our understanding and correct some of our inevitable mistakes.

Love and justice in civil society and culture

John Paul II's call for 'a civilisation of love' might be regarded as senti-mental tosh, if he had not shown the world in deed, word and symbol his commitment to freedom, justice and peace, crucial characteristics of love. A brief digression on the Pope's achievements in the world might confirm the power of his words. His contribution to the liberation of Poland and other countries under the tyranny of the USSR witnesses to his regard for political freedom as does his later promotion of human rights. In the later part of his pontificate, his encyclicals *Laborem Exercens*, *Sollicitudo Rei Socialis* and *Centesimus Annus*, celebrating the centenary of the first social encyclical, included criticism of free market capitalism as well as Marxism. Together with his visits to the poorer countries and his pleas for debt cancellation for the poorest and for fair trading regulations, the Pope proved one of the major advocates of the global anti-war campaign. In his final years his anti-war stance became more pronounced as evident in his persistent opposition to the war in Iraq.

However, love and justice in society and culture belong to a much older and broader tradition, Christian and secular, than that represented by the era of John Paul II. And we must not forget his overlooking some of the achievements of the enlightenment and democracy, particularly in the western world. The relations between religion, morality and law are indeed more complex in the present mixed democracies than the Pope seemed to realise. And the witness of the Church to the truth, as it sees it, may not be simply imposed by the Church on the democratic state, where other visions of the truth have a claim on voters and legislators. The interplay of love and justice, of the preaching and promotion of the Reign of God and its values, tasks for the Church, do not readily translate into political choices and civil legislation. Recent documents and regulations on the responsibilities of Catholic legislators, in the United States of America for example, failed to recognise the dangers, to the Church itself as well as to the state, of attempting to restrict unduly the freedom of voters and legislators, and to turn complex political programmes into one- or two-issue agendas, with heavy emphasis on gender and sexual matters. The exclusion of some Catholic politicians from the Eucharist on the basis of their distinguishing between their private moral conviction on abortion and their acceptance of the law of the land at this point, did not really exemplify either love or justice. Such ecclesial behaviour was further undermined by particular church authorities ignoring the positions of other candidates for public office on the legitimacy of capital punishment or of the war in Iraq, equally condemned by the highest authority in the Church.

In response to the deprived and exploited, to the poor and the sick, many church leaders and agencies gave both powerful witness and effective help in a striking combination of love and justice. That too has a long Christian history. In recent decades as the poor of the world became more visible and audible through mission and media, the mutual inhabitation of love and justice exercised a significantly transformative effect on ecclesial and indeed political aid programmes. It is in this area that the Christian insight that love without justice is ineffectual and justice without love inhuman is so important.

Among the many spheres in which such insight might be pursued, a neglected one is that of artistic achievement, the realm of what is sometimes grandly described as 'high culture'. Without the space, the technical (pictorial) equipment or the competence to pursue this at any great length or depth, one might reflect on love and justice in the form and matter of a single poem. As hinted in the introduction, ethics, moral theology and theology in general have been diminished by their distance from artistic creativity and aesthetic analysis. This applies in particular to ethical dimensions of love and justice in all human relationships and communities.

The poem selected here is by an Irish and Cork poet, Sean Dunne, who died prematurely in the 1990s before he was forty. In its free yet disciplined form, it reveals even in the abbreviated version quoted here what Yeats described as poetry, 'truth seen with passion', in word, image and rhythm. Its combination of practical love and sense of injustice needs no prosaic commentary.

Refugees at Cobh
We were sick of seeing the liners leave
    With our own day in, day out, so when
When the boats edged with refugees to Cobh
    It was worth the fare to travel
From Cork to glimpse on railed decks.
    They seemed like ourselves …
They hadn't a word of English but we gave
    What we could: sheets and rationed tea,
Sweets, blankets, bread, bottles of stout.
    The night they sang for hours
We heard their music pour over the islands,
    And none of us recognized the words …
And then moonlight fell on silence.

    So strange to see emigrants to Ireland
Huddled near posters telling us to leave
    The broken farms for New York streets
It was our Ellis Island: hunched
    Lines of foreigners with bundles
Staring at the grey cathedral …
    In time we turned them away. Most stood
As still as cattle when the ship drew out
    And the pilot boats trailed after it.

Still we turn them away, we Irish who depended for so long on not
being turned away. The love which gave what it could in Cobh is still
active in Ireland as elsewhere but it lacks the sustenance and substance
of justice in dealing with the new refugees, asylum-seekers and immigrants. Poets and artists often see further and deeper than politicians and
church leaders, would-be guardians respectively of justice and love in
the world.

Love and justice with their associates, human rights, freedom and
peace, belong together in a truly human society, its politics and
economics, but have to be worked out in detail in its structures and
practices.

Such talk, like 'This Poem', is dangerous. And the danger reaches
back to the biblical poem of Genesis 1—3 and the first creative act of
God. The risks taken in that divine initiative involved deeper risks still
as finally God sent his own Son. His execution did not stay the divine
hand and the sending of the Spirit inaugurated the New Creation, the
Reign of God preached by Jesus. That Reign or Kingdom is still in the

making, in its dangerous making. A theology which would serve it cannot avoid the danger and the risk and yet it must attempt in its ham-fisted way to reflect and promote the love and justice intrinsic to the tri-une God. Above all the words of that God, the poem that is that God, can and should seriously affect your heart.

Chapter Four

Assessing Our Inheritance: John Paul II and the Dignity of Women
Julie Clague

As Benedict XVI begins his papacy, it is a good time to assess the legacy to the Church of his predecessor and great friend John Paul II's writings on women. John Paul wrote more on the nature and role of women than all his papal predecessors combined, and went further than any previous pope in affirming women's dignity, in campaigning for an end to unjust sex discrimination, and in constructing a sacramental theology of femininity that he believed shed light not only on women's nature and roles, but also on Catholic doctrine and ecclesiology.

In so doing, he widened discussion of women beyond its traditional location in Catholic social teaching on work and family life and propelled it into the realm of fundamental theology, on areas touching central Catholic truths. What John Paul sought to achieve was no less than a Christian articulation of the indispensable role of women in human and salvation history.

As a result, John Paul's writings on women are at once impressive, enormously ambitious and highly controversial. One suspects that a full evaluation of their enduring significance to the life of the Church could take years. It is beyond question, however, that John Paul's writings on women are helping shape the new era that the Church has entered.[1] This brief discussion cannot hope to do full justice to John Paul's extensive and complex theology of woman, but in confining discussion to themes involving women's dignity, it may still be possible to indicate the substantial nature of John Paul's contribution to Catholic teaching, and the nature of the challenge that he has set Catholics who read his work – whatever their sex or ecclesiological station – as they carve out the future direction of the Church.

The equal dignity of the sexes
All of John Paul's teaching on women stemmed from an unshakable conviction concerning the equal dignity of the sexes. In this respect he continued the tradition explicitly articulated since the time of Pope Pius

XII, but also found, implicitly, in the writings of Popes Leo XIII and Pius XI.[2] However, John Paul augmented and amplified these teachings, reiterating them throughout his pontificate.[3] Wherever human dignity was trampled and humane existence threatened, John Paul was an articulate champion of the rights of the oppressed, and much of his teaching on women must be read in this light.

He became increasingly vigorous in his condemnation of the various forms of oppression of women. He recognised that throughout human history, it was women who have suffered most from the effects of sin.[4] He deplored the objectification of women, and the sexual exploitation and violence they suffer at the hands of men, especially through the commercialised evils of pornography and prostitution.[5] He rejected the tendency in some cultures to discriminate in favour of boys to the detriment of girls in education and other spheres, recognising the damage this does to a girl's sense of dignity by reinforcing patterns of inferiority.[6] He called for an end to all discrimination, speaking out against the marginalisation experienced by women such as widows and unmarried mothers, and he appealed for help for women scarred by the trauma of war.[7]

Women, he believed, are right to seek liberation from male domination, and he viewed the achievements of the women's liberation movement as substantially positive.[8] With the insertion of the distancing and qualifying term 'new' he would even adopt the phrase 'feminism'.[9]

Like many of his predecessors, he frequently drew attention to the dignity of women who devote their lives to their families through their important but all too often under-appreciated and economically jeopardised roles as mothers and carers; and he argued in favour of social recognition of the value of motherhood in order to support those women around the globe struggling to balance its demands with paid employment.[10] Nevertheless John Paul considered it entirely proper for women to be engaged in public and professional life on a par with men and he supported women's efforts to gain equality with men in terms of equal pay and employment opportunities.

Furthermore, he argued that the social, political and economic advancement of women is not only a legitimate goal, but also a necessary condition for a more humane society.[11] No reader of John Paul's writing on women can fail to see how gender justice must be a central focus for any agency – Catholic or otherwise – working for human development and social transformation.

Examining the past with courage[12]

It is clear, however, that for much of its history humankind has failed not only to promote but also to recognise the full dignity of women. A growing moral awareness and consensus about the wrongness of exclusionary and discriminatory practices on the grounds of sex emerged as late as the twentieth century, and then in the face of continuing opposition from many quarters. Almost without exception, the churches were not in the vanguard of these social changes.

In his *Letter to Women* John Paul paid tribute to the female trailblazers who saw through conventional morality and campaigned to overturn the patterns of inequality written into socially approved sex roles:

> I cannot fail to express my admiration for those women of good will who have devoted their lives to defending the dignity of womanhood by fighting for their basic social, economic and political rights, demonstrating courageous initiative at a time when this was considered extremely inappropriate, the sign of a lack of femininity, a manifestation of exhibitionism, and even a sin.[13]

Sadly, in this climate of hostility to the achievement of women's rights, the Catholic Church has all too often been part of the problem rather than part of the solution. In acknowledgement that, historically, members of the Church have been party to the disempowerment of women and guilty of their mistreatment, John Paul issued in his letter an unprecedented public apology expressing sorrow and regret for Catholic culpability that made headline news around the world.

The actual words of the apology are revealing and merit further attention.

> Unfortunately, we are heirs to a history which has conditioned us to a remarkable extent. In every time and place, this conditioning has been an obstacle to the progress of women. Women's dignity has often been unacknowledged and their prerogatives misrepresented; they have often been relegated to the margins of society and even reduced to servitude. This has prevented women from truly being themselves and it has resulted in a spiritual impoverishment of humanity. Certainly it is no easy task to assign the blame for this, considering the many kinds of cultural conditioning which down the centuries have shaped ways of thinking and acting. And if objective blame, especially in particular historical contexts, has belonged to not just a few members of the Church, for this I am truly sorry. May this regret be transformed, on the part of the whole Church, into a renewed commitment of fidelity to the Gospel vision.[14]

One might contrast John Paul's realism about the historical role of the Church with the somewhat triumphalist and idealised portrayal presented in the Second Vatican Council's closing *Message to Women*: 'The Church is proud to have glorified and liberated woman, and in the course of the centuries, in diversity of characters, to have brought into relief her basic equality with man.'[15]

While the real picture offers more shadow than light, it is clear that this reading of the Church's past is not an attempt to mislead. Rather, it reveals a common tendency on the part of the Church to compress complex and often ambivalent historical processes into a homogeneous and harmonised account, through which the Church is able to align and identify itself with historical developments and moral insights that bring to life the gospel message. In reality, rather than being directly responsible for the insight, the Church has found herself evangelised by it.

An obvious case in point would be the Church's conversion to the use of human rights language as a means of expressing the dignity of the person. The question of how the Church makes sense of the history it inherits (though much neglected) is of fundamental importance for all theology, and John Paul's writings provide some interesting lessons in this regard.

From the earliest days of his pontificate, John Paul had considered the dawn of the third millennium a crucial punctuation mark in time's litany, and it was in this context that he began to examine the Church's past in order to turn its mind to repentance and reform.[16] In *Tertio Millennio Adveniente*, he discussed the sins committed against Christian unity and the violence and intolerance shown to non-Catholics throughout the centuries.[17] Later he would apologise to other groups, including Jews, the Eastern Orthodox Church and indigenous Americans.

In these various apologies John Paul's intention was not solely to express regret for the more widespread and frequent misdemeanours of the Catholic flock. This is no average Catholic's list of sins for the confessional. Rather, John Paul was drawing attention to systemic sins of the Church that were supported and even encouraged by Vatican sanction and for which, therefore, there lies some institutional responsibility. Clearly, institutions do not sin; it is the people within them who find themselves trapped in a tangled web of wrongdoing.

The complicity of individuals in propping up sinful structures was given powerful expression in John Paul's post-synodal *Apostolic Exhortation on Reconciliation and Penance*, and it seems particularly apt in this context:

> ... such cases of social sin are the result of the accumulation and concentration of many personal sins. It is a case of the very

personal sins of those who cause or support evil or who exploit it; of those who are in a position to avoid, eliminate or at least limit certain social evils but who fail to do so out of laziness, fear or the conspiracy of silence, through secret complicity or indifference; of those who take refuge in the supposed impossibility of changing the world, and also of those who sidestep the effort and sacrifice required, producing specious reasons of a higher order.[18]

What is at stake here is what John Paul referred to as the 'structures of sin' created by individuals who 'introduce these structures, consolidate them and make them difficult to remove. And thus they grow stronger, spread, and become the source of other sins, and so influence people's behaviour.'[19] The Pope's apology to women rightly refers to the personal sins of individual members of the Church, but the very fact of a papal apology is sufficient indication of ecclesiastical contrition for failing on an ecclesiastical scale.

It should be noted that prior to John Paul's papacy, admissions of error or apologies for past failings on the part of the Church were unheard of. Indeed, many Catholics (whether aware of the historical evidence or not) would resist the suggestion that their Church might previously have erred. By raising awareness of the Church's past failings and asking for forgiveness, John Paul offered humanity a more credible and realistic witness of a Church of sinners on its pilgrim journey in search of the truth.

'We are heirs to a history which has conditioned us'[20]

Some may complain that John Paul's focus on the sins of the past too readily neglects the faults of the present, and that by situating the Church's wrongdoings within the historical context of widespread intolerance, a further distancing aspect is introduced which excuses Catholic failings and mitigates the impact of his apology to women. Notwithstanding the former objection, let us turn to examine this significant feature of the Pope's apology, which also characterises his treatment of other sins of the past: namely, his explicit admission that historical and cultural conditioning can influence Christian beliefs, morals and actions.

Acknowledgement that human assumptions and value systems can be shaped by the prevailing customs and mores of time and place – while taken for granted in academic study – is new to Catholic reflection. By introducing the idea, John Paul wished to underline the historical ubiquity (as opposed to the uniqueness) of the erroneous notions and norms promoted within the Church. According to this view, just as a racist culture breeds racists, humans are everywhere subject to an osmotic process of moral inculturation that, like background radiation, can silently seep into a person's moral make-up. As unwitting recipients, it is by no means easy for humans to discern the extent to which their personal views and behaviour are tinged or permeated by such forces, nor the extent to which humans can become aware of the role of such conditioning and 'cleanse' themselves from malign influences.

This raises difficult questions when considering the degree of moral responsibility individuals have for wrongdoing, and it was in order to draw attention to the difficulty of retrospectively assigning moral culpability for sexism in a sexist age that John Paul appealed to the existence of historical and cultural conditioning in his apology to women.

He makes a similar appeal in *Tertio Millennio Adveniente*:

> Another painful chapter of history to which the sons and daughters of the Church must return with a spirit of repentance is that of the acquiescence given, especially in certain centuries, to intolerance and even the use of violence in the service of truth. It is true that an accurate historical judgment cannot prescind from careful study of the cultural conditioning of the times, as a result of which many people may have held in good faith that an authentic witness to the truth could include suppressing the opinions of others or at least paying no attention to them. Many factors frequently converged to create assumptions which justified intolerance and fostered an emotional climate from which only great spirits, truly free and filled with God, were in some way able to break free. Yet the consideration of mitigating factors does not exonerate the Church from the obligation to express profound regret for the weaknesses of so many of her sons and daughters who sullied her face, preventing her from fully mirroring the image of her crucified Lord, the supreme witness of patient love and of humble meekness.[21]

Again John Paul points to the existence of social forces that might reduce but not remove individual culpability for wrongdoing. While he refrains from considering what these forces might be, it seems highly likely that the influence and power of the Church played a part in shaping the cultural climate that allowed such wrong-headed views to prevail. In any case, John Paul is careful to avoid determinism, which otherwise would render the concept of personal freedom impossible and human morality absurd. While one's historical and cultural setting may influence one's behaviour, it does not determine it. John Paul maintains that, at least for some 'great spirits' it is possible to see beyond one's own horizons and 'break free' from cultural constraints and social expectations.

Eternal nature and historically conditioned nurture

John Paul's appeal to the existence of historical and cultural conditioning adds a new dimension to Catholic discussion of historical contingency, but it does not negate or supersede previous and rather different recourses to the concept in Catholic teaching. In 1975, concerned to reiterate and uphold the Church's moral standards in a climate of sexual hedonism, the Vatican issued a *Declaration On Sexual Ethics* stating that Christian norms of human sexual behaviour are not subject to the contingencies of time or place. Rather, humans are able to discern the existence of certain moral laws that, because they are written into the nature of every human person, are always and everywhere applicable.

Those people are in error who assert that 'so-called norms of the natural law or precepts of sacred scripture are to be regarded only as given expressions of a form of particular culture at a certain moment of history'.[22] The Declaration expresses a firm belief in a common humanity, certain essential features of which are shared by all, thereby transcending the vicissitudes of history. These enduring truths about the human person are embedded in human nature and expressed in sacred Scripture, and whereas historical and cultural conditions do not determine our behaviour, these inbuilt 'givens' must. The Church therefore draws on these resources of natural law and sacred Scripture to discern God's will for humanity.

It is clear, however, that the Church has not found this process unproblematic in its long history. Over many centuries it believed the Bible and the order of nature revealed the inferiority of women. The *Declaration on the Admission of Women to the Ministerial Priesthood* admits that 'in the writings of the Fathers one will find the undeniable influence of prejudices unfavourable to women'. Similarly, Scholastic doctors 'in their desire to clarify by reason the data of faith, often present arguments on this point that modern thought would have difficulty in admitting or would even rightly reject'.[23]

Armed with the knowledge that prejudice might have clouded their judgements, these shapers of Church teaching can hardly command our complete confidence. While the Church now concedes that readings of Scripture and human nature previously deployed to support views of the inferiority of women were deficient, it maintains Catholic sexual norms derived from these sources remain secure. Nevertheless, given similar distortions and theological justifications about other groups, such as enslaved peoples, one proceeds with a rightful but respectful caution when interpreting these sources.

The example of Jesus: upholder of women's dignity

However, if as *Inter Insigniores* attests, members of the Church – even its most gifted leaders and scholars – have been guilty historically of holding the characteristically prejudicial views of their times, the same Declaration refutes the view that Jesus was subject to the same limitations.

> It has been claimed in particular that the attitude of Jesus and the Apostles is explained by the influence of their milieu and their times. It is said that, if Jesus did not entrust to women and not even to His mother a ministry assimilating them to the twelve, this was because historical circumstances did not permit Him to do so. No one however has ever proved – and it is clearly impossible to prove – that this attitude is inspired only by social and cultural reasons. As we have seen, an examination of the gospels shows on the contrary that Jesus broke with the prejudices of His time, by widely contravening the discriminations practised with regard to women.[24]

While Christians can live, however uncomfortably, in the knowledge that their tradition has exhibited prejudice against women, for many it would be a theological bridge too far to imagine that Jesus Christ himself might have, for example, pondered the superiority of his maleness. Such a hypothetical scenario would raise deeply challenging theological questions touching central Christian affirmations about Christ's sinless state. At the same time, however, to believe Jesus floated free entirely from his historical setting, somehow divinely immunised against the social ills (such as patriarchy) of the world he inhabited, would raise equally problematic questions about his incarnation as a fully human person. Between this theological Scylla and Charybdis a middle course must be steered: Jesus fulfils the role of the 'great spirit' immersed in the world but 'breaking free' of its sinful shackles.

In John Paul's writing these themes of *Inter Insigniores* are developed and become a central part of his theology of women. In Jesus a new era of the dignity of women is inaugurated, which John Paul explicitly identifies with Christ's redemptive mission.[25] 'Jesus of Nazareth confirms this dignity, recalls it, renews it, and makes it a part of the gospel and of the redemption for which He is sent into the world. Each word and gesture of Christ about women must therefore be brought into the dimension of the paschal mystery.'[26]

In an extensive midrash, which he aptly describes as a 'meditation' rather than exegesis,[27] John Paul portrays Jesus in his earthly ministry as an innovator, a promoter of the dignity of women who offers spiritual (as opposed to social) liberation.[28] Jesus' 'words and works always express the respect and honour due to women ... This way of speaking to and about women, as well as his manner of treating them, clearly constitutes an "innovation" with respect to the prevailing custom at that time.'[29]

Thus, Jesus' nature triumphed over any deficiencies of nurture. Unhindered by his patriarchal environment he promoted women's dignity, setting standards that subsequent Christians, trapped in the structural sin of patriarchy, would often fail to attain. While exegetes may shudder at the ease with which this portrayal is sketched, it functions to serve a number of purposes. In rediscovering the truth of the equal dignity of the sexes, modern-day Christians are returning to its aboriginal source in the gospel message of which previous ages lost sight.

We will correctly discern 'the path to be followed in undertaking the tasks connected with the dignity and vocation of women ... only if we go back to the foundations which are to be found in Christ, to those "immutable" truths and values of which He Himself remains the "faithful witness" (cf. Revelation 1:5) and teacher'.[30] Furthermore, such a powerful advocate of women's dignity could hardly base apostolic selection on criteria prejudicial to women.

> In calling only men as His Apostles, Christ acted in a completely free and sovereign manner. In doing so, He exercised the same freedom with which, in all His behaviour, He emphasized the dignity and the vocation of women, without conforming to the prevailing customs and to the traditions sanctioned by the legislation of the time. Consequently, the assumption that He called men to be apostles in order to conform with the widespread mentality of His times, does not at all correspond to Christ's way of acting.[31]

Catholic Christianity has always affirmed the special significance of the twelve in the ministry of Jesus and clearly assumes the non-arbitrary nature of Jesus' selection criteria. If acting in a free and sovereign manner, without cultural or historical constraints, there must be other reasons for Jesus choosing to discriminate in favour of males in selecting the twelve. What could these reasons be?

Since we have received no record of what motivations might have inspired the earthly Jesus we cannot know with certainty on what basis his choice of the apostles was made. One possibility might be that Jesus' aim was of the 'select the best person for the job' variety and that the best people, by chance, were all male. Another would be of the 'only males can do this job; which males shall I pick?' sort. For John Paul, the divine plan, disclosed through the mysteries of creation and redemption, would permit only the latter possibility.

Sacramental sexuality

John Paul's theological anthropology was anchored in the divinely ordained, historically durable 'givens' of complementary sexual differentiation, expressed as the distilled essences of 'masculinity' and 'femininity'.[32] For women (and presumably men), human activity is always a function of their distinct nature and the (feminine) gifts embedded within it.

Woman 'must understand her "fulfilment" as a person, her dignity and vocation, on the basis of these resources, according to the richness of the femininity which she received on the day of creation and which she inherits as an expression of the "image and likeness of God" that is specifically hers'.[33]

This lens of understanding allows John Paul to see a sacramentally charged, theologically significant, sex symbolism at work in the world as part of the redemptive plan. In the Church this is expressed through the marian and the petrine principles, which stand as fixed and symbolically ordered poles within the sexually differentiated ecclesiastical economy of 'service': 'These role distinctions ... must be understood according to the particular criteria of the sacramental economy, i.e. the economy of "signs" which God freely chooses in order to become present in the midst of humanity.'[34]

Thus, when Christ 'entrusted only to men the task of being an "icon" of His countenance as "shepherd" and "bridegroom" of the Church through the exercise of the ministerial priesthood', he could not do otherwise for, if he were to have chosen women, the symbolism would simply not work.[35]

Thus, because Jesus hand-picked only men as his apostles, Catholics are to believe that gender was a significant aspect of his choice, that the act of discriminating in favour of men was neither arbitrary nor innocently naive but filled with meaning, and that by so doing he was establishing a precedent of not selecting women that he intended his followers to perpetuate through an exclusionary practice of ordaining only men to a sacramental priesthood.[36]

Whither human dignity?

Whence, in this discussion of women's dignity, we are presented with a parallel. Jesus, paragon of human dignity promotion, intentionally selects only men to be in his inner circle of the twelve. The Church, upholder of women's dignity, permits only men to be ordained priests. While the gospel message is one of inclusivity, an island of apostolic exclusion exists for women that does not exist for men. While Catholicism promotes the active involvement of women throughout the social and political order, they are actively prevented from involvement in priestly ministry within their Church.

Somehow, the equal dignity of the sexes – usually considered synonymous with notions of inclusion and non-discrimination – is to be considered compatible with exclusion and discrimination. How can this be?

This line of argument should not surprise those familiar with Catholic statements on women. Both Leo XIII and Pius XI viewed the subordination of wife to husband as divinely ordained and entirely compatible with women's dignity.[37] According to Pius XI, a wife's subjection to her husband is 'established and confirmed by God' and 'does not deny or take away the liberty which fully belongs to the woman both in view of her dignity as a human person, and in view of her most noble office as wife and mother and companion ...'[38]

And he cautioned against the dangers that can arise when 'false teachers ... assert that such a subjection of one party to the other is unworthy of human dignity', that 'the rights of husband and wife are equal' and that 'the emancipation of women ... ought to be effected'.[39] By contrast, John Paul spoke of 'the rightful opposition of women to what is expressed in the biblical words "He shall rule over you" (Genesis 3:16)', and was emphatic that the subjection of wives to husbands is not God's design but a consequence of sin: 'the words of the biblical text directly concern original sin and its lasting consequences in man and woman.'

The loss of equality marks 'the disturbance of that original relationship between man and woman which corresponds to their individual dignity as persons ... only the equality resulting from their dignity as persons can give to their mutual relationship the character of an authentic "*communio personarum*".'[40] Human dignity is served not when husbands subjugate their wives, but when their relationship is one of equality, mutuality and reciprocity – a realisation that has emerged (and is still emerging) all too slowly in the Church and wider world.[41]

Here we see the shifting ground on which the supposedly foundational principle of human dignity stands. Portmanteau-like, the concept has been filled with various meanings for assorted purposes at different moments of the Church's history. While the equal dignity of the sexes, often expressed by John Paul in concrete terms through the language of human rights, was considered a sufficiently robust sine qua non to be employed by him to justify an end to exclusionary and discriminatory practices within public and professional life, its persuasive power is strangely enfeebled when applied by others to female participation and representation within the institutional Church. This worrying fluidity in what human dignity entails cheapens its currency and undermines its moral force.

Like Pius XI on the subordination of wives, John Paul taught that exclusion of women from priestly ministry does not impinge on their dignity.[42] Likewise, he identified this practice with the divine will: the reservation of priestly ordination to men 'is to be seen as the faithful observance of a plan to be ascribed to the wisdom of the Lord of the universe'.[43]

However, it is difficult to see how the equal dignity of the sexes is promoted (rather than merely asserted) when, for women but not for men, the norms of behaviour that usually guarantee human dignity are put aside. It seems more the case that, with regards ordination – unlike the normal participatory values and duties of treatment that apply in wider social life – certain considerations (related to the sacramental economy of sexuality) are identified with God's intent, and are therefore of such overriding importance that they relativise the demand to respect human dignity.

If this is the case, it would require of the Catholic a suspension of moral disbelief with regards human dignity that is unsustainable. The danger of such a position is that divine fiat appears to play the voluntarist card to trump human morality – a concept of God that many would find untenable and intolerable. Tragically, and precisely because of the many merits found in the reciprocity of female–male relations, the 'complementaritism' employed in justifying an exclusionary priesthood has created a church where, in the realm of ecclesiastical function, separatism (not collaboration) is presented as a virtue. This ecclesiastical apartheid is a deeply rooted structural sin that wounds men as well as women, and is deeply damaging to the credibility and witness of the Church.

Worryingly for the future direction of the Catholic Church, one of Pope Benedict's last outputs as Prefect of the Congregation for the Doctrine of the Faith: the wishful *Letter on the Collaboration of Men and Women in the Church and in the World* – despite its title – embodies this separatist attitude by echoing John Paul's essentialist contrast between the sexes and inserting the now commonplace reminder of the reservation of priestly ministry to males, thereby missing the opportunity of offering a healing vision of collaborative ministry.[44]

Questions for the future

John Paul has bequeathed an important legacy to the Church in his teachings on the equal dignity of the sexes. In a world that is far from female-friendly they constitute a rallying call to justice for the socially engaged Church. The theological anthropology that underpinned John Paul's understanding of the dignity and vocation of women has received a more mixed reception. Perhaps this is only to be expected, given the widely differing and vigorously invoked understandings of sex and gender that have emerged in the last half century. In due course a number of those views will no doubt appear as yet more products of their times, quietly discarded by future generations. It is this ambivalent and controversial inheritance that Benedict and his flock must negotiate in order to transform the culture of sexual separatism into a genuine (as opposed to token) culture of collaboration.

In the third millennium the Catholic Church has much work to do on the thorny subject of sex and gender. The future will reveal much about the Church's attitude not only to women but to its own self-understanding: to its use of Scripture, to its appeal to the natural law and to its rich but ambivalent tradition. In their search for the truth, the pilgrim people of God seek to make sense anew of the Christian inheritance into which they are inculturated.

Notes

1. The clearest indication of the ongoing influence of John Paul's theology of women is to be found in the *Letter On the Collaboration of Men and Women in the Church and in the World* (31 May 2004), issued by the Congregation for the Doctrine of the Faith, signed by its then Prefect Cardinal Joseph Ratzinger and approved by Pope John Paul II.
2. Cf. Pius XII, 'The Dignity of Woman' (14 October 1956); Pius XII, *Women's Duties in Social and Political Life (Questa Grande Vostra Adunata)*, Address to Members of Various Catholic Women's Associations, 21 October 1945 (London, CTS), p. 4; John XXIII, *Encyclical Letter On Establishing Universal Peace in Truth, Justice, Charity, and Liberty, Pacem in Terris* (11 April 1963) n. 41; Vatican II, *The Pastoral Constitution on the Church in the Modern World, Gaudium et Spes* (1965) nn. 9 and 29; Paul VI, *Apostolic Letter on the Occasion of the Eightieth Anniversary of the Encyclical Letter 'Rerum Novarum', Octagesima Adveniens* (14 May 1971) n. 13; Pius XI, *Encyclical Letter on Christian Marriage, Casti Connubii* (31 December 1930) 27; Leo XIII, *Encyclical Letter on Christian Marriage, Arcanum Divinae Sapientiae* (10 February 1880) n. 11.
3. John Paul II, *Apostolic Exhortation on the Role of the Christian Family in the Modern World, Familiaris Consortio* (22 November 1981) n. 23; John Paul II, *Apostolic Letter on the Dignity and Vocation of Women on the Occasion of the*

Marian Year, Mulieris Dignitatem (15 August 1988) n. 1; John Paul II, *Apostolic Exhortation on the Vocation and Mission of the Lay Faithful in the Church and in the World, Christifideles Laici* (30 December 1988) n. 49; John Paul II, *'Women: Teachers of Peace', Message for the World Day of Peace* (1 January 1995) n. 1; Pope John Paul II, *Letter to Women* (29 June 1995) n. 1.

4. *Mulieris Dignitatem* 10 and 14; *'Women: Teachers of Peace'* 4.

5. *'Women: Teachers of Peace'* 5; *Letter to Women* 5.

6. *'Women: Teachers of Peace'* 8.

7. *Familiaris Consortio* 24; *Christifideles Laici* 49; *'Women: Teachers of Peace'* 10.

8. *Mulieris Dignitatem* 10; *'Women: Teachers of Peace'* 4; *Letter to Women* 6.

9. John Paul II, *Encyclical Letter on the Gospel of Life, Evangelium Vitae* 25 (March 1995) n. 99.

10. For example, John Paul II, *Encyclical Letter on Human Work, Laborem Exercens* (14 September 1981) n. 19; *Familiaris Consortio* 23; *Mulieris Dignitatem*, esp. nn. 17–19; *'Women: Teachers of Peace'* 6, 7 and 9; *Evangelium Vitae* 99; *Letter to Women* 4.

11. *Familiaris Consortio* 23; *'Women: Teachers of Peace'* 4 and 9; *Letter to Women* 4 and 6.

12. 'Yes, it is time to examine the past with courage, to assign responsibility where it is due in a review of the long history of humanity', *Letter to Women* 3.

13. *Letter to Women* 6.

14. *Letter to Women* 3.

15. Second Vatican Council, 'Closing Messages' (8 December 1965).

16. Cf. John Paul II, *Apostolic Letter on Preparation for the Jubilee of the Year 2000, Tertio Millennio Adveniente* (November 1994) nn. 23 and 33.

17. *Tertio Millennio Adveniente* 34–5.

18. Cf. John Paul II, *Apostolic Exhortation on Reconciliation and Penance in the Mission of the Church Today, Reconciliatio et Paenitentia* (2 December 1984) n. 16.

19. John Paul II, *Encyclical Letter for the Twentieth Anniversary of 'Populorum Progressio', Sollicitudo Rei Socialis* (30 December 1987) n. 36.

20. *Letter to Women* 3.

21. *Tertio Millennio Adveniente* 35.

22. Sacred Congregation for the Doctrine of the Faith, *Declaration on Certain Questions concerning Sexual Ethics, Persona Humana* (29 December 1975) n. 4. The Declaration reminds Catholics of the wrongness of all non-marital, homosexual and masturbatory sex.

23. Sacred Congregation for the Doctrine of the Faith, *Declaration on the Admission of Women to the Ministerial Priesthood, Inter Insigniores* (15 October 1976) n. 1.

24. *Inter Insigniores* 4 (see also n. 2).

25. *Mulieris Dignitatem* 12–13.

26. *Mulieris Dignitatem* 13.

27. *Mulieris Dignitatem* 2 and 25.

28. *Mulieris Dignitatem* 12–16, 25–6.

29. *Mulieris Dignitatem* 13.

30. *Mulieris Dignitatem* 28.
31. *Mulieris Dignitatem* 26.
32. Cf. *Mulieris Dignitatem* 7; *Christifideles Laici* 50; *'Women: Teachers of Peace'* 3; *Letter to Women* 7–8.
33. *Mulieris Dignitatem* 10.
34. *Letter to Women* 11.
35. *Letter to Women* 11 (cf. *Inter Insigniores* 5).
36. Cf. *Christifideles Laici* 51; John Paul II, *Apostolic Letter on Reserving Priestly Ordination to Men Alone, Ordinatio Sacerdotalis* (22 May 1994) n. 2; *Letter to Women* 11.
37. Pius XI, *Casti Connubii* 27; Leo XIII, *Arcanum Divinae Sapientiae* 11.
38. *Casti Connubii* 28 and 27.
39. *Casti Connubii* 74.
40. *Mulieris Dignitatem* 10.
41. Cf. *Mulieris Dignitatem* 24.
42. *Ordinatio Sacerdotalis* 3.
43. *Ordinatio Sacerdotalis* 3. Cf. 'This norm, based on Christ's example, has been and is still observed because it is considered to conform to God's plan for his Church', *Inter Insigniores* 4.
44. CDF, *Letter on the Collaboration of Men and Women in the Church and in the World* (2004), esp. n. 16.

PART TWO

IN GOOD FAITH: THE REALITIES OF SEXUALITY

Chapter Five

Breaking Our Silence

Ann Smith

'Speak for us,' they challenged
As we shared our stories under the African sun.
Speak for us, for we
Already burdened with the pain and poverty and powerlessness
Of AIDS among us
Can't match the might of Rome's Goliath-men
Who, claiming God-shaped creeds and rights,
Forge rules till they become our millstones,
While they walk free and light and tall
With the air of those who know and trust their truth
And only their truth
God-given – so they claim – for them, to them and through them.
And with their truth they bind and shame and judge us.

Speak for us, for these Goliath-men who never know our lands or live
  our truths
Claim powers to loose or bind, everywhere, in every time, unswerving,
  immune.
Speak for us to these kingdom-eunuchs
Who carve their kingdom rules on slabs become our tombstones
Safe in their ivory tower cocoons
Deaf to our truth of kingdom-not-yet-come
Though groaning for birth among us.

Speak, they urged, but not in guarded tones as is your norm till now.
No more your whispered words confined to safety zones
As if their utterance brings shame, or death, or worse.
Our truth made yours begets your power,
Our voice made power may yet sway
The minds and hearts of these Goliath-men
So resolutely stony-faced
Yet all the while tottering
On their crumbling feet of clay.

Let our truth-before-power ring out, bringing them light,
Bringing us life.

Speak out, speak now,
Boldly, loudly, expertly,
Faithful to the truth of life, not rules.
Our leaders' mumbled efforts quickly fade
As Roman purse-strings tighten.
Those who, undeterred, proclaim their people's truth
Fast find themselves a solitary voice.
Their erstwhile peers turned back, they tread a desert course
Prophetically loyal, brave, pained by their abandonment, and so alone.
But you are strong and free
And versed in Goliath tongues, as in ours.
Speak for us ...

***

I paused, we paused.
The I become we, the we with I.
We and I paused and pondered and questioned.
What then of all we've said behind closed doors?
What of daring words and lofty thoughts
Spoken to inspire and challenge and support
Yet left untended and uncharted
Hanging in the air of friendly far-off places
Vaporised by the heat of friendly far-off suns?

Our fear-filled whispers turned to judge us
And call us to account
For measured words and guarded silence when shadows of Goliath-men
        fell close
For ways once wise now serving only
To collude, entrap, betray, play safe.
What use our insights tested only by like minds?
What point discernment that we've veiled?
Our Janus-mouths voiced yes and no, old and new,
Past and future-present,
Brought hope, confusion, joy and loss
As we too wavered, bowed
Whenever soutaned Goliath shadows loomed,
They and we both caught by fear not of what we can't or won't
But of what we can.

And as the we with I pondered
We re-membered
We re-vived
The stories of those robbed of name and voice and choice.
Stories of women made to do the bidding of whoever held the power
Of purse, or home, or state
Or sometimes even life itself.
Stories too of men dehumanised,
Crushed by markets and labour and wars and pressures
To perform, and power-form, self-form and conform,
And of those taunted and mocked and hounded
Merely because the creed they hold
Or the life they live
Or the love they dare to name
Is different.
Stories of the young robbed of skills and hope and vision,
Of the old robbed of memories and security.
Stories always of power over powerless,
Rich over poor
North over South.
And through it all, silently, stealthily, the viral night took hold,
Spreading its rule where power already reigned
Smashing the last defence of the poor and powerless and rejected.

In response, solution-peddlers roam.
Day on day they broadcast spell-fixed formulas,
Unfurl their banners promoting life and hope and remedy
To all who buy their wares
– Only theirs and always theirs.
Black-clad Goliaths preach their rules
That once for always label
Good and bad, right and wrong, law and sin.
Grey-suited Goliaths with no less zeal proclaim a different infallibility
Found in finest crafted latex, only, always, simply.
Each plies their trade in light of day.
Their stereo-polar slogans drench the air and promise safety fast and
    sure
To all who follow them.
With dusk, Goliaths black and grey withdraw
Retreating to their safe and moneyed homes
To worship at their graven altars
Of righteous truth or mammon-driven profits

And rest in virgin or companioned beds
Appetite sated, cares at bay.
While in the streets they've left
The hunger pangs, the pains of violence,
The need for hope and love.
Give passage to the viral thief as dark enfolds
The power of daylight creeds by now worn thin.

***

'Come join my song' God Spirit urged.
Tell out my hymn of truth
– Shaped not by rules or dictates,
Nor glossy adverts pitched to sell
But by my law of love.
Sing of my truth of love
That begets each and all my people, uniquely mirroring my image
As I carve and hold each in the palm of my hand
And celebrate their rainbow-spectral beauty
And name each as my own
And call them to myself.
I delight at all that I have called to being and see that it is good,
Different and good.

Hymn too the truth of God-authored science
To be proclaimed, not hidden or disowned,
Recognised, not distorted,
Unfolded in every age, not time-frame frozen once for always.

My hymn sings too of freedom,
Covenanted with all creation,
Offering choice and liberation,
Loosing chains,
Sighting the blinded,
Enabling the bent walk straight and firm
As all are called to do.
A freedom that gifts each God-imaged self.
A freedom that tithes each self for others.

Another verse sings loud of justice
That enriches the poor,
Restores the bowed and exploited,
Accepts all those rejected

And voices those made silent,
While transforming the de-throned mighty
That they too might make my justice come
For each. For all
With each. With all.

My final verse proclaims *Shalom*
That each might be restored to wholeness
Healed, at-oned
With who you are
For you, for others, in me.

Come share this song that's old as time,
Tell out this hymn that's ever new.
Sing it by day, by night
In ivory towers, in sun-baked lands.
Sing loud with outcasts now my prophets.
Sing loud with leaders no longer mute.
Let this sound transform and heal, renew, make whole.
For wherever, however this hymn finds voice
I will delight to breathe my love to life
And see the beauty of God's Reign brought forth
This song's my Word, my sole beloved Word.
Come birth my Word to flesh.

***

God Spirit's song is out, it's sung.
Her hand re-formed our stuttered utterances.
Her Word made ours,
Echoed and found echo
In many and varied hearts and minds
In many and varied lands.
And even in the recesses
Of ivory towers and marble halls and conference rooms
Some have been heard to hum this tune though very *sotto voce*
– Just in case a censor swoops, or boardroom colleagues sneer.

Yet once again the shadows loom
Now of self-appointed Goliaths
Mandated not by rank or office
But by their fortress-stagnant sense of truth and right
And always binding duty to defend

Claimed by the privileged, enlightened few.

Their drumbeat booms a rallying war-cry monotone
To threaten, intimidate, isolate, destroy.
As with poisoned arrow vile they scorn, despise and pour contempt
On all who'd sing a new re-Worded tune,
To drown out once for all
That Spirit-crafted hymn for life
– A hymn they label death.

What's sung is sung, it will not be unsung.
That Word now fleshed cannot be unbirthed.
The I with we cannot disown, unspeak
Our truths made Truth,
Our words en-Worded.
For who or what would we become
Sucked into the lifeless vortex
Of these Goliath-drummed chill shadows?
What too of those already virus-burdened,
If we are silenced
Or choose retreat,
And seek once more the safer ground?

The drum beats on
The drummers deafened by their boom
To the deeper, richer melody
That's gained momentum, gathered strength
As disparate voices add their polyphonic harmonies
That resonate their rainbow-spectral lives.

Still the shadows fall and loom
To gag and silence, to swallow into darkness
All who would sing this different tune,
Or any tune but theirs.
And fear still grips, though not so tightly now,
And others jeer though not so fully now.

We wait, I wait
And hope and grieve and ache and celebrate and fear.
And in the hope-fear-pained and joyful waiting,
In twilight-anxious-eager groan-filled watching,
I-we dare to dream

This richer tune will chase the viral night
And dissipate Goliath shadows
Bereft of power drawn from rules and banners.
That it will trumpet signs of God-shaped Reign
Come among us, though not completely now,
Becoming, through each Godsong-pregnant moment,
But not yet fully here.

'Speak for us' they challenged.

Chapter Six

Good-Faith Learning and the Fear of God

James Alison

The virtue of fear of God is little mentioned nowadays.[1] I invoke it because typically those who enter into some sort of moral discussion imagine that we are starting off from the standpoint of the good guys. Those who are moved by fear of God fear lest our own irresponsibility, our own hardness of heart and defect of vision perhaps be carrying us down a route that is too easy, one that is ever more free of voices which question and challenge us. So fear of God obliges us to a certain athletic tension with respect to our own way in case it leads us into disaster.

In order to situate more exactly the reason for this invocation at this time, I would like to bring to your attention Gitta Sereny's book *Into That Darkness: From Mercy Killing to Mass Murder*. In this magnificent text Sereny shows the slow route to moral corruption undergone by a local Austrian policeman, Franz Stangl, who went on to become the Camp Commander of the extermination camp at Treblinka. Stangl would preside over the death of about a million people without committing a single act of personal violence, convincing himself that he had no other option owing to the harshness of the situation.

However, it is not because of the interviews with Stangl that I highlight this text now, but because of the author's study of what happened in Germany when Hitler was planning his programme of murdering mentally and physically handicapped people.[2] A former priest, who had become a Nazi official, was charged with obtaining from a distinguished Catholic moralist a formal written opinion concerning the probable reaction of the Church towards the policy of forced euthanasia which was to be introduced by the government. The opinion, whose five copies have disappeared completely, was written by the very distinguished moralist, Professor Mayer of Paderborn. According to the sworn testimony of those who read it, it gave to understand that the killing of the mentally handicapped might be admissible.

Apparently, knowledge of the tenor of this document reached high within ecclesiastical spheres. From the silent reaction of those spheres,

Hitler deduced that his programme of the killing of such patients would not provoke an enraged reaction from the Church. Having feared that the Catholic population, at the instigation of their hierarchy, would rise up against these measures, he saw that this wouldn't happen, so he could begin his programme. Which he then did.

Of course, after the war, when there was an attempt to clarify the circumstances of the opinion and of who knew what before the introduction of the euthanasia policy, there were many cases of amnesia and declarations of not having known what was going on. Such forgetfulness and ignorance were difficult to believe because there had been a few brave and isolated voices among church leaders of the time who preferred to go to prison rather than keep quiet.

Thus, seduced by the possibility of a détente with a hostile regime, some notable Catholic figures felt it appropriate to compromise a moral doctrine which had hitherto been implacably opposed to allowing any exception to the prohibition of the murder of handicapped people. The result of this seduction was the murder of thousands of utterly vulnerable and unprotected people, the loss of credibility on the part of ecclesiastical authorities, and, at the end, the absolute professional shame of those who had allowed themselves to be so seduced.

Civil challenge

The reason for recalling this in the context of fear of God is because of the possible symmetries which exist with what is going on currently. If I had been in Germany at that time and in those circumstances, it would be very rash of me to think that I would likely have behaved better than my brethren in the faith who compromised. That is to say, it is much more probable that I would have been of the conformist party, and not of the brave party whose members were, over the long term, fully justified.

Well, here we have something similar. Nobody doubts the Church's traditionally implacable opposition in the face of any attempts to legitimise sexual and affective relationships between same-sex couples. Yet behold, encouraged by the growing good will shown by the civil governments in our own and other continents, some of us, amongst whom I count myself, are proposing that we let drop a link in the chain of that implacable opposition, and are suggesting that it is quite possible that the Church can, without any damage to its divine doctrine and mission, change its characterisation of gay and lesbian people. By changing its characterisation, it can change also its position with relation to the civil laws which normalise the lives of such people.

I would be very stupid if I were not to ask myself whether, should I reach the age of 81, like Professor Mayer of Paderborn at the time of the

1967 Frankfurt euthanasia trial, I would not run the risk of being found to be in the most absolute shame and discredit through having made myself an accomplice and a partisan of something which might, over time, come to be seen as a moment when our societies headed off down an insidious and sinister pathway. And, of course, none of us knows now what exactly will be the effects of the proposed changes to the law or the civil code in our countries. Ecclesiastical voices, with prophetic tones, predict severe damage to our social life, and consider, along with the highest representatives of Islamic thought, that the very foundations of society are threatened by the extension of the category of civil marriage to same-sex couples.

Other voices point out that there is no sign of any such damage being produced in those countries or states where the law has already been changed. Instead these voices affirm that not to extend the right to full civil recognition is to carry on producing an evil in the degree to which people are being condemned to the category of second-class citizens without any objective basis. Where there is discrimination without objective basis, and those who do the discriminating begin to be aware of the baselessness of their discrimination, they have ever less excuse for the evil they are perpetuating. Whatever the case, should the ecclesiastical argument be right, we would need much more time to measure the social consequences of the extension of civil marriage, although it is very difficult to say how these consequences would be measured.

That's why fear of God is so important. Whether we like it or not, we are in new territory. It is for this reason that I would like to work very slowly, showing step by step the links in my argument so that, where what I say is crazy, this may be rectifiable before it is too late. That is to say: mine is an attempt to talk about matters gay in the midst of the Church in such a way that what I say is capable of discussion and of being contested.

I consider it important to signal in advance what it is that I think I am doing, since it is notorious that if the characterisation of gay and lesbian people upheld by the Vatican congregations be true, then it is to be doubted that gay or lesbian people who accept themselves as such would be capable of rational discourse about the matter. According to the official characterisation, such a person would have accepted as part of their 'I' something which is nothing but an objective disorder. This would have corrupting consequences in their self-presentation and in their capacity for reasoning.

A parallel would be trying to talk to someone who is drunk. While someone is in that state, none of us would think that that person is capable of reasoning or of moral responsibility. In fact, we would show a marked lack of sanity ourselves if we were to speak 'to' such a person, trying to engage his 'I'. Rather, while the drunken state lasts, his 'self' is temporarily beyond being engaged by us, and we would do well to talk 'about' him so as to work out who gets to swipe his car keys, and who will take him home and put him to bed.

A straight line

So I know in advance that seen from such a perspective, this attempt of mine to speak in the midst of the Church is no more than an attempt by a drunk driver to show the traffic cops that he's able to walk in a straight line. Normally the very fact of having a go is a sign that the driver is not altogether there. I would merely ask those who maintain the perspective of the Vatican congregations that they take my attempt to walk in a straight line as a sign of good faith, and treat it as some sort of cry for help. That is to say, I'm asking that I not be considered an enemy of the faith, or an infiltrator who is sapping the foundations of the Church, introducing weird heresies. In the worst-case scenario, I'm a deranged fool attempting a piece of reasoning, but at least with nothing hidden, all in the full light of day. And if the perspective of the Vatican congregations turns out to be true, then I dare say that there are many of us who are similarly deranged and we are going to need very well-developed pastoral help so as to enable us to return to our right minds.

Thus to my first premise in this attempt. Currently the Church, including its gay and lesbian members, finds itself in a situation where there is a serious conflict between two elements of Catholic doctrine which hadn't appeared to be in conflict before, but which for a few years now have been producing a very strong disturbance in the life of many of the faithful. The two elements are as follows: on the one hand the Church's traditional teaching about original sin and grace, and on the other, the traditional teaching about sexual acts between people of the same sex.

The first element is well known. The Church teaches that at the fall, and therefore in the real living out of all of us, our human nature was very seriously damaged, but that this damage did not destroy our human nature. The distinction is important. If our nature had been destroyed, that is, if we are radically depraved, as is taught by some of the churches which are heirs to the Protestant Reformation, then salvation would come to us as something without any continuity with our nature, with our past, and there would be no organic continuity between 'who I was' before accepting salvation and 'who I will turn out to be' when all is revealed. However, since our nature was seriously damaged, but continues to be human nature, salvation does reach us in the form of a process of the perfecting of our nature. As a result of this, 'who I will turn out to be' has, according to the most traditional Catholic teaching, reaffirmed at the Council of Trent, an organic continuity with 'who I was'.

Thus, what is normal within the living of the Catholic faith, what is normal in the process of growth in grace, is always starting from where one is, knowing that no part of human desire or living out is intrinsically evil, that is to say, incapable of being ordered or healed, only capable of being wiped out. Nevertheless, all our desire is damaged in the way we receive it and live it out: it is seriously distorted. But we can trust that even what is most base within a person's life is capable of being transformed into something which will be a reflection of the divine splendour. What is normal, then, in Catholic anthropology, is to regard no human desire, heavily distorted or addicted to evils of various types though it may be, as a radically perverse entity but rather to see it as something which can in principle be returned to flowing towards what is good.

This, I should say, is an essential part of the Catholic faith. Without this, the whole of Catholic teaching concerning grace, mercy, forgiveness and the sacraments would have to be altered radically. Furthermore, it seems to be part of that *sensus fidei* which Catholics have as an instinct that we understand that the mercy of the Church consists above all, and always, in starting from where one is, and not causing an obstacle to grace by insisting that one has to become something else before being able to receive grace.

The second element in this conflict is the teaching about sexual acts between people of the same sex. Until fairly recently it did not appear that there was a conflict between this teaching and the doctrine of original sin and grace, since the teaching about sexual acts was just that: a teaching about acts and nothing else. It was taught that what was forbidden were any sexual acts whatsoever between people of the same sex, with different reasons brought forth, in different periods, to justify the prohibition.

A false dichotomy

However, what all the reasons took for granted was that such acts would be a perversion of a human nature which tended of itself, and always, towards what we would nowadays call some form of 'heterosexuality'. In prohibiting the acts, nothing was being said about the condition or being of the person, and it was understood that the prohibition didn't affect the *being* of the person, only the acts. That is to say, it used to be possible to say in good conscience to a person who had engaged in such acts that they should desist, and instead seek their flourishing, which they would only achieve if their desire were to return to its normal riverbed. It was, for example, normal to suggest to young men who had confessed acts or thoughts of this nature that they should hurry up and get married so as to be cured. At a time when 'gay' hadn't yet been invented, and there were only 'sodomitical acts', there didn't seem to be a conflict between the teachings about grace and about those acts.

The problem is that over the last several decades these two teachings do appear to have entered into conflict. And the reason is a change in society which has come upon us all, Catholics or not. The change consists in the ever increased recognition during the second half of the twentieth century that it is really not possible to make such a clear-cut distinction between acts and being as had been traditional. It seems that there exist some people, a minority which occurs more or less regularly in all societies and cultures, as well as in the groupings of other animals, who just are 'like that'. This doesn't appear to be an individual aberration, but it just is the case that there is a class of people with the common and recognisable characteristic of a lasting and stable emotional and erotic attraction towards the members of their own sex.

Moreover, if you remove from the psychological profiles of a hundred people only the detail concerning each one's sexual orientation, there is absolutely nothing in the profiles which would allow you to indicate in a regular and accurate way what the orientation corresponding to the profile in fact is. That is to say, the presence of an orientation towards a person of the same sex does not appear to bring along with it any emotional or psychological configuration, even less any deformation, which is not found equally among people of the majority orientation.

The conflict between the two elements of Christian teaching raises its head, then, because while the discussion was about acts and not being, it was thought possible to say to someone at the same time 'Don't do that!' and 'Flourish, brother!' because it was thought that the acts didn't flow from what the brother was. However, it has become ever more problematic if it is understood that someone is just 'like that' for, in part at least, his flourishing will be discovered starting from what he is.

Now this conflict is by no means a merely academic matter. It is lived, very intensely, by many young people for whom working out whether it is a matter of 'I'm just like this, and so I must be this in the richest way possible' or whether it is rather a matter of 'I'm not like this, but I suffer from very grave temptations which in some way I must overcome' is a gravely tortured experience. Evidence suggests that more and more young people are overcoming this conflict by working out that they just are 'like that'. It is on that basis they are going to risk constructing a life.

Being like that

Faced with these conflicts, the Vatican congregations decided to respond. If they conceded that 'being like that' is simply part of nature – part of God's creative project – then it is evident that the acts which flow from that way of being could not be intrinsically evil. Indeed they might be good or bad according to their use and circumstances, as is the case with heterosexual acts. So, they were faced with one of two possibilities: either recognise that 'being like that' is neutral, which means, in the case of everything created, positive, so the absolute prohibition of the acts falls; or deny that 'being like that' exists, except as a defect of a radically heterosexual being, and because of this the traditional absolute prohibition of the acts can be maintained.

Please notice that there are two logical barriers which the ecclesiastical argument cannot jump without falsifying its own doctrine. The first is this: the Church cannot say, 'Well, being that way is normal, something neutral or positive, the Church respects it and welcomes it. The Church only prohibits the acts which flow from it.' This position would lack logic in postulating intrinsically evil acts which flow from a neutral or positive being. And this would go against the principle of Catholic morals which states that acts flow from being – *agere sequitur esse*.

The second barrier is this: the Church cannot say of the homosexual inclination that it is a desire which is in itself intrinsically evil, since to say this would be to fall into the heresy of claiming that there is some part of being human which is essentially depraved – that is, which cannot be transformed, only covered over.

Faced with these two barriers, ecclesiastical logic did a backward double-flip worthy of an Olympic gymnast so as to arrive at the following formulation: 'The homosexual inclination, though not itself a sin, constitutes a tendency towards behaviour that is intrinsically evil, and must therefore be considered objectively disordered.' With this phrase, the Vatican congregations sought to maintain the absolute prohibition of the acts without describing the desire as intrinsically evil.

Nevertheless the price of this definition is very high. It obliges its defenders to insist that the homosexual inclination, independently of any acts flowing from it, is something objectively disordered. And the kind of objectivity they have in mind is deduced not from what can be known through experience, but is an a priori which depends on the Church's teaching concerning marriage, namely the a priori of the intrinsic heterosexuality of all human beings. From the presupposition of the intrinsic heterosexuality of all human beings, it is deduced that the person whose inclination is towards those of the same sex is a defective heterosexual.

Let us not delude ourselves here. This characterisation of the gay or lesbian person as a defective heterosexual is absolutely necessary for the maintenance of the prohibition, as the authors indicate with the 'must be considered' of their phrase. The problem is that, for the characterisation to work properly within the doctrine of original sin and grace, it would have to be the case that the life of grace would lead the gay or lesbian person to become heterosexual in the degree of his or her growth in grace. That is to say, in the degree to which grace makes us more patient, faithful, generous, capable of being good Samaritans, less prisoners of anger, of rivalry and of resentment, just so would it have to change the gender of the persons towards whom we are principally attracted.

The problem is that such changes do not seem to take place in a regular and trustworthy way, even amongst the United States groups which promote them with significant funds and publicity. The senior representatives of such groups admit that at most, and only in some cases, a change in behaviour is produced. The fundamental structures of desire continue to be towards persons of the same sex.[3]

This then is the conflict: for the prohibition of the acts to correspond to the true being of the person, the inclination has to be characterised as something objectively disordered. However, since the inclination doesn't alter, unlike desires which are recognisably vicious, the gay or lesbian person would have a desire which is, in fact, intrinsically evil, an element of radical depravity in their desire. And we would have stepped outside Catholic anthropology. Or, on the other hand, the same-sex inclination is simply something that is, in which case grace will bring it to a flourishing starting from where it is, and with this we would have to work out which acts are appropriate or not, according to the circumstances, and we will have stepped outside the absolute prohibition passed on to us by tradition.

Which truth?

What I want to underline here is that this is a conflict between elements of Catholic doctrine lived by many people. So when people say to gay and lesbian people 'you should just be obedient to the teaching of the Church' it is no frivolity to reply 'sure, but which one? To the uninterrupted teaching about grace and original sin? Or to the recent characterisation which the Vatican congregations now consider necessary in order to maintain the traditional prohibition? Because both together, at the moment, it's not clear how that can be done.' And since all parties to the discussion are in agreement that the teaching on grace is the most important, the conflict is reduced to one concerning the characterisation. Either it is true to affirm that the homosexual inclination is objectively disordered, or it is not.

One side must have got it wrong, and one side must have got it right. And the field of possible error is in the area of what really is. The whole argument turns on the veracity or otherwise of the characterisation of what is. Either being gay is a defective form of being heterosexual, or it is simply a thing that just is that way.

This brings us to the next step. If it were the case that the homosexual inclination truly is a disfiguration of a fundamentally heterosexual structure of desire, then there would be no conflict between the two teachings. There would only be a conflict between the truth and the grave disfiguration of desire in people who don't want to recognise their perversity. This would be a very deeply rooted conflict, of course. However, if it were the case that the homosexual inclination is simply a thing that just is 'like that', and is not a disfiguration of anything, then the official characterisation, and along with it the absolute prohibition, is false. And the deeply rooted conflict would be one between the truth and the grave disfiguration of the intelligence and desire of the forces which do not want to recognise this emerging truth.

And here I return to the fear of God. I consider that it is very dangerous to say, 'one of us is wrong, and since it is certainly not I, it must be you.' Instead I would like to delineate a position which would allow us to seek the truth together and in good faith. I propose it for your consideration, so that it can be seen whether or not what it postulates be legitimate. I do this through some theses, along with some accompanying observations.

My first thesis is this: I consider that the Catholic doctrine of original sin offers in principle the possibility that, over time, we come to learn something about our being human in such a way that a change is undergone not by the doctrine of grace but by its anthropological field of application. Let me explain: if we were to follow the position which Trent regarded (rightly or wrongly) as the Reformed one, human beings are so depraved in our nature that we cannot learn anything true from ourselves, from what is around us, or from waves of change in society. The unique access we have to truth is through revelation, and wherever there is a conflict between the apparent truth known naturally and revelation, then it is revelation which wins out, since our corrupted nature cannot serve as a criterion for truth.

If we were to follow the Catholic position, however, then even though human beings are gravely damaged in our natures, something can indeed be known, even though it be with much difficulty and by sorting through many misconceptions, concerning what is true starting from ourselves and what surrounds us. Furthermore, when there is a conflict between apparent truth known naturally and revelation, the apparent truth known naturally is indeed capable of acting in the role of criterion for our knowledge of divinely revealed truth. It is for this reason that Catholic theology speaks of a 'natural law', because we consider that creation and the new creation have an organic continuity between them which is in principle knowable by the exercise of reason.

From this we deduce the following: if the teaching of the Church were the position labelled 'Reformed', then there would be no possibility of our learning anything authentic concerning, for example, whether the homosexual inclination is a defect in an intrinsically heterosexual being, or if it is something which just is like that. The only thing we could do would be to insist on the characterisation deduced from revelation. However, since the Church's teaching is not this, but is subtly different, then in fact we cannot reject, on purely a priori grounds, the possibility that we human beings might reach, through a difficult path, one interwoven with many false leads, the understanding that what seemed to be a defect in something is not. Rather it is merely a normal occurrence within created matter, with its own tendency to flourishing.

This means that there are no reasons of faith which stand in the way of our carrying on in our search for which of the two positions is closer to the truth. Both parties can participate in the discussion and in the process of learning in good faith.

Pathologies of desire

My second thesis, which follows on from the previous one, goes thus: authentic objectivity about what human beings are can be reached by means of careful study and discernment of the lives of people over time. Since what is now is not totally bereft of continuity with what we shall be in the new creation, then in principle, and with due attention to circumstance, the tendency to corruption or to flourishing which can be detected by means of study and discernment of the lives of people over the long term, does indeed point towards what the person really is. So if it were true that all humans are, by the mere fact of being human, intrinsically heterosexual, then there would be detected in those who, not recognising this, live as if they were gay or lesbian, a growing corruption of their human nature which would affect all the areas of their lives. In the same way there would be detected in people who are apparently of homosexual inclination, but who hold fast to their intrinsic heterosexuality, a growing flourishing in all areas of their life.

Given that we are questioning pathologies of desire, let us take an analogy from the same field. By means of study, we have come to distinguish between people who steal, and people who are kleptomaniacs; between people who take measures to slim, and people who suffer from anorexia; between people who consume alcohol and people who are alcoholics. In each case we know how to distinguish between those acts which, good or bad as they may be in themselves, are not part of an objectively disordered inclination, and those acts which are part of an inclination which we would call objectively disordered. We punish the thief, but we seek treatment for the kleptomaniac. We congratulate the person who goes on a diet, but we seek to help the anorexic.

And we know, furthermore, that our distinction is objective: that kleptomania, anorexia and alcoholism are not only minority behaviour patterns, but conditions which, if they are not controlled, put the health and flourishing of the person into danger. In the same way it should be possible to detect if self-acceptance as gay tends to put in jeopardy a person's health and flourishing, or if, in the case of people who have these desires but do not accept them as part of their being, it is rather this non-acceptance which puts their health and flourishing into danger.

With this I am discounting the following possibility. This would be to affirm that, 'however much we study, human opinions are always so relative that we will never be able to demonstrate anything, so we must stick with revelation, which is the only source capable of objectivity. Besides, revelation in this area would concern a future created heterosexuality which would only be brought to fruition in the heavenly wedding banquet, so any signs of homosexual flourishing now are not revelatory of anything at all.' To discount this is to accept in principle the possibility of saying that belief in the intrinsic heterosexuality of all the members of the human race does not form an obligatory part of the foundations of the Catholic faith, however much it may have been a common presupposition until recently.[4]

This is because we are in principle capable of reaching objectivity about the matter without depending on a doctrinal a priori. We may indeed discover over time that all human beings are intrinsically heterosexual, and that any appearance to the contrary is an illusion. But should we find this not to be the case, then there would be no problem for Catholic doctrine as such, since Catholic doctrine doesn't depend on what might turn out to be a false or uncertain anthropology.

If it were the case that not all human beings are intrinsically heterosexual, then extending the opportunity to marry to same-sex couples would present no threat to the existence of heterosexual marriage, and there would be no logical reason why same-sex couples should be deprived of that opportunity.

I hope that both parties could come to accept these theses in principle. Which would allow me to advance a third thesis. Since we are in a field where reality is greater than the positions which are currently held as certain, or, to put it another way, where truth is ahead of all of us and obliges all of us to allow our perceptions to be expanded by study and knowledge, there remain to be established the criteria which would allow a common agreement concerning what might constitute flourishing in the case of people of homosexual inclination.

For example, there are things which are no longer in question. There is no sort of empirical evidence to suggest that a person of homosexual inclination be, for that reason, either more or less capable of exercising whatsoever profession. A person's excellence as pilot, gardener, nurse, teacher, surgeon, accountant, postman or priest seems to be in no way affected by their sexual orientation. Nor is there any evidence to suggest that the habitual sexual practices corresponding to the inclination affect those exercises of excellence except in cases of compulsive behaviour, which are certainly no monopoly of those of homosexual inclination.

One would have to say that the fact that 'the children of this world', normally so astute at perceiving the sort of excellences which would allow them an advantage over others, have not detected that the presence of gay people in their companies, their armies, or their professions, lessens their competitive advantages begins to speak strongly in favour of 'being gay' making no difference at all in the field of professional, economic and social viability. This would suggest that there begins to be a strong probability that the homosexual inclination of itself does not lead to any diminishment of human flourishing.

However, it would, in my view, be insufficient to allow the matter to be considered resolved on this evidence. It might be the case that social and economic forces were happy to use a characteristic, let us say, of personal instability, or a habit of maintaining appearances, so as to have a strong and loyal employee who could be used in the service of a profession for a certain time, but who could finally be sacked as he or she burns out through lack of a healthy basis of personal living.

Personal flourishing

For it is not only social and economic flourishing which must be considered, but personal flourishing. And it is here that we would have to work out what are to be the criteria for flourishing. My suggestion, some more or less adequate questions, would be of this sort: does a person of homosexual inclination who accepts himself as such tend, because of this, to be more capable of personal responsibility, of developing interpersonal relationships in a serene manner, of truthfulness, of compassion, of acting in a non-possessive way, of overcoming rivalries, and of generosity extended over time, or less?

There would be two fields of comparison. The first would be between those of undoubted heterosexual inclination on the one hand, and those of a homosexual inclination, whether accepted or not, on the other. If it could be demonstrated as a stable, repeated and consistent result that people of homosexual inclination tend to be less capable of responsibility, of serene interpersonal relationships, of truthfulness, of compassion, of acting in a non-possessive way, of overcoming rivalries, and of generosity extended over time, then, given equality of social circumstance (a big 'if' for a group which will always and inevitably be a minority group), there would at least be a strong suspicion that there is something defective in the inclination itself. I have not yet seen a serious study which demonstrates this, but this should not rule out the possibility of closer study.

The second field of comparison would be between people of homosexual inclination who accept that their inclination is part of their being, and that their flourishing flows from this, people who in a certain technical language were referred to as 'egosyntonic', on the one hand; and on the other, people who deny that their inclination is part of their 'I', being rather a heavy yoke to be borne and the cause of severe temptations which must be overcome, people who in that same technical language were referred to as 'egodystonic'. If it could be demonstrated as a stable, repeated and consistent result that the former tend to be less capable in all the previously described areas than the latter, then we would have very good evidence to suggest that the homosexual inclination, far from being a thing which just is 'like that' is instead some sort of defect, and when it is treated as such, then the true nature of the person tends to flourish. And if not, not.

Now, of course, there may be other suggestions about the type of criteria which should be employed, and I welcome their being raised. My thesis is precisely that the appropriate criteria are yet to be established.

What is clear, however, is that for anyone who is interested in the truth, this matter can no longer be put off. It seems that even now the Vatican congregations are discussing among themselves the criteria for admission to seminaries. One of their points of interest is exactly this one. If it is true that those who are 'egodystonic' are those most capable of flourishing, because they correspond more closely to the reality of being human, then it would be worthwhile to undertake a massive education campaign concerning this among young people, clearly demonstrating all the evidence so that those who have allowed themselves to become 'egosyntonic' either become dystonic or do not present themselves as candidates for the priesthood. But if it is not true, if it is the case rather that the egosyntonic are more likely to flourish, then it is very much in the interest of the whole Church, which traditionally has a considerably higher proportion of men of homosexual inclination among its clergy than that which appears in the general population, that its own employees dwell in truth.

So my fourth and last thesis is simple. It is that we can no longer put off seeking the truth of this matter in the Church. It is something for our new Pope, Benedict XVI, to consider. I draw his attention to some words of his predecessor, John Paul II:

> [Many] cases of 'social' sin are the result of the accumulation and concentration of many personal sins ... It is a case of the very personal sins of those who cause or support evil or who exploit it; of those who are in a position to avoid, eliminate or at least limit social evils but who fail to do so out of laziness, fear, or the conspiracy of silence, through secret complicity or indifference; or, of those who take refuge in the supposed impossibility of changing the world, and also of those who sidestep the effort and sacrifice required, producing specious reasons of a higher order.[5]

Now the validity of this teaching is independent of what turns out to be the truth about the homosexual inclination. If the inclination is an objective disorder, then those who are certain that it is must consider that the fact of hiding this reality tends to produce a very grave social ill. They should provide both funds and human resources in a convincing educational programme, starting from well-elaborated and well-trusted empirical data which demonstrate the truthfulness of their position and make it more and more difficult to ignore. They will have, as a matter of urgency, to exclude from seminaries and houses of religious formation all those people, whether 'formators' or 'formandi' who are not fully convinced by the true characterisation, since it would be very cruel to allow people who believe that their way of being is compatible with Christian living to remain in their delusion, wasting their time and their life uselessly.

The traditional ecclesiastical ambiguity in this sphere, the usual 'don't ask, don't tell', will have to be changed into something much more rigorous. The fact that there seems to be a growing conviction everywhere that this position is wrong should encourage rather than discourage the desire to make truth resplendescent in the world.

If, on the other hand, the homosexual inclination is something that just is 'like that', nothing more, the late Holy Father's phrases are no less urgent, and have a special field of application within ecclesiastical structures. For there can be very clearly detected within them dishonest social realities which are the fruit of many personal sins, situations of evil where many people have failed to tell the truth through fear of its consequences. People who have more than a strong suspicion that being gay is not an objective disorder, and who might well have committed themselves to building up the common good in their respective societies, but who fail to face up to the lie 'out of laziness, fear, or the conspiracy of silence, through secret complicity or indifference'; the attitude 'of those who take refuge in the supposed impossibility of changing the world, and also of those who sidestep the effort and sacrifice required, producing specious reasons of a higher order'.[6]

The enemy of the truth in this matter is not so much the stridency of voices opposed to change, but the silence of those who have more than a strong suspicion that the official position is nothing more than the production of a 'specious reason of a higher order'. I pray that we be gifted with both fear of God and with mercy towards the cowardice in our own and others' hearts so that we may have the courage to seek the truth together, and the charity to leave no one in the place of shame in which Professor Mayer and the ecclesiastical superiors who knew his position, dwelt in silence and complicity.

Notes

1. For greater clarification of the relationship between *fear of God* and the virtue of hope of which it is a formative part cf. Josef Pieper, 'Hope', and especially section V, 'Fear as gift' in *Faith, Hope, Love* (San Francisco: Ignatius, 1997).

2. I refer to pp. 60–77 of the London: Pimlico, 1995 edition of *Into That Darkness*.

3. I am basing this judgement of mine on my own experiences with such groups, on conversations with Jeremy Marks and other leaders of the formerly ex-gay group Courage (UK), and on Wayne Besen's book *Anything but straight* (New York: Harrington Park Press, 2003).

4. This is not, of course, to question that as a matter of common sense, human reproduction is intrinsically dependent on the biological complementarity of the sexes.

5. John Paul II, Post-Synodal Apostolic Exhortation *Reconciliatio et Paenitentia* (1984), para. 16.

6. ibid.

Chapter Seven

Teenage Pregnancy: Are the Churches to Blame?

Jane Fraser

The United Kingdom has the worst record on teenage pregnancy in Europe. Around 41,000 teenagers under the age of 18 in England become pregnant each year, including nearly 6,000 who are under 16. While some of these young people and their children go on to have happy and fulfilled lives, many do not. All too common are stories of unfinished education, poor employment prospects, low income and poor housing. This in turn results in poor physical, emotional and spiritual health for both the young parents and their children. Those who choose to terminate their pregnancy face fewer long-term consequences, in the form of regret for their decision or social disadvantage, but concerns for the individual by her social and faith communities are, nonetheless, also significant.

The response of the British government was to introduce a teenage pregnancy strategy in July 1999, with the aim of halving the number of teenage conceptions over a period of ten years and increasing by 60 per cent the level of teenage parent participation in education, training and employment so as to reduce the risk of long-term social exclusion. A comprehensive programme of national and local initiatives has produced encouraging progress on meeting these very challenging targets.

By way of contrast, there has been no significant policy initiative from the major faith communities. The independent advisory group to the government's Teenage Pregnancy Unit has two members who were appointed as faith advisors on the basis of our faith perspective and pro-fessional experience of these issues, myself and Martin Pendergast. Our remit is to enable faith communities to recognise the important part they have to play in ensuring the targets of the teenage pregnancy strategy are met as well as playing our own individual part in shaping that strategy.

The first step was to undertake a mapping exercise to identify faith organisations that might support the Teenage Pregnancy Unit's aims. Those we sought out covered both bodies with a religious focus and charities. Contact was then established through a twice-yearly inter-faith forum. A significant feature of what has emerged so far is that develop-ment has been piecemeal, often arising from local initiatives, driven by the motivation of individuals and local groups in response to the identi-fied need. In some instances this has been done in the face of a lack of encouragement by those in positions of authority within their faith group.

Given that the major faiths in this country are generally perceived as placing great importance on the maintenance of high standards of sexual morality, this lack of clear engagement in the issue of high rates of teenage pregnancy and the churches' possible culpability is one that needs to be taken seriously. There is an historical background to this situation, as well as factors inhibiting current engagement. But there are also remedies, based on examples of good practice.

The long view

Christian churches in Britain have a long history of either sheltering or supporting 'fallen women' (more usually prostitutes but also those who had sexual relations outside of marriage). These have included the unmarried mother and her 'illegitimate' child. However, it was not until the nineteenth century that this concern became more formalised into a network of organisations and institutions that expressed, on the one hand, an active Christian concern for the plight of the women and/or their children and, on the other, a desire for reform and reintegration into mainstream society.

Prior to this there were many notable examples of humanitarian concern leading to the establishment of institutions. Most famous were Thomas Coram's Foundling Hospital established in 1739 and The Magdalen Hospital, opened in 1758 by Robert Dingley. Although these founders were laymen, their motives were religious as well as humani-tarian. Religious training was regarded as a fundamental part of the process of reclamation.

The Magdalen, for example, had its own chapel and chaplain and quickly won the respect and support of the Church. This led to the estab-lishment of other charities with a similar purpose during the nineteenth century and so a 'combination of piety, complacency and, withal, a genuine desire to help, so characteristic of nineteenth century rescue work, was … firmly established'.[1]

The Poor Law Amendment Act of 1834 reflected the attitudes and assumptions held by devout Christians (among others) that it was the woman's responsibility to resist temptation not the man's to refrain from offering it, and that, should she fail, the woman should suffer the full consequences of her fall. However, the increasing economic and social distress of unmarried mothers and their 'illegitimate' children was a source of concern to the growing Evangelical Movement and, by the middle of the nineteenth century, a number of compassionate initiatives had begun to emerge. Notable among these were the Female Aid Mission and the London Moonlight Mission.

At the same time, the Clewer House of Mercy, the Wantage Sisters of St Mary the Virgin and penitentiaries and similar institutions were being founded by Tractarians and Anglo-Catholics. The Catholic Children's Rescue Society and, later, the Church of England Children's Society were just two examples of organisations set up at this time by the churches to care for destitute children, many of whom were 'illegitimate'.

This multiplication of effort highlighted the need for coordination. A role for the institutional Church in controlling and guiding what had hitherto been largely spontaneous and individual efforts began to emerge. The Church Penitentiary Association was formed and pursued this aim mainly by distributing grants only to those institutions that were 'under the management of self-devoted women with the ministration of a chaplain of the Church of England in spiritual matters and its application signed by the bishop of the diocese'.[2]

From another wing of the Church, not specifically Anglican, came the Reformatory and Refuge Union, founded in 1856 by the seventh Earl of Shaftesbury. Their Female Penitentiaries' Special Fund was used to give direct and practical help to women and girls in need and to pay women missionaries to 'go out into the streets at night distributing tracts and speaking kind words to the unhappy creatures they found there'.[3] The Female Mission also sponsored institutions of a kind that were a key feature of moral welfare work until the mid twentieth century. These could be described as a 'Refuge for Deserted Mothers and Home for their Illegitimate Infants' and offered short-term care to the nursing mother.

Following this, they would also offer long-term care to the child, which might take the form of foster care, while the mother went out to work. The mother was thus expected to contribute to the child's upkeep, an early recognition of the possibility of rehabilitating the mother through her child.

Although 'self-devoted women', backed by concerned and compassionate men, were undertaking much-needed rescue work as an expression of their Christian concern for 'fallen women' and the unmarried mother and her child, the concept of prevention was not to emerge until Josephine Butler and Ellice Hopkins brought new insights to bear on what was seen as 'this social evil'. They wanted to create a society with a single moral standard for both men and women and, in parallel with this, a judicial system that would be impartial in its dealings with both sexes. They also wished to make it less easy for girls to 'go wrong', encourage men to refrain from seducing them, and to substitute compassion for hostility and condemnation to them.

The repeal of the Contagious Diseases Act was a successful attack on the double moral standard that was prevalent at that time. It could also be seen as an attack on the mores of a society that outlawed the prostitute so completely that even the common processes of justice were not considered applicable where she was concerned.

Butler and Hopkins were also involved in the battle resulting in the passing of the Criminal Law (Amendment) Act of 1885 which, as well as suppressing brothels, raised the age of consent to 16 in order to protect girls from sexual exploitation and early pregnancy. Ellice Hopkins was encouraged by Dr James Hinton to 'rouse educated women, and through them their husbands and their sons, to a sense of their duty with regard to the social evil'.[4]

Her work led to the foundation of the Church of England Purity Society and the White Cross Army (not specifically Anglican), which later amalgamated in 1891 to form the popular White Cross League. It demanded from its members high standards of personal conduct and a 'chivalrous respect for womanhood'. They were expected to work towards raising the tone of public opinion in respect of sexual behaviour and to combat the prevailing double standard of sexual morality. At the same time, women were being urged not to leave to chance the instruction of their sons about 'the facts of life' and to instil in them a sense of responsibility about sexual relationships.

This new approach to the problem of immorality, creating pressure for reform, ran alongside continuing work by those committed to rescue work. There was, though, increasing criticism of the harsh and rigid treatment often given to girls in such institutions. Mrs Bramwell Booth, who oversaw the activities of the Salvation Army in this regard, stated that she could not imagine herself becoming any better for a long stay in such harsh surroundings.[5]

The basis of rescue work was essentially religious, undertaken for the love of God and motivated by a belief in the worth of each human soul. It was not, however, until the end of the nineteenth century that the Church began, slowly and tentatively, to accept direct responsibility for work done in its name, a process that was not completed until the early twentieth century when training of workers and a statement of the ideals and principles underlying rescue work were drawn up.

The new social conditions created by the First World War prompted a new approach, reflecting the effect of the war on the economic and social position of women, relationships between the sexes, and attitudes generally. Some women were able to exploit the increased opportunities for acceptable substitutes to marriage and family, but for many the large numbers of 'surplus women' generated restlessness and frustration. The spread of information about contraception and its greater use meant that, at least among the more educated, there was a reduction in the risk of unwanted children. A steady decrease in the legitimate birth rate and the loss of so many lives in the First World War stimulated a desire to develop all forms of maternity and child welfare work and, in particular, focus attention on the problem of the higher death rate among babies born out of wedlock. Local authorities were now empowered to give grants to voluntary organisations catering for the unmarried mother and her child. This made increased residential provision possible, while the accompanying inspection led to improved standards.

The National Council for the Unmarried Mother and her Child was formed in 1918 and set out to reform and educate public opinion towards a constructive rather than a punitive approach to the unmarried mother. They insisted on the responsibilities of fathers as well as mothers, campaigning for realistic affiliation orders and advocating that wherever possible, mother and child should remain together. However, at the same time there was a growing movement that sought to provide a normal home and family for the child, though this came at the cost of complete separation from the mother through legalised adoption. This culminated in the passing of the Adoption of Children Act of 1926.

One of the major features of 'moral welfare' work with unmarried mothers during and immediately following the Second World War was the central role played by the Christian churches in providing Mother and Baby Homes for unmarried mothers before and during their confinement. Afterwards the churches acted as agents for the adoption of these women's babies. Partly because of social stigma and partly because of economic reality, only rarely was an unmarried mother able to move towards caring for the baby herself.

With the introduction of reliable methods of contraception in the mid 1960s and the greater sexual freedom associated with the knowledge that sexual intercourse need not necessarily lead to pregnancy, attitudes towards pre-marital sexual relationships and illegitimacy changed dramatically. This, coupled with greater economic prosperity and full employment, led to a decline in demand for Mother and Baby Homes and a growing tendency for unmarried mothers to keep their babies.

With the growth of the welfare state after the Second World War came the recognition that the state had a primary role to play in providing social and medical care, regardless of social status. Voluntary organisations, including those sponsored by the churches, continued to have a role in highlighting unmet need, pioneering innovative services or catering for their own or a restricted group of people. Hence, during the post-war years, Christian organisations experienced in 'moral welfare' work with unmarried mothers provided a significant proportion of the adoption placements until the necessary knowledge and expertise was acquired by the (then) local authority Children's Departments.

Without the basis of rescue work and the need to campaign for reform and recognition of the needs of this stigmatised group, the motivation and credibility of the Christian churches in relation to pre-marital sexual relationships and its consequences was almost completely extinguished. Moral crusades against abortion and teenage sexual relationships continued to be promoted by some Christian groups and individuals but direct responsibility for such work was not taken up again by the institutional Church in any of the main Christian denominations.

Moreover, with the values base of the social work and other caring professions (both Church and secular) largely focused on prevention, self-determination, care in the community and respect for the beliefs and culture of the individual, much of the missionary zeal had gone out of work with those facing unplanned pregnancies. It is hard to imagine a campaign such as that promoted by the White Cross League attracting such extensive, popular support now as it did in the 1890s. The reasons for this are many and varied, some arising from the need to respect a wide range of cultural and faith-based values in Britain, some from medical and legal developments that have separated sexual intercourse from the inevitability of pregnancy and/or childbirth, and some from the teachings of the churches (or what they are perceived to teach).

When the Abortion Act was passed in 1967, it became possible for many women facing an unplanned pregnancy to consider a termination of the pregnancy as an alternative to either struggling to care for the child alone or placing the child for adoption. Abortion avoided the long-term consequences that moral welfare work aimed to address and as a result, church-sponsored social work gradually lost its main focus on the consequences of sexual behaviour.

However, despite this, none of the options open to the young woman facing an unplanned pregnancy was an easy one, each having the potential to create problems. Those providing abortion services or acting as referral agents soon became aware of the need for careful counselling. The services that emerged at this time give a valuable insight into the changing role of the churches in response to the rising number of teenage pregnancies. The consequences of the Abortion Act illustrate the current dilemma.

No easy answers

The Christian faith holds that human life is sacred and thus to be cherished and respected. Taking a human life, therefore, is only to be condoned in exceptional circumstances. Consequently, many Christians, most notably those who hold to the teaching of the Catholic Church, believe abortion to be a sin. The churches, however, vary in their teachings about the circumstances under which a termination of pregnancy might be deemed to be acceptable, based partly on the need to preserve the life of the mother and partly on an understanding of the stage at which life begins.

Prior to the twentieth century this was believed to be at the stage of 'quickening' (when the foetus is first felt to be moving) but as modern medical diagnostic techniques have identified how advanced development is during the first weeks *in utero*, the debate has moved to identify life, or the potential for life, either at conception or at implantation. Further debate centres on the stage at which the foetus becomes viable independently of the mother.

Although there is evidence that abortion was almost as common prior to the passing of the Abortion Act in 1967 as in the following years, the growing number of legal abortions has caused considerable concern among Christians, in particular among Catholics. The Society for the Protection of Unborn Children (SPUC) was established initially to oppose the liberalising of abortion legislation but has continued to campaign on this issue and to work with women facing an unplanned pregnancy with the aim of promoting alternatives to abortion. The Catholic Church does not sponsor it but a large proportion of its supporters are from that denomination.

Running parallel with this development was the establishment of the Brook Advisory Centres by Helen Brook who was a Catholic concerned to make provision for young people who were sexually active but who wished to avoid an unwanted pregnancy. Her primary motivation was the avoidance of unwanted pregnancy and abortion through education and the provision of reliable contraception.

Both of these organisations offered advice to those facing an unplanned and possibly unwanted pregnancy. Both organisations contained Christians whose professional concern was motivated by their faith, as well as some of other faiths or none. Although Brook Centres focused on the needs of the young and unmarried, the main difference between the two organisations was in the values that motivated them and their attitude towards abortion. Those who attended SPUC for advice about a problem pregnancy would be encouraged to avoid a termination of pregnancy. Those who attended Brook Centres would be encouraged to consider all options open to them and to decide on that basis what, for them, was the better (or least onerous) solution.

About two thirds of the young people thus counselled at Brook opted to continue the pregnancy and a third asked to be referred for consideration for an abortion.[6] This proportion has remained fairly constant over the years. The attitudes and values espoused by SPUC were based on a desire to turn people away from abortion. The attitudes and values espoused by Brook Centres were based on a desire to enable young people to evaluate critically the options open to them, based on accurate information and personal circumstances, to grieve for the ideal that cannot now be realised in this situation, and thus to offer the opportunity to learn from and grow within the process of following the decision through.

Counselling at Brook Centres was undertaken by qualified and experienced social workers or psychologists whose work was subject to peer review, training and supervision. Those who were of a Christian faith (mainly from Protestant denominations) had, in the early days of this work, given careful thought to the moral dilemma thus posed, whereby they might find themselves supporting someone who had chosen to seek a termination of the pregnancy, whereas they themselves, if faced with a similar situation, would see this as contra-indicated by their faith. As professionals working in a secular setting and as Christians, their focus was on the need for these young women to explore what, for them (and, as far as possible, the father of the child), was the 'right' solution, in the sense of having the greater potential for good. As one of those social workers explained:

> If the death and resurrection of Jesus Christ is the basis for our understanding of how good can come from evil and nothing is too evil that it cannot be redeemed, it has a very powerful message for a young person facing a problem pregnancy when, in effect, they 'cannot do right for doing wrong'. There is no ideal solution, for each solution to the problem falls short of the ideal. Hence the young woman needs to be encouraged to seek what for her seems to have the greater potential for good. I believe she should then be supported by her church community in realising that potential for good.
>
>   Freedom of choice lies at the root of this approach and is based in the freedom to choose good or evil that God gave to humanity at our creation as embodied in the story of Adam and Eve in the Garden of Eden. It is also based on the supreme example of humanity's freedom of choice in the risk God faced in allowing His people to choose to accept their Messiah or reject Him.[7]

What is of particular relevance to the churches' involvement in work with teenage parents and those at risk of pregnancy is that Brook Centres grew in number and credibility among young people throughout the latter part of the twentieth century, offering advice on relationships and contraception. Although not an abortion referral agency, its professional approach to counselling those facing a problem pregnancy was then taken on by district health authorities when setting up similar services. Moreover, the educational materials produced by Brook, and based on their experience of listening to young people and responding to their needs, were increasingly seen as brand leaders with credibility amongst young people and those working with them on issues related to their sexuality.

On the other hand, educational work and written materials produced by SPUC were seen as actively promoting one particular position on the subject rather than a balance of perspectives and were, at times, alleged to be factually inaccurate. Their acceptance in educational circles was, therefore, limited.

At present, one in three women experience an abortion at some stage in their reproductive lives. Young people are therefore aware that this issue has a direct relevance to their lives in that they may know a sister, cousin, aunt or friend who has sought this solution to an unwanted pregnancy. They therefore have real difficulty in identifying abortion as inherently evil but see it, rather, as a distressing and potentially harmful consequence of unplanned pregnancy or unprotected sexual intercourse. They are therefore unlikely to heed the condemnation of abortion promoted by SPUC and the Vatican.

What is more likely to resonate with them is a realistic presentation, based on credible scenarios that raise awareness of the fact that a young woman facing an unplanned and unwanted pregnancy may have to choose between options, all of which she may see as morally wrong. We have already considered the premise that most Christians see abortion as in principle to be avoided (as, indeed, do people of other faiths). Bringing up a child without adequate material, emotional and social resources may also be seen as sinful given the primacy of the child afforded by Jesus in the gospels.[8] What is less frequently acknowledged is that, in some cultures within the UK and some socio-economic groups, giving up responsibility for one's flesh and blood through adoption is also seen as morally reprehensible.

Although this may seem like a 'no win' situation, it does highlight the need to consider the circumstances and the conscience of each person when faced with a complex dilemma with implications for the young woman's future spiritual, emotional, social and physical welfare. This, then, in my opinion, should be a focus for the Church's professional engagement in what could be termed a twenty-first-century equivalent of nineteenth-century rescue work.

Engaging with the solution

If, however, the Church is to regain a position of strength and authority in relation to prevention of the circumstances leading to the unacceptably high rate of teenage pregnancy in the UK, it needs first to be engaged in the solution. To return to my previous analysis of developments following the Abortion Act, it was only through active engagement in providing services for young people who were already sexually active, and then listening to their needs, that Brook was able to develop educational materials that were seen as credible by young people. At the same time they met the needs of teachers and other professionals working with them who required resources that engaged young people in the process of considering information and viewpoints in order to understand the issues for themselves.

Indeed, for twenty years, most of this material was written by the author, a priest in the Church of England, based on her previous professional role as a counsellor in a Brook Centre. The Christian churches would do well to consider fostering more vocations to priestly ministry within the youth work, health and sex education professions as a mark of their commitment to young people's moral and sexual development. It is my experience that many youth workers in the Church and voluntary sectors are acutely aware of the need for such work but feel ill equipped to engage in it. They are also fearful of the possibility of a negative reaction from their sponsoring body. Given the high proportion of youth work sponsored by church-based organisations and groups, this is a sad reflection on the role of such bodies around sexual matters and the need to invest in training to a professional standard.

This is not to deny the valuable role that can also be played by voluntary initiatives. The Mothers' Union in Wakefield, for example, ran a highly successful crèche for teenage mothers to enable them to access education on the same premises as their babies. A high standard of care was provided under the supervision of a qualified nursery nurse but the informal friendships of the Mothers' Union volunteers and the practical advice and support offered gave the young mothers an unthreatening insight into Christian family life and values.

Christian churches, on the whole, promote the ideal of abstinence from sex before marriage and faithfulness within it even if, at the same time, they accept its diminishing role within a committed relationship. However, throughout the Church's history this is an ideal that has more often been honoured in the breach than the observance. The situation has been exacerbated in modern times by a combination of early physical maturity, extended education and delayed marriage and child-bearing trends, as well as the development of reliable forms of contraception.[9] [10] The response of Christian groups has varied from promoting the use of reliable forms of contraception to the promotion of abstinence through pledges. As with abortion, the difference in approach has largely, but not exclusively, been along denominational lines, with Protestants being more comfortable with the use of contraception than Catholics.

However, this has not always been the case. Historically almost all Christians were opposed to birth control on the grounds that it challenged God's unique authority over issues of life and death. This stance has since been abandoned by almost all church leaders in the Protestant traditions as well as, in practice, by large numbers of the Catholic laity. However, amongst young people and those on the fringe of the Catholic Church, the prohibition of all but 'natural' methods of birth control can lead to a lack of confidence in seeking contraceptive advice when it is needed to prevent an unplanned and possibly unwanted pregnancy.

Although 86 per cent of parents feel strongly that there would be fewer teenage pregnancies if more parents talked to their children about sex, relationships and contraception,[11] attitudes of young people vary markedly from their parents' generation even among those of faith. Professor Leslie Francis' research of adolescents in England and Wales[12] found that only 14 per cent of adolescents saw pre-marital sexual intercourse as wrong and this figure only rose by 1 per cent among the Christians in the survey. The Church needs to take account of what these young people are telling us.

The Church's credibility is also weakened by the fact that the Bible has so little to say that is clear and unambiguous on this subject, and there is such a brief church history of what we regard as the tradition of abstinence before marriage. For example, pre-marital cohabitation in the form of 'betrothal' was more usual and a range of informal marriage practices was widespread until the passing of the Hardwicke Act in 1753.

Breaking the pledge

What is of particular concern is that although the promotion of abstinence before marriage through such schemes as the US *True Love Waits* does initially delay sexual activity, when the young people who sign the pledge fail to adhere to it (as 88 per cent eventually do[13]) they are around one-third less likely to use contraceptives as they are not 'prepared for an experience that they have promised to forego'.[14] The result is that abstinence programmes are associated with an increase in the number of pregnancies among the partners of young male participants.[15] Churches that promote such programmes are therefore more likely to be associated with the cause of the high rate of teenage pregnancy than with a solution to it.

In contrast there is strong evidence concerning the effectiveness of comprehensive sex and relationship education, linked to accessible services, which encourages young people to delay sexual activity but also encourages them to use contraception if they do have sex.[16] Moreover, a consistent theme in current research is that parents are a preferred source of sexual education but that many young people recognise that they don't currently have that sort of relationship with their parents or are too embarrassed to contemplate such discussions.[17] Enabling parents to undertake this role and complement comprehensive school sex education programmes should therefore be the preferred approach if the churches see preventing teenage pregnancy as a priority, as it is also a key factor in delaying first sexual intercourse and improving contraceptive use.[18]

The Church seems to have returned to the tradition of 'betrothal' that persisted well into the nineteenth century in western society. It is now unusual for young couples getting married in church not to have already established a sexual relationship. Young people of the Christian faith are more likely to express their commitment to their partner in a mutually exclusive and faithful sexual relationship than their parents were when they were young and unmarried (as evidenced in comparative figures for age at first sexual intercourse).

They are more likely, too, to rejoice in that intimacy and do so without fear or shame when avoiding the risk of pregnancy or infection. It would appear, therefore, that the Church needs to focus on fostering commitment and encouraging the development of young people's skills in negotiating relationships, in building the friendships and social intimacy skills they need before embarking on a sexual relationship within a relationship of commitment if they are to be able to aspire to the Christian ideal of mutuality, faithfulness and respect. Certainly, research into what young people themselves want consistently reflects this view.[19]

Research does not suggest that providing young people with sex and relationship education and contraceptive advice increases sexual activity.[20] There are now a few examples of Christian bodies promoting personal and sexual relationship education from a faith perspective. The Christian education charity Care has developed its own pro-marriage sex education pack for schools, *Evaluate,* which preaches delaying sex rather than chastity and is based on the fact that early sexual activity (under the age of sixteen) is associated with significantly higher levels of regret, of non use of contraception and conception before the age of eighteen.[21] The Catholic archdiocese of Birmingham, under the leadership of Father Joseph Quigley, has produced a more comprehensive package of personal and sexual relationship education, *All That I Am*. He comments:

> I'm convinced that trying to lower the teenage pregnancy rate is intimately related to trying to improve young people's self-esteem and their understanding of their dignity. If we reduce the ways of looking at development simply to strategies of saying 'no', we are failing to understand the issue of dignity and the gift of sexuality.[22]

The scheme includes both a primary and secondary curriculum and is backed by a programme of support for teachers delivering the course. It is hoped that schools sponsored by other denominations may use the programme to tackle these issues.

Young people today see themselves as having a right to choose what, for them, is compatible with an innate sense of what is right. And yet this is not a free for all in the values sense. We know from research conducted in the mid 1990s,[23] [24] that religion persists as an important predictor of adolescent values over a wide range of areas, including sexual and relationship values. The same research casts serious doubt on the often-held assumption that religion is so privatised and marginalised in the modern world of young people that the faith dimension of their social and sexual values is irrelevant.

I believe that it is therefore incumbent on the Church to speak to them about their sexuality in terms that relate to their experience of growing up in the new millennium, that we listen to the moral values that they espouse and aspire to and involve ourselves in meaningful dialogue with them both within our churches and in the secular setting of schools, youth groups and young people's advice centres. Hopefully, this should lead to the churches once more being seen as providing a solution to the problem of teenage pregnancy rather than being, at least to some extent, to blame.

Notes

1. Quoted in M. Penelope Hall and Ismene V. Howes, *The Church in Social Work* (Routledge & Kegan Paul 1965), p. 15.
2. *Annual Report of the Church Penitentiary Association, 1876–1877.*
3. *Report of Reformatory and Refuge Union, 1866.*
4. Rosa M. Barrett, *Ellice Hopkins* (Wells, Gardner, Darton & Co. Ltd 1907).

5. Madge Unsworth, *Maiden Tribute* (Salvation Army Publicity and Supplies 1949), p. 37.
6. Figures quoted in the Annual Reports of Birmingham Brook Advisory Centre, 1975–1980.
7. J. Fraser, 'What do young people want to say to the churches about their sexuality?', *CSCS Newsletter* 19 (Winter 2002/3) as a report of a Churches Together in Britain and Ireland (CTBI) Consultation.
8. Matthew 18:4f.; Mark 9:36; Luke 9:48.
9. Average age at first marriage is now around 30 years and less than 1% of people marrying are virgins. See *Population Trends no. 119* (London: The Stationery Office, Spring 2005).
10. Average age at birth of first child is 29.5 years. See *Population Trends no. 118*, (London: The Stationery Office, June 2004).
11. BMRB International, *Evaluation of the Teenage Pregnancy Strategy: Tracking Survey. Report of Results of Benchmark Wave* (January 2001).
12. Leslie J. Francis, *The Fourth R for the Third Millennium: Education in Religion and Values for the Global Future* (Lindisfarne Books 2001).
13. Alan Guttmacher Institute, *Sex Education: Needs, Programs and Policies: Occasional Report* (New York: The Alan Guttmacher Institute, April 2004).
14. A. DiCenso, G. Guyatt, A. Willan and L. Griffith, 'Interventions to reduce unintended pregnancies among adolescents: systematic review of randomised controlled trials', *British Medical Journal* 324 (7531):1426 (2002).
15. ibid.
16. UNICEF, *A League Table of Teenage Births in Rich Nations*. Innocenti Report Card No. 3 (Florence: UNICEF Innocenti Research Centre, 2001).
17. John Coleman, *Key Data on Adolescence* (Trust for the Study of Adolescence 2005).
18. C. Swann, K. Bowie, G. McCormick and M. Kosmin, *Teenage Pregnancy and Parenthood: A Review of Reviews. Evidence Briefing* (London: Health Development Agency, 2003).
19. BMRB International, *Evaluation of the Teenage Pregnancy Strategy: Tracking Survey. Report of Results of Benchmark Wave* (January 2001).
20. D. Kirby, *Emerging Answers: Research Findings on Programs to Reduce Unwanted Teenage Pregnancy and Parenthood* (Washington DC: National Campaign to Prevent Teen Pregnancy, 2001).
21. K. Wellings, K. Nanchahal, W. Macdowall, S. McManus, R. Erens et al., 'Sexual Behaviour in Britain: Early Heterosexual Experience', *Lancet* 358:1843–50 (2001).
22. Fr Joseph Quigley, quoted in *The Birmingham Post*, 8.2.2002.
23. L. J. Francis and W. K. Kay, *Teenage Religion and Values* (Leominster, 1995).
24. R. Gill, *Churchgoing and Christian Ethics* (Cambridge, 1999).

Chapter Eight

Educating in a Time of HIV/AIDS

Jon Fuller SJ and James Keenan SJ

Let us consider a fact. Although the AIDS epidemic has historically had its greatest impact in sub-Saharan Africa, where 25 million of the world's 42 million HIV-infected persons reside,[1] a troubling pattern of growth in the giant Asian countries of India and China portends an even more frightening future for the global epidemic as the virus establishes a foothold in the region.

In September 2004, Richard Feachem, Executive Director of the Global Fund to Fight AIDS, Tuberculosis and Malaria, reported that the number of infections in India had probably surpassed the previously highest number of 5.6 million infections in South Africa. In March 2005, the United Nations warned that unless large-scale effort for prevention, HIV testing and treatment are put rapidly into place in China, that country will likely count 10 million infections by 2010.[2] [3] These statistics, like so many others about HIV/AIDS, make us realise how much the virus is outdistancing our response to it.

If the pandemic is continuing to advance relentlessly despite current prevention and treatment efforts, we must examine ourselves critically, confronting the world, the Church, and the academy by asking how, in 2005, after 24 years' experience, can we be doing so poorly in the face of this epidemic? For those of us who work in educational institutes, we must especially ask: how well are we teaching?

This was the central question posed at a plenary session of the XVth International HIV/AIDS Conference held in Bangkok in July 2004 by Dr Mary Crewe of the Centre for the Study of AIDS at Pretoria University, South Africa. She asked what educational institutions should do when 42 million people are currently living with HIV/AIDS and an additional 25 million have already died.[4] In light of such obvious failure, can we continue to educate as we do, or ought we to aim at a more transformative model of moral education?

In promoting the latter, Dr Crewe reminds us that more than a third of all people living with HIV/AIDS are young people between the ages of 15 and 24, and almost two-thirds of these are girls. Why is it left to young girls, Dr Crewe asked, to bear the burden of the HIV/AIDS pandemic? But as she poses this question in South Africa, those of us in the North are left with another question. How do we in the industrialised world teach 15 to 24-year-olds at a time when their own generation in the developing world is so vulnerable?

Dr Crewe advocates a way that educators in the developing world and in the industrialised world can collaboratively work together toward a radical overhaul of awareness education, 'so that this epidemic might transform whole school systems for the better'. She argues that the values we must highlight are three: 'social integrity, gender equality, and compassion'.[5] We will return later to these three values, but for now we want to focus on the relevance of education in a time of HIV/AIDS.

As we entertain this question, that is, as we seek to recast our educational institutions so as to transform our cultures and social structures, we must never lose sight of the primary concern that directly affects our students. To them, she says, we need to give a vision 'that they are valuable, rather than vulnerable'.[6]

Twin conversations

So what significant steps have been taken in our respective fields of inquiry, and which outstanding challenges remain? The call to have a more integrated bioethics has been motivated by a recognition of the need to produce greater gender, economic, political and social equity. The ramifications of trying to meet these complementary needs have completely overtaken the field of bioethics, as HIV/AIDS has prompted theological and philosophical bioethicists to rethink their entire discipline.

As a result, bioethicists are no longer singularly engaging physicians as their primary interlocutors, and they are also no longer looking to the physician's office or operating room as the primary object of ethical analysis and concern. For the first time, discourse with public health officials has become a priority, since contemporary medical ethics is more interested in public health and in major population groups than it is in particular physicians and their individual patients. This is a shift from the private, yet interpersonal, to the social and the structural.

This does not mean, as Daniel Callahan and Bruce Jennings remind us, that ethicists want to lose their first dialogue partners. It is not that the public health official is replacing the physician, but rather that ethicists now realise a need to be in dialogue with both, with more recent emphasis being placed on the importance of the former.[7]

Moreover, in maintaining these two conversations, it should not be misconstrued that the physician's world is simply a microcosm of the public health official's world. As Thomas Aquinas and Josef Fuchs often remind us, the descent into the particular is always an encounter with more and more variables. In other words, while public health officials approach the social with insights about demographic patterns and epidemiological impacts which are fundamental generalisations, the physician can counter with very detailed, experiential narratives for each patient. The former are not simply summaries of those latter narratives, any more than the narratives are only encapsulations of the generalisations. Together their perspectives, the private and interpersonal as well as the social and institutional, inform bioethicists – as moral educators – to have a better grasp on human health.

Callahan and Jennings note that this turn to public health is due to two main insights: first, the sad awareness that the preventable transmission of infectious diseases, HIV/AIDS especially, is occurring at ever greater rates; and second, that 'the health of populations is a function more of good public health and socioeconomic conditions than of biomedical advances.'[8]

Regarding this second point, we recognise that by engaging the public health official primarily we might lose some of the 'excitement' and 'allure' of traditional, clinical bioethics. Along with clinicians, bioethicists can also get caught up by their interest in the researcher. The world of the stem-cell debate and genetics, for instance, becomes very technologically glamorous. But public health forces us into the ordinary, the routine, the basic. It is what Giovanni Berlinguer calls an 'everyday bioethics',[9] or what Maura Ryan refers to as a 'bioethics from below'.[10]

When we appreciate the shift from the clinical world to the public health world, we need to revisit the relevance of the so-called four principles of biomedical ethics that Tom Beauchamp and James Childress have articulated: benevolence, non-maleficence, autonomy and justice.[11] These four principles, which are often referred to as the 'Georgetown mantra', have dominated bioethics for over 25 years. Though they have been claimed to be universally applicable, in fact they are as local in their origin as in their relevance. They reflect a vision of bioethics that is steeped in western values, and which is largely focused on the professional relationship between physician and patient.

Why not? This perspective was born of philosophers working next door to their own university's health-care facility. Thus benevolence and non-maleficence pertain to particular physicians and to other members of the health-care guild, and depend very much on models dominant in the industrialised world. In this perspective autonomy is any patient's fundamental right, and justice can become a bit of a 'remainder' concept, addressing whatever issues the previous three did not. For the most part, in this framework, justice considers whether the physician's particular patient gets fairly treated. Rightly or wrongly, these principles still dominate discussions between bioethicists and clinicians, but they fail when we explore the universe of discourse between bioethicists and public health officials.

When we attempt to broach the topic of justice not with the individual First World physician but with the developing world public health official, justice becomes not a remainder concept but rather, as we shall see, the basic conceptual framework for the bioethical discussion. When conversing with public health officials, we are by necessity required to consider entire populations, their access to treatment, and prevention strategies for everyday illnesses that include infectious diseases. Thus, just as public health officials cannot imagine a hermeneutics of the Georgetown mantra as being relevant to their primary sphere of moral education, neither can we. Now we need a hermeneutics that takes us into the world far beyond the clinician's office.

This search for a new hermeneutics is at the same time a search for a new language, for language is central to understanding how we conceive HIV/AIDS and the world in which it thrives. As Albert Jonsen notes, 'The public language ... of AIDS is as important as the science.'[12] Together with public health officials, bioethicists are now searching for language that allows them to grapple with issues long since ignored or overlooked.

The challenge, then, is to look not only at the health of the patient, but to the conditions that make some persons more vulnerable to this infection than others, at the contexts that make the transmission of HIV more probable, and at the structures that assist or hamper persons in accessing information regarding both prevention strategies and treatment. In other words, unless we reflect on the social, economic, religious and political infrastructures in which people at risk for HIV/AIDS live, there can be no adequate hermeneutics for the ethics of health in the age of AIDS.

Before turning to the landmark contributions by the late Jonathan Mann, we need first to examine the claims of two other major figures who lead us in a similar direction. First, Paul Farmer, a physician and medical anthropologist who divides his time between Haiti and the Harvard health-care institutions of Boston. He has consistently looked at the inequity of social institutions and how they embody virulent pathologies of power. Reflecting on the deep connection between poor health and poverty, he sees the root causes of disease as being more connected to economics than to biology. He is particularly vigilant about the structural violence which is frequently visited upon women and girls.[13]

From a different perspective, global economist Jeffrey Sachs looks at how disease affects social structures. Disease makes people poor.

Disease keeps people within a downward-spiralling economy. While poverty certainly creates the conditions by which people are at risk for poor health, disease destroys their ability to escape from the very context that made them susceptible to ill health in the first place.[14]

He writes:

> Disease is not only a tragedy in human lives, disease is disaster for economic development ... the major reasons why many of the poorest countries in the world, particularly but not exclusively in sub-Saharan Africa, are stuck in poverty is that the disease barrier is so great that it is blocking many different normal avenues of economic advance.[15]

Farmer and Sachs do not contradict one another: rather, they keep us on track to see the deep and interlocking connections between poverty and disease. It was this interconnection between poverty and disease, particularly with respect to HIV/AIDS, that prompted Jonathan Mann to challenge the hermeneutical context for doing public health in a world of HIV/AIDS.[16]

In 1997 Mann, first director of the United Nations Global Programme on AIDS (predecessor to UNAIDS) had the foresight to make the connection between human rights and public health. He did this by first drawing attention to the connection between poverty and illness:

> The vast majority of research into the health of populations identifies so-called 'societal factors' as the major determinants of health status. Most of the work on this area has focused on socio-economic status as the key variable, for it is clear, throughout history and in all societies, that the rich live generally longer and healthier lives than the poor ... A major question arising from the socioeconomic status-health gradient is why there is a gradient.[17]

In response to this question, Mann reflected on the inability of public health to integrate into a solution what it realised was central to the problem:

> While public health may cite, or blame, or otherwise identify the societal-level or contextual issues – which it acknowledges to be of dominant importance, both for influencing behaviour and for determining health status more broadly – it does not deal directly with these societal factors.

Mann then gave three reasons for this paradoxical inaction:

1. 'Public health has lacked a conceptual framework for identifying and

analyzing the essential societal factors that represent the conditions in which people can be healthy.'

2. 'Public health lacks a vocabulary with which to speak about and identify commonalities among health problems experienced by very different populations.'

3. 'There is no consensus about the nature or direction of societal change that would be necessary to address the societal conditions involved.'

He concluded by rueing the ineffectual babble that public health officials inevitably uttered without these critical tools:

> Lacking a coherent framework, a consistent vocabulary, and a consensus about societal change, public health assembles and then tries valiantly to assimilate a wide variety of disciplinary perspectives, from economists, political scientists, societal and behavioral scientists, health systems analysts, and a range of medical practitioners. Yet while each of these perspectives provides some useful insight, public health becomes thereby a little bit of everything and thus not enough of anything.

Bridging the gap

Mann appreciated in the language of human rights its integral comprehensiveness and its moral urgency. That is, human rights language could link global campaigns for the right to access available medical treatments with equally effective and strategic movements to obtain greater equality in political, economic and social forms of life. He therefore proposed that public health had a desperate need for the conceptual framework of human rights to analyse and effectively respond to the unprecedented nature and magnitude of the HIV/AIDS pandemic:

> Modern human rights, precisely because they were initially developed entirely outside the health domain and seek to articulate the societal preconditions for human well-being, seem a far more useful framework, vocabulary, and form of guidance for public health efforts to analyze and respond directly to the societal determinants of health than any inherited from the past biomedical or public health tradition.

What tangible changes have resulted from this language change? First, the Declaration of Commitment on HIV/AIDS at the United Nations General Assembly Special Session on AIDS (UNGASS) of June 2001, the UNGASS Declaration, provided public health officials and AIDS activists with a common language of discourse to be used not only with their surgeons general or ministers of health, but also with their kings, presidents and prime ministers. The language of human rights provides a bridge between the political and the medical.[18]

Second, this linkage of disciplines led to another building of bridges: imagining access for all, and eventually conceiving this as a moral imperative. While the 1998 international HIV/AIDS conference in Geneva had as its theme 'Bridging the Gap', at this conference it was really only AIDS activists who kept trying to challenge different sectors within the health-care community to imagine the possibility of treating already infected persons from the developing world with the drugs that in 1996 in the industrialised world brought new hope even to late-stage patients.

Even though the talk was of 'bridging the gap' between North and South, the Geneva meeting became known as the conference to 'mind the gap'. Many saw the gradient for access to care in the developing world as so steep that not even the late Evel Knievel could have heroically brought it together with one of his famous motorcycle leaps. In fact, some proposed that anti-retroviral therapies were really only appropriate for the industrialised world, arguing that developing world patients' inability to find appropriate water and to 'understand times of administration', made provision of these drugs completely unimaginable.

By the Durban International AIDS Conference in 2000, however, public health officials and clinicians faced the once unimaginable. It was there that the question of universal access would finally be brought to centre stage, and it would be there that Peter Piot, Executive Director of UNAIDS, would for the first time challenge the world to think not in terms of millions of dollars in aid, but in billions.

> We are hearing and heeding the ever-louder call of people living with HIV to place the issue of access to treatment at the center of the world's moral agenda ... Today we need billions – not millions – to fight AIDS. We need at the minimum $3 billion per year for Africa alone for basic prevention and basic care. And this figure is ten times what is being spent today ... But also let's not forget that each year African countries are spending $15 billion in debt repayment. That's four times more than they spend on health and education ... Let this be the conference the world remembers for solutions, for mobilization, and for breaking the silence.[19]

Third, at the 2002 Barcelona International AIDS conference, concrete proposals for drug access were finally being proposed by public health activists, economists, government officials and UNAIDS. Successful programmes in Thailand, Haiti, Costa Rica and Brazil were specifically studied and invoked as examples of normative solutions. Paolo Teixeira of the Brazilian STD/AIDS programme explained why and how his nation came to the decision that antiretroviral therapies should be made universally available to all HIV-infected citizens, and singularly credited the language of human rights as the cogent means for validating the policy: 'What we have been doing is to put into practice principles that have long been recognized by the international community. At their very core is the Universal Declaration of Human Rights, adopted more than 54 years ago.'[20]

Certainly there continues to be debate about human rights language: whose rights, how are they articulated, how are they applied, who guarantees them, and – invariably - who determines the answers to any of these questions? Nevertheless, in responding to these central issues it is precisely the vocabulary of human rights and its conceptual framework that allow these critical discussions to occur, and make possible the development of coherent, equitable and effective policies for HIV prevention and treatment.

We cannot imagine that achievements attained thus far in responding to the pandemic could have been possible without this shift in conceptual framework. Its effectiveness has been proven, and for this reason we believe that it is a key asset in the armamentarium of moral educators for teaching about and responding effectively to our world infected by HIV/AIDS. The language of human rights provides us a way to communicate within and across disciplines not only to analyse properly the socioeconomic conditions relevant to the transmission of HIV, but also to forge consensus and to galvanise the political will to eradicate effectively these conditions.[21]

Common good

As mentioned earlier, Catholic theological ethicists and bioethicists have paralleled these developments by bringing the language of the common good, social justice, solidarity and the option for the poor into their discourse.[22] This again arises from the shift of interlocutors, focus, context and language. In many ways Lisa Sowle Cahill pioneered this shift, and colleagues and students have appropriated her initial insights and subsequent developments.[23]

The new language of Catholic bioethics engages the traditional language of Catholic social justice at the same time that it makes the former more social and more attentive to issues of power and distribution of resources than was previously held. In a word, our language helps us to bridge the gap between conceptual analysis and social change: we do this because bioethics must be effective. Like public health officials, we need to realise that questions of vulnerability to disease and access to information and treatment really need to be understood in their social settings. We cannot make the claims of what is fair unless we have the linguistic instruments to understand why there are inequities or, to use the language of Mann, why there is the 'gradient'.

Concomitantly, we need to recognise that just as those writing on Catholic bioethics were turning to the Catholic social tradition, simultaneously those writing on sexual ethics in a time of HIV/AIDS also made a similar shift. Here we can think of authors from Europe and Africa, like Kevin Kelly (another contributor to this book),[24] Stuart Bate,[25] and Paulinus Odozor,[26] who have seen in the Catholic social tradition an important resource for developing a just sexual ethics that appreciates particularly the importance of gender equity. Here, then, we see an integration of Catholic bioethics, social ethics and sexual ethics, long looked for over the past hundred years.

But all these efforts lead us to ask the second and final question: if we have been developing the tools of analysis for ethical action, and if ethicists along with those from the medical and pubic health communities are working to respond to the plight of those affected by HIV/AIDS, why is this epidemic still outdistancing us?

We want to suggest, as was repeatedly pointed out in Bangkok, that the fundamental problem is not a lack of resources that could be appropriately directed, but rather a lack of political will and leadership to make such commitments. This lack of political will seems at times to be sheathed by a fearful protectionism more interested in its own 'moral integrity' than in the welfare and survival of those most threatened. After fleshing out this argument, we will conclude by comparing this interest in 'preserving purity' with a contrasting historical example: the relevance of mercy as it was lived in Europe at the end of the fifteenth century in responding to the outbreak of syphilis.

Moral integrity?

Several key claims point to the strategies by which stable populations are, in effect, quarantining themselves against the virus and against the 'values' (or lack thereof) that they identify with the virus.

First, HIV/AIDS is perceived as a multi-layered threat, an insight that cannot go unmentioned. At a first level, because HIV is an infectious (though not easily transmissible) virus, every society's self-understanding finds it necessary to perceive the virus as inevitably coming not from within 'our society', but from outside of it. The first person in any society to contract the virus had to have acquired it from a member of another society. For this reason (as is true in the history of syphilis), one repeatedly hears about the 'entry from outside' of HIV/AIDS into any culture, and of the need to document its foreign source.

Second, the virus particularly thrives where there is instability, a notion that we believe is extremely important. Those who are viewed as being 'marginalised' in any society are commonly described as those most at risk of acquiring HIV infection, but we would contend that this characterisation doesn't quite get to the core of vulnerability to becoming HIV-infected. HIV/AIDS breeds specifically where there is social instability, whether that means those who are affected by civil strife, military incursions or liberation armies in Uganda, Haiti, Sudan or the Congo; those who are refugees in any part of the world; those who are the victims of natural disasters; those in the prisons of Russia; those married to South African or Indian truck drivers who themselves live in very unstable worlds; those in debt-ridden nations on the verge of economic collapse; heads of families forced to migrate for employment, and those at home who await them; those who are drug addicts, whose own apprehension of themselves is itself unstable; those who are forced into sexual activity to support their children, their families, or their school fees; those who are overseas workers and fishermen; those who engage in clandestine homosexual activity in homophobic societies; or those girls and young women who are faithful to their marriages or to other stable sexual relationships but whose husbands or partners put them at risk because of external sexual liaisons.

In short, if we want to find persons at risk of the virus or who already are infected by it, they are not simply marginalised people. They are people who are vulnerable precisely because their lives and their social settings lack the stability needed to live safely in a time of HIV/AIDS.

Jeffrey Sachs, in his recent *Time* magazine essay, emphasises the importance of this concept of instability. He writes:

> Since September 11, 2001, the US launched a war on terrorism, but it has neglected the deeper causes of global instability. The nearly $500 billion that the US will spend this year on the military will never buy lasting peace if the US continues to spend only one-thirtieth of that, around $16 billion, to address the poorest of the poor, whose societies are destabilized by extreme poverty.[27]

Peter Piot argues in a similar direction. 'A first and crucial way in which the AIDS pandemic is exceptional is that an 'epidemic equilibrium' or plateau is nowhere in sight – not globally, not at the level of epidemics in most countries, and not over the long term.'[28] This instability or lack of equilibrium is a chaotic world in which the very structures needed to fight the virus are lacking.

Third, against this threat of instability, more stable societies and institutions (including churches) have attempted to create protective barriers. Again, Piot reminds us that 'the barriers to prompt and effective action are immeasurably magnified by taboo, denial and prejudice.'[29] This strategy is remarkable because in an almost perverse way these defensive barriers on the part of leaders in strong, stable cultures are antithetical to the attempts of ethicists, public health officials and clinicians to keep the most vulnerable persons uninfected.

As opposed to supporting those public health preventive strategies (condoms, needle exchange, preventive education) which protect HIV-vulnerable individuals, some leaders and members of their societies perceive that the better and more important shields are those that keep risky individuals distanced from 'the general population', or that are perceived as protecting social mores and orthodoxy from contamination.

For instance, on 20 April 1998 the Clinton Administration declined to lift a nine-year-old ban on federal funding for needle exchange programmes despite the finding by government agencies that such programmes effectively reduce HIV transmission, do not encourage drug abuse, provide a bridge to general medical care and to drug treatment and detoxification, and ultimately save lives.[30]

General Barry McCaffrey, then director of the White House Office of National Drug Control Policy, actively urged the administration not to lift the ban, saying that doing so would send the wrong message to children: 'As public servants, citizens and parents, we owe our children an unambiguous "no use" message.'[31]

Though researchers[32] and major newspapers had endorsed needle exchange programmes,[33] and though supportive arguments from religious and ethical sectors were subsequently offered,[34] including from the Society of Christian Ethics (which comprises the United States' theological ethicists),[35] McCaffrey's protectionist argument of our children and of our public image won the day. That is, even though scientific studies and moral principles were able to defend needle exchange programmes, the chance that a 'mixed-message' might be heard by youth living in stable societies trumped any other argument.

In this way, the United States, allegedly in the name of morality, created a barrier which isolated the unstable world of drug-users from the rest of society and from interventions that could have saved the lives of drug-users themselves, and also of their sexual partners and their children. Unfortunately, this and other barriers are not uncommon, and can be seen in many countries where citizens can identify those most at risk for HIV infection as those that also threaten society's values. (More recently, Human Rights Watch was compelled to launch a campaign against US efforts to suppress funding for needle exchange programmes within the United Nations system – or for any programmes referred to as focusing on 'harm reduction'.[36]

Fourth, this isolation is often backed by a deep moral judgemental-ism, whether explicitly stated or not. Donald Messer in his new book, *Breaking the Conspiracy of Silence: Christian Churches and the Global AIDS Crisis*, examines compelling data from the HIV/AIDS pandemic and finds a church leadership that stands pathetically aloof, righteous and judgemental. He appeals to several surveys, among them an infor-mal one taken at a World Council of Churches gathering in Harare, Zimbabwe, in 1998, in which 68 per cent said they believed the pan-demic to be a punishment from God. Only 48 per cent were willing as leaders to respond to church members with the virus, and only 25 per cent would educate youth about related issues of sexuality and drug use.[37]

This 'morality' of exclusion, moreover, identifies as morally compro-mising and not clinically helpful the very instruments which have in fact been shown to be capable of providing HIV/AIDS protection (condoms, needle exchange, and more-than-just-abstinence-based education). Just as some believe that unstable individuals need to be cordoned from society, so too, they believe, should these instruments. For this reason, any society that tolerates or welcomes these instruments is perceived as putting their population at risk.

Fifth, moral judgementalism depends powerfully on the capacity to blame. This blame is deeply tied to the belief that those living in unstable situations cannot be trusted, and ought not to be admitted to the stable 'inner circle' of society. Moreover, since their condition is in many cases presumed to be their own fault, it does not merit the sympathetic and supportive response that occurred, for example, with victims of the Indian Ocean tsunami. (Some estimates of the number of lives lost in the tsunami approach 300,000, which generated billions of dollars of support within weeks. Although HIV/AIDS causes the same number of deaths every 37 days, the will to commit concomitant resources to pre-vent such loss of life simply does not exist. We must ask, why are we unable to respond similarly to human lives threatened by HIV/AIDS?)

The biblical tradition of Job, whose narrative contradicts the deep-seated belief that we are the authors of our own troubles, apparently has no claim here. Attempts to humanise those already HIV-infected by illustrating that almost anyone can get HIV appear to have had the opposite effect.[38] For example, though the infections of famous 'inno-cently infected' Americans such as Ryan White, Arthur Ashe and Elizabeth Glaser's daughter tangibly convey that anyone could become HIV-infected and that blame is therefore inappropriate, still their stories led many to believe that we must as a result be all the more protective against the threat, distinguishing the 'innocent' infected from those who are blameworthy.

Thus, the face of AIDS is rarely perceived as being innocent. This attitude can be seen all too well in the offhand comment of a good friend of ours, a law enforcement official, who commented 'I equate AIDS patients with the prisoners I have in my cells. I see them as a threat.' Rather than being able to identify with the HIV-infected, we become more convinced that, like Ryan White's playmates, we must keep our distance.

Sixth, silence is frequently integral to a strategy of protecting orthodoxy, and is particularly problematic when questions of sexuality are addressed. Public health officials remind us that if anything, we need to more directly and clearly bring discussions of sex and sexuality into the open. However, HIV prevention programmes that only permit discussion of abstinence can actually put adolescents at increased risk for HIV, other STDs and pregnancy if and when they do initiate sexual activity. One recently cited study of 12,000 young people suggested that while those taking sexual abstinence pledges indeed delayed initiation of intercourse by an average of 18 months, 88 per cent still went on to have sex before marriage, but only 40 per cent of pledged males used condoms when they eventually had sex as compared with 59 per cent of those who did not take the pledge.[39]

Breaking the silence

What does breaking the silence afford? At the Bangkok HIV/AIDS Conference, studies of men who had risky sex with other men and then later with unknowing female partners were reported from Africa, India and the United States. Two other panel presentations broke a long-held taboo by disclosing male homosexual practices in Africa. This led, in turn, to the question of whether an HIV-infected person had a moral responsibility to inform his or her sexual partner. By thus bringing these sexual practices into the open, people were able to discuss the challenges to prevention strategies.

When the question, 'What do faith-based organisations need to do in the face of HIV/AIDS?' was posed to the leading theologian at the conference, Kenya's Musimbi Kanyoro, she answered: 'Break the silence on sex!'[40]

What we see in this sixfold strategy is not merely a lack of political will, but an actual active resistance to any real engagement with root-cause issues. This resistance is based on deep-seated fears of becoming contaminated at a variety of levels, and occurs among other citizens as well as church people, and also, the leaders of both. When we compare this isolationism with the developing strategies of ethicists, public health officials, clinicians and researchers, we find a gap between these two mindsets as broad and as deep as the gap between those at highest risk for acquiring HIV infection and those seeking to be distanced from them.

If bridging the gap is what we must do, how do we do it? First, we must advance greater dialogue among advocates of these two very different strategies. Through education and respectful conversation we must find appropriate means to build common ground, and especially to name and to raise up as models effective bridge-builders. As a negative example, in an editorial attacking the late Pope John Paul II's record on AIDS prevention, *The Lancet* lamented the lack of communication between the Vatican and UNAIDS.[41] In response, the Reverend Robert Vitillo, special advisor on HIV and AIDS to Caritas Internationalis, wrote that since 1999, Caritas and UNAIDS have in fact been working together through a Memorandum of Understanding – the only such MOU which UNAIDS has established with any faith-based organisation.

But other initiatives are also in evidence. Here we think especially of the work of CAFOD (the Catholic Agency for Overseas Development of the bishops of England and Wales) through its brave and well-argued attempts to confront the contemporary Catholic tendency to retrenchment and purity as opposed to the risks of mercy;[42] of Yale Divinity School's Margaret Farley's initiative to create opportunities for discourse between women from the USA and from Africa so as to address the pandemic;[43] and, finally, of Bishop Kevin Dowling's relentless efforts to move his brother bishops in South Africa to endorse effective prevention strategies and to promote a healthy and realistic discourse on sexuality.[44]

In his attempt to bridge the gaps, Donald Messer confronts the churches' need to advance AIDS prevention. He specifically challenges them to ask whether the messages of mercy, forgiveness and compassion have not been compromised by an agenda driven by purity, law and judgement. Messer argues that not only is the welfare of those at risk of HIV infection being threatened by these approaches, but that the very integrity of the Christian character is also being jeopardised.

Messer insists that AIDS is not a dirty word, and exhorts us to follow the example of Jesus. He outlines and examines seven stages to a platform for a call to action: challenge the sexual practices of men; provide behavioural change education for men and women; reach out to the most impoverished women; reject patriarchal structures of Church; champion human rights legislation and eradicate gender inequities; help women to protect themselves against HIV/AIDS and receive proper health care;

protect the well-being of children.

Echoing both Mary Crewe and the eminent Irish moral theologian Enda McDonagh (another writer in this book),[45] British moral theologian Kevin Kelly has proposed a new theology of AIDS and of sexuality that will reawaken us not only to the needs of those infected or at risk of becoming infected, but indeed to the very kenotic essence of the Church.[46]

The quality of mercy

Toward that end, we need then to draw our attention not only to those at risk, but also to those who create the barriers which exclude those at risk. We must remind them that for their own sakes they must bridge this gap. This is what the gospels command, whether in the last judgement of Matthew 25 or in the Lucan Good Samaritan parable. In these and other instances, Christ's fundamental command is to be merciful. And as we see in the Good Samaritan story, the call to be merciful often requires us to sacrifice our desire to maintain purity.

What is mercy? The willingness to enter into the chaos of another. Moreover, as a virtue it claims to embody the heart of Catholic moral education.[47] On this note, then, we close by commenting on the Church's merciful historical response in the face of another dangerous epidemic transmitted through sexual relations: the syphilis epidemic at the end of the fifteenth century.

In 1497, the Compagnia del Divino Amore (Confraternity of Divine Love) was founded in Genoa in 1497 by Chancellor of the Republic, Ettore Vernazza, as a group of laity and clergy committed to working for those suffering from shame: the poor, the prostitute and the syphilitic. Victims of syphilis, having been abandoned both by their families because of shame and by hospitals because of fear of contagion, found a welcome in the confraternity's Hospitals for the Incurables.

In 1499 they built the first of these in Genoa. In 1510 St Gaetano da Thiene built a hospital for the incurables in Rome at the Church of St James on the via Flaminia, so as to care for the pilgrims who fell victim to syphilis on the pilgrimage to Rome. In 1517, the confraternity built 'the Hospital of Mercy' in Verona. Shortly thereafter, Gaetano went to Vicenza to reorganise 'the Hospital of Mercy' there to serve the syphilitic. In 1521 the Ospedale degli Incurabili was opened in Brescia. In 1522 Gaetano opened a hospital, still standing today, in Venice. In the same year a Confraternity chapter was founded in Padova and within four years they opened their hospital for syphilitics. In 1572, a hospital opened in Bergamo and in 1584 another in Crema.[48]

As did Christians in the early sixteenth century, we also find ourselves confronted with an 'incurable disease'. No one today remembers the narratives of those who excluded the victims of syphilis by establishing physical or social barriers of protection based on moral judgements of blame. Rather, history teaches us about the self-understanding of those who realised they were compelled by Christ's demand for mercy to identify with the burden of those at risk and to provide them with effective relief, comfort and companionship. They welcomed the incurables into their more stable world.

As educators in a time of HIV/AIDS, we are learning to appreciate the critical importance of attending to the concepts of justice, human rights, the common good, and the option for the poor. If we can be faithful to the need for a broadening and deepening of our approach, assuredly we will be able to develop a more competent and comprehensive strategy that encompasses bioethics, sexual ethics, public health policy and medical care. Similarly, by retrieving the lessons of mercy, we might be able to coax those who are afraid and entrenched in isolation into extending their hands and their resources from their firm and stable centres of faith and morals to those who live unstable lives in unstable settings. That movement, animated by mercy, is certainly what we need today, not only for those living in chaotic lands, but just as importantly for those living in the stable ones of faith and culture.

Notes

1. UNAIDS, 2005.
2. 'India surpasses South Africa as Country with most HIV cases, Global Fund Director says', Kaisernetwork.org, 16 September 2004 (available at http://www.kaisernetwork.org/daily_reports/print_report.cfm?DR_ID=25766&dr_cat=1).
3. 'China: Business urged to help fight AIDS', *New York Times*, 19 March 2005 (available at http://www.nytimes.com/2005/03/19/international/19briefs.html?).
4. Mary Crewe, 'A pep-talk too far: Reflections on the power of AIDS education' (12 May 2005), http://www.csa.za.org/filemanager/list/6/.
5. http://list.s-3.com/cgi-bin/wa.exe?A2=ind0407&L=caba&F=&S=&P=2720.
6. http://www.plusnews.org/AIDSReport.ASP?ReportID=3647 (12 May 2005).
7. Daniel Callahan and Bruce Jennings, 'Ethics and public health: forging a strong relationship', *American Journal of Public Health* 2 (2002), pp. 169–76.
8. ibid. p. 169.
9. Giovanni Berlinguer, 'Bioethics, health and inequality', *Lancet* 364 (2004), pp. 1086–91.
10. Maura Ryan, 'Beyond a Western bioethics?' *Theological Studies* (March 2004).
11. Tom L. Beauchamp and James F. Childress, *Principles of Biomedical Ethics*, 5th edn (Oxford University Press 2001).
12. Albert Jonsen, 'Foreword' in *The Meaning of AIDS*, ed. Eric Juengst and Barbara Koenig (New York: Praeger Publishers, 1989).
13. Paul Farmer, Margaret Connors, and Janie Simmons (eds), *Women, Poverty and*

AIDS: Sex, Drugs and Structural Violence (Monroe, ME: Common Courage Press, 1996); Paul Farmer, *Pathologies of Power: Health, Human Rights and New War on the Poor* (Berkeley: University of California Press, 1998); *Infections and Inequalities: The Modern Plagues* (Berkeley: University of California Press, 2002). See also Paul Farmer and David Walton, 'Condoms, Coups, and the Ideology of Prevention: Facing Failure in Rural Haiti' in *Catholic Ethicists on HIV/AIDS Prevention*, ed. J. F. Keenan (Continuum 2000), pp. 108–19.

14. Jeffrey Sachs, *Macroeconomics and Health: Investing in Health for Economic Development. Report of the Commission on Macroeconomics and Health* (Geneva: World Bank Organization, 2001); Jeffrey Sachs and John Luke Gallup, *The Economic Burden of Malaria, Centre for International Development* (Harvard University, February 2002).

15. Jeffrey Sachs, *Winning the Fight against Disease: A New Global Strategy*, Keynote Address to the 2003 Fulbright Scholar Conference (2 April 2003), p. 1.

16. See also Jon Fuller and James Keenan, 'The language of human rights and social justice in the face of HIV/AIDS', *Budhi: A Journal of Ideas and Culture* 8 (2004), pp. 211–33.

17. Jonathan Mann, 'Medicine and public health, ethics and human rights', *The Hastings Center Report* 27 (1997), pp. 6–13. See also J. Mann, 'Human Rights and AIDS: The Future of the Pandemic' in *Health and Human Rights*, ed. Jonathan Mann (New York: Routledge, 1999), pp. 216–26.

18. 'Declaration of Commitment on HIV/AIDS, Global Crisis – Global Action', United Nations General Assembly Special Session on HIV/AIDS, 25–27 June 2001.

19. Peter Piot, opening ceremony, XIIIth International AIDS Conference, Durban, South Africa.

20. Paolo Teixeira, quoted by Carmen Retzlaff in 'One step ahead of us', *IAPAC Monthly* (publication of the International Association of Physicians in AIDS Care), reporting on the Barcelona AIDS Conference (October 2002), p. 285.

21. See also, *AIDS, Health and Human Rights: An Explanatory Manual* (Cambridge, MA: The Francois-Xavier Bagnoud Center for Heath and Human Rights and International Federation of Red Cross and Red Crescent Societies, 1993); *Health and Human Rights in Times of Peace and Conflict* (Cambridge, MA: The Francois-Xavier Bagnoud Center for Heath and Human Rights, 2000).

22. Certainly the language of human rights is not inimical to the language of Christian theological ethics. In his landmark work, *The Idea of Natural Rights: Studies on Natural Rights, Natural Law and Church Law* (Atlanta: Scholars Press, 1997), Brian Tierney demonstrates that the idea of natural rights originated with the late eleventh- and twelfth-century decretal formulas by which theologians and canonists tried to articulate the rights of popes, bishops, clergy and other church members, not as inimical to the life of the Church but as constitutive of the Church. In the Church as in the developing world, rights language is generally not used as some sort of voluntaristic assertion of power or entitlement over and against others; rather, it can spring from a community of faith looking to see how its members can best protect the good of the whole Church and of its individual members.

23. Lisa Sowle Cahill, *Bioethics and the Common Good* (Milwaukee: Marquette

University Press, 2004); 'Theology, bioethics, and social change', *Journal of Religious Ethics* vol. 31, no. 3 (December 2003), pp. 363–98); 'Genetics, commodification, and social justice in the globalization era', *Kennedy Institute of Ethics Journal* 11 (2001), pp. 221–38; 'Genetics, Individualism, and the Common Good' in *Interdisziplinäre Ethik: Grundlagen, Methoden, Bereiche*, ed. Adrian Holderegger and Jean-Pierre Wils (Wien: Herder, 2001), pp. 378–92.

24. Kevin Kelly, *New Directions in Sexual Ethics: Moral Theology and the Challenge of AIDS* (London: Geoffrey Chapman, 1998).

25. Stuart Bate (ed.), *Responsibility in a Time of AIDS* (Pretoria: SACBC AIDS, 2003).

26. Paulinus Odozor, 'Casuistry and AIDS' in *Catholic Ethicists*, pp. 294–302.

27. Jeffrey Sachs, 'The End of Poverty', *Time* (6 March 2005).

28. Peter Piot, 'Why AIDS is exceptional' (8 February 2005) at http://www.aidsmatters.org/archives/100-Why-AIDS-is-Exceptional.html (20 March 2005).

29. ibid.

30. http://www.ndsn.org/marapr98/harm1.html (20 March 2005); (Amy Goldstein, 'Clinton Supports Needle Exchanges But Not Funding', *Washington Post* (21 April 1998), p. A1; Sheryl Gay Stolberg, 'President Decides Against Financing Needle Programs', *New York Times* (21 April 1998), p. A1; Marlene Cimons, 'Decision Against Funding Needle Plan Draws Fire', *Los Angeles Times*, Washington Edition (21 April 1998), p. A4; Lynda Richardson, 'U.S. Refusal to Finance Needle Exchanges Angers Agencies', *New York Times* (22 April 1998), p. A27).

31. Christopher Wren, 'White House Drug and AIDS Advisors Differ on Needle Exchange', *New York Times* (23 March 1998), p. A10.

32. Peter Lurie, A. Reingold, B. Bowser et al., *The Public Health Impact of Needle Exchange Programs in the United States and Abroad*, prepared for the Centers for Disease Control and Prevention (October 1993). http://www.caps.ucsf.edu/capsweb/publications/needlereport.html (20 March 2005).

33. Peter Lurie and E. Drucker, 'An opportunity lost: HIV infections associated with lack of a national needle-exchange programme in the USA', *Lancet* 349 (1997), pp. 604–8; Lawrence Gostin et al., 'Prevention of HIV/AIDS and other blood-borne diseases among injection drug users: a national survey on the regulation of syringes and needles', *Journal of the American Medical Association* 277 (1997), pp. 53–62.

33. Editorial, 'AIDS Prevention Efforts Should Include Syringe Programs', *Dallas Morning News* (22 April 1998); Editorial, 'Sticking It To Needles', *USA Today* (22 April 1998); Editorial, 'Clean Needles, No Money', *Washington Post* (23 April 1998), p. A24; Editorial, 'Cowardice on Clean Needles', *New York Times* (22 April 1998); Editorial, 'Cop-Out on Needle Exchanges', *Los Angeles Times*, Wash. Edition (22 April 1998), p. A10.

34. For instance, Jon D. Fuller, 'Needle Exchange: Saving Lives', *America* (18 July 1998); Editorial, 'Needle Exchange Saves Lives', ibid.

35. http://www.stadtlander.com/cdc/CDCHIVSTDTBPreventionNewsUpdate WednesdayJanuary192000.html#g5 (20 March 2005).

36. 'U.S. Gag on Needle Exchange Harms U.N. AIDS Efforts' (3 March 2005), at

http://hrw.org/english/docs/2005/03/02/global10250.htm (20 March 2005).

37. Donald Messer, *Breaking the Conspiracy of Silence: Christian Churches and the Global AIDS Crisis* (Minneapolis: Fortress Press, 2004), pp. 5–7.

38. http://www.aegis.com/news/ads/1991/AD911666.html (20 March 2005); http://www.tucsonweekly.com/tw/04-06-95/review3.htm.

39. Nicholas D. Kristof, 'Bush's Sex Scandal', *New York Times* (16 February 2005), p. A27 (also available at http://www.religiousconsultation.org/News_Tracker/ Bush_sex_scandal.htm).

40. See also, Vincent Lynch (ed.), *HIV/AIDS at Year 20000: A Sourcebook for Social Workers* (Boston: Allyn & Bacon, 2000).

41. 'The Pope's Grievous Errors', *The Lancet* 365.9463 (12 March 2005).

42. http://www.cafod.org.uk/policy_and_analysis/commenteditorial/hiv_debate/ tablet_article (20 March 2005).

43. Margaret Farley, 'Partnership in Hope: Gender, Faith, and Responses to HIV/AIDS in Africa' in *The Mighty and the Almighty: Foreign Policy and God* (Yale Divinity School 2004), pp. 16–20.

44. Jon D. Fuller and James F. Keenan, 'Church Politics and HIV Prevention: Why Is the Condom Question So Significant and So Neuralgic?' in *Between Poetry and Politics, Essays in Honour of Enda McDonagh*, ed. Linda Hogan and Barbara FitzGerald (Dublin: Columba Press, 2003), pp. 158–81.

45. Enda McDonagh, 'Theology in a Time of AIDS' at http://www.cafod.org.uk/ resources/worship/theological_articles/theology_in_a_time_of_aids (21 March 2005); 'The Reign of God: Signposts for Catholic Moral Theology' in *Catholic Ethicists*, pp. 317–23.

46. Kelly, *New Directions in Sexual Ethics*.

47. James Keenan, *The Works of Mercy: The Heart of Catholicism* (Lanham, MD: Sheed & Ward, 2005).

48. Alessandro Massobrio, *Ettore Vernazza. L'apostolo degli incurabili* (Roma, Città Nuova, 2002). See http://64.233.179.104/search?q=cache:c5ecaoY-d4QJ: lettere2.unive.it/deltorre/corso/materiali/Scuole.rtf+%22Compagnia+del+ Divino+Amore%22+sifilide&hl=en (21 March 2005).

Chapter Nine

Families Valued

Eva Heymann SHCJ

The idea of working with people with HIV/AIDS came to me in 1987, at the end of a 30-days retreat. I had recently retired and so had been praying and thinking about my future work.

Initially, the thought did not attract me. I suppose I felt scared. I realised that it would involve me with the gay community and I was ambivalent about that. I remember thinking: 'Not I Lord ...' My fears were rooted deep within me. They stemmed from an internalised awareness that the gay person was *persona non grata* in society at large and certainly not acceptable within most Christian churches. Would I too become isolated and perhaps infected with the virus? We cannot always name what we are most afraid of. Our inner darkness can conceal it from us.

However, the idea would not go away so I wrote to the provincial of my congregation, asking her views and hoping that she would suggest that I should explore other paths. Instead she replied by return of post, full of enthusiasm and encouragement to go ahead.

My early explorations led me to Father Bill Kirkpatrick, whose ministry to people with HIV/AIDS on hospital wards was and remains unique. Bill is a sensitive listener and a compassionate priest. Back then when clergy, medical personnel and many others were afraid to go near anyone who had HIV/AIDS, Bill would sit for long periods, often in shared silence, by the bedside of patients diagnosed with the virus. He would visit them at home after their discharge. He prepared their funerals together with partners, family and friends.

His total acceptance of each person in their own right, regardless of their medical diagnosis or their sexual orientation, was a rare gift at a time when others were afraid of catching the virus. Bill's commitment and compassion inspired me and led me to contact the Terrence Higgins Trust (THT), the first support centre for people with HIV/AIDS in London. I attended training courses there and was accepted as a volunteer counsellor.

A totally new experience was unfolding for me. Working within a predominantly gay community was a shock to my system. I had never even heard the word mentioned in my community, nor in my family. At the end of my first day, I went home realising that it was I who was an 'outsider', weighed down by my anti-gay prejudices, which I had unconsciously absorbed in the society in which we live and from the traditional teaching of the Church.

At THT I was working alongside a warm-hearted, conscientious and committed group, mostly gay men and a few women, all of whom were dedicated to the service of people with HIV/AIDS. At the top of the building were the offices of Frontliners – a group of men who had been diagnosed with HIV/AIDS. They were deeply involved in supporting the ever-increasing number of people infected and affected by the virus.

Outsiders

Gradually I realised that the most important lesson I had to learn was an acknowledgement within myself that I belonged to a society which ostracised the gay and lesbian community. This was a process which led me to see that in vilifying anyone, society itself becomes more de-humanised than the people it is rejecting and at times persecuting. I learned that fear was not only an inhibitor, but more infectious than any virus.

The people I worked with at THT enabled me to lose my own fear relatively quickly. They accepted me long before I could fully accept them. It was an important process for me, and vital for anyone who works with those on the margins of society.

Where was the Church? This was the question I kept asking myself in those early days. The image that remains with me was of standing in a thick fog and searching for a light that would give direction. Slowly I started to link with others who echoed my cry: 'Where are you?' It was not that we felt the absence of Christ, for he was visibly amongst us in the men, women and children who lived with HIV/AIDS and those who were affected by their diagnosis. But fog can disable our sense of direction. It generates fear.

This was highlighted for me one evening when I received a phone call from a nurse on the HIV ward at the Mildmay Hospital in East London. She asked if I knew of a Catholic priest who would be available straight-away to give the sacrament of communion to a patient. His family were with him, including an uncle who was a priest. He had arrived from abroad knowing that his nephew, Paul, was in hospital but not that he was on an AIDS ward. He was horrified when he discovered this and said that he could not possibly say Mass at the bedside. He was appalled to hear that Paul was gay. The priest's fear of catching the virus had been evident and he had left the family to book into a hotel for the night.

I rang several priests, but at such short notice none was able or agreeable to meet the spiritual needs of this family. Ultimately I telephoned a Jesuit community and spoke with one of the priests who assured me he would go to the hospital immediately. He said Mass for the family and gave the Blessed Sacrament to each one present.

The following morning, he happened to be doing the *Thought for the Day* meditation on BBC Radio 4. He reflected on his experience of the night before. It was a wonderful gift to all of us who worked as volunteers and often found ourselves in difficult situations.

One of the organisations I encountered was Catholic Aids Link (CAL), chaired by Martin Pendergast. At its monthly meetings, we discussed how we might challenge the institutional churches to become more actively involved with those who were living with the virus and those who were supporting them. CAL included priests and members of religious congregations as well as lay people.

During one of these meetings, we coined the phrase: 'The Body of Christ has AIDS'. Some members of CAL were shocked by this and felt that its use would be counter-productive, but we were not put off. Using it on our fliers to advertise HIV/AIDS workshops, we discovered it could be effective.

Shock tactics

There are, I believe, times when it is necessary to use shock tactics to pierce the curtain of fear, stigma and ignorance. This was one of them. We had already tried in many different ways to involve our institutional churches in reaching out to people living with AIDS but the nationwide response we had hoped for had not materialised. We needed to become more visible and proactive in challenging our churches as well as ourselves, to allow Christ's mercy, love and spiritual healing to be activated in us and through us. This was often happening with individuals at grass-root levels but was rarely visible in the hierarchy of the churches.

With this in mind, a banner with the words 'The Body of Christ has AIDS' was taken to Rome. It was unfurled by a priest with HIV/AIDS at a conference there when Mother Teresa was speaking. He was escorted from the hall and the banner removed. It caused headlines around the world. Using shock tactics is not the way we usually approach the leaders of our churches, but I remain convinced that it was right to do so at that particular moment in time, as a way of highlighting the urgency of the need for all churches to combine in supporting people with AIDS, their partners and friends. We had to break down the false image of 'them and us' so that 'we' could become the inclusive and operative word for all Christians and other faiths to work together.

We still have a long way to go, especially in terms of the hierarchies of our Christian churches.

Deaf to Christ

There were many moments of anger during the early years of my involvement. I will never forget the occasion when a group of us had arranged a Mass to be celebrated with people with HIV/AIDS, their families, friends and carers. Father Jim, a priest with AIDS, had been invited to concelebrate. He was already vested when the officiating priest said he could not possibly concelebrate with him. Even as I recall this experience today, almost 20 years on, I can still feel the depth of my anger that the institutional Church could be so far removed from Christ, so deaf to his cry: 'I have come that they may have life and have it abundantly ...'

During that Mass many tears were shed – of anger and anguish – but it was the priest who had been rejected whose embrace during the kiss of peace brought us back into union with the suffering of the body of Christ and gave us the hope to continue to challenge prejudice.

Fear of infection and society's attitude towards homosexuality were not the only obstacles which needed to be addressed. There were whole families out there suffering and in need of help. The parents of a young man who had died of AIDS had approached THT and asked if a support group could be formed for others in their situation. I was asked to lead this group in its monthly meetings.

The couple who had started it all off talked to me about the isolation they felt in their own social circles, where it was not possible to speak openly about their son's illness and death. The pain of isolation and rejection was, they said, an additional burden on them at the time when they were told that their son was terminally ill. There was no support from their local churches.

Mutual support

The membership of the monthly meetings grew rapidly. On the whole it was parents of people living with AIDS who attended, but we also had brothers and sisters who came to the meetings to get advice about how they might best help and to find out what kind of support was available from church groups. Predictably, the latter was virtually nonexistent.

One mother told us that when she heard that her son was diagnosed with HIV, she was afraid that she would no longer be allowed to be a eucharistic minister in her (Catholic) church, as people might be afraid they could catch the virus from her if they drank from the chalice she had used. This mother felt that neither the parish priest nor members of the congregation would support her and her family in countering such ignorance and facing up to the problems they were encountering. The Family Support Group gave her an opportunity to share her fears and realise that she was not alone in this situation.

As the group grew in confidence and trust in each other, it was energised to reach out to the wider family of society. On one occasion, a young music teacher arrived. She explained that she was working with a prisoner who was HIV-positive. She taught him cello. He was isolated from other prisoners, she told us. She had come to the group to ask if they could give her advice on helping the young man to get in touch with his family who did not know of his HIV status. He wanted to tell his mother, but was afraid she would break under the burden of such news. We encouraged the teacher to tell her pupil that his mother would be welcome at our group where she could talk with others in similar situations.

Sadly, we enjoyed little if any support from parish communities at this point in time. Undoubtedly it was fear which was the strongest barrier to a truly Christ-like response to the growing number of people infected and affected by HIV/AIDS. What could be done? There were, we knew, no easy answers. It was a fraught situation for all concerned.

Our attempts to involve the hierarchy in our efforts were not very successful. A group of Catholics contacted Cardinal Basil Hume and asked if he would meet us to discuss ways to involve the Church in supporting people with HIV/AIDS. At first this suggestion was refused, though a meeting was subsequently set up.

We went along as a group of about thirty people. The cardinal and other representatives of the hierarchy were present. We had been asked to choose just four of our number who could speak for three minutes each to explain why we needed support from the Church. This was not the kind of framework for communication we had envisaged. However, I think all of us were impressed by Cardinal Hume's evident distress when faced with the earnest requests for help from people who were already in advanced stages of AIDS.

As a result of this meeting, he invited the speakers to meet him again. He also gave his personal support to individuals and small groups. He was generous in providing grants for people with HIV/AIDS and their carers to go on the yearly interfaith pilgrimages to Lourdes.

Subsequently there were some signs of the Catholic Church's willingness to reach out to people with AIDS, but no concerted policy was developing. It was yet another lost opportunity for the Catholic hierarchy to reflect on the prophetic call of the Church and to allow the inclusive love of Christ to be extended to all its members.

During the 1990s there was a marked change in the statistics of the virus. The rapidly increasing numbers of heterosexual people infected with HIV demanded ever more pastoral as well as medical and social care, but fear of the virus was if anything even more deeply rooted than before. Pious churchgoers could no longer point a finger at a minority of the population. They had to acknowledge that the rate of infection was not confined to the gay community.

Parish failure

This could have been an opportunity for ecumenical participation, but for this to be truly effective, it would have needed Christian parishes and other faith groups to become more involved in reaching out to individuals and families. We may not have had a cure for HIV infection, but with the combined support of the leadership of the churches, we could have tackled effectively fear and prejudice. This would have represented a breakthrough for the many families who had no access to spiritual and social support at a time of profound shock and distress.

Yet we failed and therefore caused literally untold suffering. I know of several families where this failure of the Church to stand by them has been the root of long-term psychological breakdown. Take the case of Paul, aged 13, a bright, intelligent boy, who was left without spiritual and emotional support at the time of his father's AIDS-related illnesses and his eventual death. Paul refused to go to school because he was frightened what would happen to him if his friends discovered that his father had AIDS. He avoided all social contact with his peers and became clinically depressed.

I was around this time given an opportunity to become involved with a multidisciplinary team at St Mary's Hospital in Paddington. They provided holistic care for children with AIDS and for their families. A clinical nurse specialist and I started a small support group for parents and grandparents of children infected or affected by the virus. It was a challenging learning experience for all of us, as working with children with AIDS evoked in me different feelings to working with adults. There were times when I felt frustrated and angry with God, the world at large and particularly with the blindness of our church leaders.

But what impressed me most of all was the courage of children and the devoted care shown by their parents and grandparents. Many of these children had been infected in the womb. I remember one eight-year-old girl who had struggled with several AIDS-related illnesses telling us that she loved to come to the hospital to see her consultant. I asked her why and she replied: 'Because he listens to me.' Wouldn't it be wonderful if all children could have a similar experience of support in their local parishes?

As a Catholic religious, who started life from Jewish roots, I long to see myself as part of a universal Church which has a dialogue with, interacts and supports, people with AIDS. We have to reach out across national and international boundaries and, in doing so, end the bondage of fear.

Dream my dreams

How can this be done as we embark on the new papacy of Benedict XVI? My response comes in the form of allowing myself to 'dream my dreams'. I have ten headings in mind. They might be seen as Ten Commandments but I know that such a title would be counter-productive, especially if suggested by a woman. So I will list them as a framework for an inter-faith response to the worldwide AIDS pandemic.

There is no order of preference, but each section highlights our inter-dependence as human beings, especially with the most vulnerable members of our local communities. At a time when the Churches in our country are diminishing in membership, a real sense of what it means to be community might inject new life into declining institutions. As members of the Body of Christ, we need to put ourselves in the shoes of our neighbour.

A listening Church

The meeting with Cardinal Hume, which I described earlier, high-lights the need for communication at all levels by and with the leaders of our Churches. It also demonstrates the need for a willingness on all sides to be open. Clear information about HIV/AIDS has to be given to all, and especially to those who are prejudiced or feel that this is not a matter which is ever likely to touch them personally. HIV affects all of us and can infect a wide range of people. A listening Church would be a humble Church, seeking information and praying for insight and direction to respond to the needs of those who are infected and affected by the virus.

A servant Church

The Churches are in a position to provide spiritual, emotional, social and practical support. Christ embodied a sense of service, especially to the marginalised, which we need to internalise in our lives and institutions. This is closely linked to my hopes for a listening Church. When we can really hear with our hearts and not merely with our ears we will be motivated by the Holy Spirit who called Christ to become a model of service to others. Then people with HIV/AIDS will discover that fear can be replaced by love.

An inclusive Church

My dream symbol of an inclusive Church would be an open door, where streams of people of all ages, nationalities and disabilities would find refuge, support and respect.

A Church connected to its grass roots

Institutions are not generally experienced as being firmly rooted in the visions and dreams of their founders. This is true of our Churches. We need to go back to our beginnings and Christ's vision for the Church, as the Body of Christ, to ensure that we nurture the body, mind and spirit of each unique person made in the image of Christ. We need healthy roots to enable us to grow in faith and love, just as trees and plants need roots to grow and withstand storms and inclement weather.

An institution with a soul

All institutions are weighed down by paperwork, hours of meetings and material concerns. This is unavoidable, but churches also have resources which other organisations lack. They can draw on a wide range of professionals who could be encouraged freely to offer their services to support families and single people coping with HIV. There are churches that do this, but it is by no means the norm.

A compassionate Church

My understanding of the word compassionate is that it means to suffer with another person. A priest who could tell a gay person who was in great physical and mental pain that his current suffering would reduce his time in purgatory (as some in my experience have) has not yet allowed the compassionate Christ to touch his own heart. A caring Church needs to offer unconditional support to its members. This is especially the case in the complex area of HIV/AIDS where many young people have to face death and dying. The availability of relatively new medicines in the West has the advantage of prolonging life, but with it come other issues, such as providing more flexible respite care and home support. The latter is an area where many parishes could be encouraged to become involved. Ongoing support for teenagers infected by the virus is an ever-growing need.

A Church that reaches out to those who are most vulnerable

In this day and age, when the gap between the materially rich and poor is visibly widening, there is also the invisible abyss that separates us from the marginalised and rejected members of the Body of Christ. The gay community is often socially and spiritually marginalised. The fact that many families affected by HIV/AIDS are afraid to seek spiritual support is an indictment on our society, especially when this happens within the Church. As a countersign to this scenario, we need to dream our dreams and ensure that in our waking moments we can rid ourselves of such incidents.

Occasionally there are rays of hope. Tom, aged 27, was in advanced stages of AIDS-related illnesses. He had friends who ensured he could be with them in the local pub every Saturday evening. At times when he was unable to walk, they provided a wheelchair: a simple but effective solution to his fear of isolation.

The Church as voice for the voiceless
This is one of my favourite dreams. It has endless possibilities. One of the most obvious applications would be to invite a person diagnosed with HIV to give the homily at a Sunday morning Mass. I have experienced this and it produced signs of real hope in the congregation.

A fearless Church
If we are truly rooted in Christ, then fear is less likely to dominate us. Fear is the nettle which we need to grasp most firmly. It can dehumanise an institution as well as individuals. I have seen the effects of this many times in my work with families affected by HIV/AIDS. I have heard sad stories of children who were not invited to their friends' birthday parties, because someone in their families had AIDS. Gradually they became more and more isolated, which affected their work at school and their whole emotional /social development. Fear is often rooted in ignorance.

To counteract this, a small group of us met at the Christian Education Centre at Crawley. Each of us was involved in supporting people with HIV/AIDS. In our preliminary discussions we planned to offer AIDS-awareness courses for one evening over a period of six weeks. The team comprised doctors, nurses, teachers, social workers and people with AIDS who gave their testimony. The aim was to diminish fear, to empower people to be well informed about HIV/AIDS and encourage them to become involved in supporting people in their family and community.

The results were amazing. At the end of one evening a lady spoke to a member of the team: 'I'd like to do some volunteer work, but I've never spoken to a gay man in my life.' My colleague replied: 'Well, you are doing so right now.' They talked for a while about her fears and anxieties. Towards the end of their conversation, my friend said to her, 'Would you like to meet someone who has AIDS?' She was still fearful, but allowed him to introduce her to one of the team. He left them to talk together. Later, as he looked back towards them, he saw her in the arms of the man with AIDS, weeping while he was consoling her. She told me later that this moment had changed her whole life.

Blessed are...

What happened during these courses was a model of how people could respond to the needs of those infected and affected by AIDS. We were a multidisciplinary team of men and women, of different sexual orientations, life experiences and interdenominational beliefs. Some were HIV-positive and some were not. These differences were in no way divisive, but they came together in something which the audience could relate to.

Towards the end of each course a person with AIDS spoke about his own fears and hopes for the future. This was always a moment of challenge. It opened our eyes and hearts to the fact that we are all interdependent creatures, utterly unique and loved by the God who created us. Fear can be overcome by that love.

Extending such programmes to every diocese would require a daunting amount of training, finance and support, but it could also be an opportunity to activate the often-dormant gifts and abilities of people who have not previously had the opportunity to connect consciously with the Beatitudes.

I would like to conclude with a prayer written by Father Bill Kirkpatrick during the early days of the inter-faith group, which met regularly at THT. Different support groups and individuals used it on many occasions.

> Loving God
> Show yourself to those who are vulnerable
> And make your home with the poor and weak of the world;
> Warm our hearts with the fire of your Spirit.
> Help us to accept the challenges of AIDS.
> Protect the healthy, calm the frightened,
> Give courage to those in pain,
> Comfort the dying
> And give to the dead eternal life.
> Console the bereaved, strengthen those who care for the sick.
> May we your people, using all our energy and imagination,
> And trusting in your steadfast love, be united with one another
> In conquering all disease and fear.

The sentiments expressed in this prayer are needed as much now as they were in the 1980s. The institutional churches have to provide a compassionate response to HIV/AIDS, rooted in a willingness to offer practical, emotional and spiritual support without fear, judgement or prejudice towards individuals with HIV/AIDS, their partners and families. The human resources for this are available. The financial means could also be forthcoming. What we still lack is the will.

Chapter Ten

The Quandaries of Nature and Grace

Mark D. Jordan

To many ears, 'vocation' is a lost metaphor. It means just profession or hobby, what you do daily for a living or what you might do with your days if there were no living to earn. Even for Catholics, who might be expected to hear the word's resonance, 'vocation' refers to church profession, a sort of career in the priesthood or under vows.

So it is worth the effort to remember that languages influenced by Christendom speak of 'vocations' because Jesus once called out to people. They responded quite literally by following him as he travelled. We rely on the metaphor of 'vocation' because Jesus called, and because before him the God of the Hebrew Scriptures called the world into being, called after the first human beings in the garden, called upon patriarchs, kings, fierce heroines, prophets and serving women. If early twentieth-century Roman Catholic theology sometimes lost itself trying to separate God's creation from churchly certification in a religious calling, more recent documents have insisted on the 'universal call to holiness in the church'[1]

During the last century, a growing number of Catholic believers judged it their vocation, in one sense or another, to secure the well-being of those people called 'homosexuals', 'inverts', 'homophiles', 'lesbians and gays', or 'queers' (to stay with polite or recently rehabilitated terms).[2] Some believers conceived the calling in secular terms and so took to legislative reform, health care, or direct political action. Others received the calling as a divine urgency to declare sacramental solidarity with this persecuted sexual minority – or to give thankful testimony about divine graces received as a member of it.

These declarations and testimonies have yet to be considered well enough as either history or theology. For many reasons, the history of the gay and lesbian movement has been told against religion, especially Christianity. The motives for excluding queer Christians included personal reactions against churchly crimes past or present, but also theoretical suspicions of religion on Marxist or Freudian grounds.

For equally strong and rather more obvious reasons, most Christian groups, notably including the Catholic Church, have written their queer members out of any official account – except perhaps as object lessons. Even so, there is a history of queer Catholicism to be told, both as medieval preacher's *exemplum* and as a theologically significant glimpse of divine action on human natures too often counted as beyond the reach – or the love – of God.

Early episodes of queer Catholicism

The story of queer Catholicism can be told from many beginnings and with innumerable episodes. Let me concentrate on two early American moments. I retell them not as representative history or as sociological sample, but as matter for a meditation on the theology of vocation.

In 1946, two schoolteachers met in Atlanta. One claimed to be an Orthodox bishop exiled from Greece for defending priests defrocked for committing same-sex acts.[3] He not only defended them, he confessed that his own desire was directed towards men – though he chose not to act on it because of the discipline of monastic celibacy.

The second teacher was Catholic. He suffered a different sort of exile. George Hyde had left a Vincentian seminary.[4] For at least a year, he had been questioning Roman teaching on homosexuality – aloud and before some of the 'competent authorities'. Much later, he recounted his views in these words: 'I told them this: "The Church is the House of the Lord ... a home for all men and women, but you would not have it so. You have built closets in every corner in which to hide the homosexual out of sight and out of hearing of the word. This is wrong. The Church is the House of the Lord, and in His House there are no closets."'[5]

At the same time that the two teachers were comparing church experiences, 12 members of a local parish, both women and men, agreed to admit their homosexuality to the pastor.[6] They were then publicly denied communion. They approached Hyde, asking him to lead discussions about their situation and their future prospects. After a few months, the group decided that the way forward was to found a church that would feed them with the Eucharist.

So the exiled bishop ordained the former seminarian on 1 July 1946, in a meeting room of the Winecoff Hotel, the rental fee paid by the owner of the hotel bar. The downtown hotel stood some four blocks from the church where the protest had been staged. On Christmas Eve, they were back in the hotel to celebrate the nativity. The handmade altar cloth came from the mother of one of the members, while a 'closeted' Catholic priest donated the candles. In the year following, the newsletter of the young community was already rejecting standard (mis)readings of Genesis chapters 18 and 19 on the sin of Sodom.[7]

George Hyde went on to do other things, in other jurisdictions. In 1957, he took the Eucharistic Catholic Church into full communion with the Orthodox Catholic Church of America, one of the many groups claiming apostolic succession through Joseph René Villatte.[8] It is not so important to judge Hyde's organisational choices as to recognise that already in 1946 some Catholics understood their vocations, both lay and clerical, as requiring the public refusal to deny homosexuals the Eucharist.

The other early episode is not mainly Catholic, but Catholic vocations figured within it. In 1964, an initiative from an urban Methodist ministry, Glide Memorial, brought together 15 leaders of San Francisco 'homophile organizations' with 15 Protestant clergy, local and national, for a weekend 'consultation'. The consultation was bold for an early effort: it included a Friday night tour of disreputable bars and participation on Saturday in a necessarily secret queer picnic.

It also presented the participants with summaries of scriptural, theological and psychological views on homosexuality. The most compelling document was a compilation of responses to a rushed and unscientific survey. Don Lucas used his position as executive secretary of the Mattachine Society, one of the largest homophile groups, to circulate a questionnaire to its national mailing list. He explained to the membership that he had been asked to present 'some of the problems and conflicts that the homosexual finds in regards to the Church ... In talking with hundreds of persons over the years I have found that a great number do have definite conflicts in regards to religion and the Church.'[9]

Though the questionnaire attempted to separate topics, many respondents ran them together – and the great majority commented more than once on personal vocation in relation to homosexuality.[10] For example, 31 of Lucas's 40 respondents wrote at one point or another about growing up in a Christian church. The denominational range was wide, from Catholicism to Unitarianism and Christian Science. By the roughest division, there were 16 Protestants, 7 Anglicans and 7 Catholics. Let me juxtapose two of the responses from Catholics, even at some length, to show the peculiar anguish of discovering queer sexuality while growing into a sense of vocation within Catholic settings.

The first response is from an adult man in Missouri who describes himself as being raised in a family '100 per cent Roman Catholic for generations back'.[11] He reports that he spent three years studying for the priesthood in seminary, but adds nothing about the circumstances of leaving or about his present occupation. He describes his spiritual situation in painful terms, even though he acknowledges that individual priests have treated him without revulsion. 'If the attitude of the Catholic Church ever did change, it would mean that I could live with the hope some day of dying in God's good graces. We are taught that to die outside our Church's exhortations and teachings is to spend eternity in torture and suffering.'

Yet this man has no hope of a change in Catholic teaching. He longs for it, but then he counts it 'so ideal' that 'it almost sounds ridiculous'. The split between longing and resignation is captured most succinctly in reflections on Catholic upbringing. 'I am firmly convinced that what good qualities of character I may possess were partially the result of the Catholic Church's teachings, which are of the most unselfish and noblest behaviour, and of the practice of this religion by those closest to me. The only bad thing resulting from this background would be the frustration and disorientation of my own personality' around sexual matters. The 'only bad thing' a 'disorientation' of personality? It is as if a knotted self were only to be expected – as if there were no way of life in which he could avoid it.

A sharper poignancy finds expression in the response of a young man who was 16 years old at the time Lucas circulated the survey. Nothing else is disclosed about him, but his voice is so vivid that Lucas reprints his written answer entire. I take three excerpts.

> One priest tells me 'go see a doctor', another tells me that 'your inclinations are abnormal because carnal love should only result in offspring', and another tells me that 'you can desire latently but it is a sin to follow through overtly!' ... I have no place to go, and it is impossible to become an atheist.

> I don't have visions. I don't see and converse with Christ every night before I go to bed. How am I supposed to know what my Creator thinks of me? The Church says that God thinks I am a 'monster'.

> I don't want to be condemned. Please don't make me feel I'll go straight to hell – at least send me to purgatory, then I'll have a slight chance to progress.'[12]

In both individuals, but particularly in the second, we read of someone split between a created nature and a doctrine that denies it grace. Both respondents want to be reconciled with the Church, as both fear (on its terms) future damnation and present exile. The only vocation offered to them seems no vocation at all – only a witness to a vocational contradiction. The contradiction pries apart the purpose written into one's creation from the vocations authorised by the Church. To separate them is to lose Catholicism.

Sacramental liberation

Around the Bay Area of San Francisco, in the turbulent first wave of 'gay liberation', some would try to heal the contradiction by offering queer Catholic vocations with more moral and sacramental freedom than the two respondents felt – or than George Hyde's congregants wanted. By 1969, a number of experimental Catholic communities had coalesced around shared liturgy and politics. The Society of Priests for a Free Ministry announced Masses on the streets in support of local men who had been fired for being gay.[13]

Two years later, the society was supplying a priest to the Catholic Community of St John the Beloved, an 'experimental parish for the gay community'. The community itself was sponsored by 'a Catholic Worker commune serving the homophile community of San Francisco'.[14] In assuming that queer people already constitute a 'community', the experimenters begin to think that queer Catholics deserve their own forms of religious expression and life. If the breakaway church in Atlanta insisted on being open to all believers including homosexuals, the later communities in San Francisco would interpret the anguish of the queer Catholics as a call to find queer Catholicism.

In early 1969, the Catholic organisation Dignity was founded in southern California – not least because of the challenge from the new 'gay church' in Los Angeles, Troy Perry's Metropolitan Community Church (MCC). Many Catholics were attracted to the MCC despite its Pentecostalist roots. They still are.

Dignity, by explicit contrast, began as a support group run by an Augustinian priest, Pat Nidorf. Nidorf advertised for 'Catholic gays' in the San Diego 'underground' newspaper in 1969.[15] Frustrated by the lack of response, he placed ads in the *Los Angeles Free Press* and *The Advocate*, then a local newsletter and not a national glossy. More people, including some who had been attending MCC, drove to San Diego for the meetings. After alternating between San Diego and LA for a time, Nidorf moved the meetings to LA to be nearer most of the membership.

In early 1971, a letter was sent to the archdiocese asking for recognition. The response was predictable: Timothy Manning, then a co-adjutor or deputy to the archbishop, rebuked Nidorf for working in the diocese, judged the principles of Dignity 'untenable', and ordered him to stop working with the group. In response, the leadership of Dignity passed to the laity who began a campaign of national outreach. A first national meeting was held in 1973, with a dozen recognised chapters and another dozen in formation.

What were the principles of Dignity that the bishop found 'untenable'? Almost a year before meeting with him, the organisation had adopted a 'Statement of Position and Purpose' based in part on recently published articles by John McNeill. It claimed, among other things, that 'homosexuality is a natural variation on the use of sex. It implies no sickness or immorality. Those with such sexual orientation have a natural right to use their power of sex in a way that is both responsible and fulfilling.'

The document also asserted, to my mind more provocatively, 'we believe that gay Catholics are members of Christ's mystical body, numbered among the people of God ... We believe that gays can express their sexuality in a manner that is consonant with Christ's teaching.'[16] Here evident variation in created sexuality implies a diversity of erotic vocations within the Church. Nature cannot be sundered from grace, so the Church must respond to nature's kinds by fostering new vocations.

From the mid-1970s, the history of Dignity has been measured – if not driven – by two documents from the Vatican's Congregation for the Doctrine of the Faith. The first document, *Persona Humana*, seemed tacit encouragement to some in Dignity so far as it admitted a permanent or unchangeable homosexuality – that is, homosexuality much like nature.[17] The second document, *Homosexualitatis Problema*, corrected this misapprehension and ordered that Dignity and similar organisations be denied access to Catholic parishes or other facilities.[18] Less important for the moment than the group's canonical vicissitudes are the different senses of vocation that they disclosed.

After 1986, when push came to shove, members of Dignity went in at least three different directions. Some stayed with the national organisation, which became a kind of ministry-in-exile. Others resumed their places in regular parishes or joined an officially approved 'diocesan outreach programme'. Yet other members took the moment as an occasion to join more encouraging Christian groups – or to abandon Christianity altogether.

The scattering marked how difficult it had become to argue that Dignity offered a haven for queer Catholic vocations. Some who left had lost patience with the hierarchy or with organised Christianity. They came to see 'queer Catholicism' as both nature and grace in chains. Others left because they could not conceive of distinguishing Catholicism from obedience to the hierarchy. For them, grace was a certain kind of authority. Before it, testimonies to nature could only yield.

Vocations in history

I have staged these episodes and experiments as variations on the deeply Catholic theme of nature and grace. Variation, not progression: the three episodes do not fall onto a single line aimed at a radiant future. They do not predict or foretell. They suggest instead that the puzzles of nature and grace, ever present in Catholic thinking, have been complicated by a third term, an authority that claims exclusive jurisdiction over the interpretation of both nature and grace. It claims jurisdiction over the interpretation of nature by invoking a particular promise of grace.

The invocation has become more strident in the last two centuries in part because nature has shown itself more complicated and uncertain than some doctrines imagined. The stridency of claims for church authority over nature is due as well, especially in sexual matters, to a fourth term. I have let the term play out in the form of my essay, but I have not yet named it. The term is history. Simple formulations of nature and grace in sex are unsettled by science, but perhaps even more by history – and especially that curious sub-field called the history of sexuality. I can illustrate the difficulties – and a possible resolution – by distinguishing various senses of my title, of the relation between homosexuality and vocation. What sense does it make to say that homosexuality can be part of a (Catholic) vocation?

The three historical moments show that some Catholics have felt a call to be active on behalf of the civil rights and churchly inclusion of queer people. This admirable struggle, which is hardly finished, is not exactly the incorporation of homosexuality into a vocation. To feel the vocation to defend queer people from persecution is not the same as having a religious vocation through homosexuality. To note what is obvious: many of the most effective activists on behalf of queer people were not and are not queer. They have felt the call to action on religious or ethical grounds, regardless of their identity. It is true that some queer people have felt – still feel – the call to action with particular force, but other activists had no personal stake beyond conscience.

Does it make sense to move beyond social justice in order to ask how homosexuality itself can be taken up into the divine calling that gives direction to one's life? Many psychologists or social workers or health-care providers would look at the question and wonder immediately whether 'homosexuality' is the sort of thing that you can receive as a vocation, in either secular or religious senses. They would object that the sexual attraction is not a fixed essence so much as a changeable passion that can shift over a lifetime. They would also note that sexual activity is only loosely related to the sense of any identity. Many men who regularly have sex with men very much resent being identified as homosexual.

Historians of sexuality would add a similar objection: acting on same-sex desire – or even experiencing it – is not one and the same thing in every place and time. In fact, 'homosexuality' as a category is not yet 150 years old. It was invented by and for certain classes of people in certain parts of the world. There has been much controversy over whether the category 'homosexuality' can be applied before 1850, outside Europe and its colonial descendants, or beyond the boundaries of the middle classes.

The term has entered Christian theology even more recently – as recently as the 1970s for the most official documents of Roman Catholicism. For a historian of moral theology, the prominence of the word *homosexualitas* is one of the most striking things about *Homosexualitatis Problema*.

I feel the force of these objections. I agree that we need to be careful of conceiving 'homosexuality' as an eternal essence. At the same time – and this is my reply – our vocations come to us through historically changeable social identities. We live our callings in relation to the shapes for human lives we find around us, even if we mean to change them. It may be that some of us are called through social identities that would have been unthinkable a century before and would be uninteresting a century afterwards. It may be that we are living through a time in which some people are being called to insist on the goodness of loving within sexes and genders. A hundred years from now it may not be. Is 'homosexuality' the sort of thing that can be a calling? No more and no less than most of the other social categories that we use to shape our lives.

It is equally important to remember that most queer Catholics had labels pinned on them before they could choose to assume them. Here another remark by Don Lucas's young Catholic is worth recalling. 'Throughout my whole life I've received the sacraments, done good and bad things, sinned and confessed. Now, since a couple of months ago, I am "against nature, which is the law of God, and unless you (referring to me) change you are doomed".'[19]

Homoerotic identities are typically assigned as condemnation long before they are chosen as liberation. If they are historically mutable, that challenges church authority before it challenges queer 'communities'.

A Catholic calling?

There remain the objections that homosexuality conceals a more important challenge, one nearer the heart of our present quandaries over nature and grace. Behind the question (can homosexuality figure in a Catholic calling?) there stands another question: how is erotic life part of any

Christian vocation?

The question leads off in many directions. To Catholic ears, for example, it can evoke another series of historical reflections. One striking change in official moral theology during the last century has been the increasingly positive value assigned to sex as part of most human lives. You can see this is in Catholic 'marriage movements', or in de facto pastoral judgements on adolescent masturbation. Or the question can be a way of asking whether our bodies and their desires can be messengers of vocation. How might our bodies reveal to us (I use the verb deliberately) what stands beyond our social identities or their sum?

The question about erotic life might also remind us to beware of easy rankings or comparisons of vocations, especially so far as the rankings always put anything related to the body on the lowest rung. So life under religious vows of poverty, chastity and obedience was held by most Catholics during most centuries to be intrinsically better than life in marriage or unvowed singleness. Even if we reject that sort of ranking, we may fall into others. We may think, for example, that being a Christian is more important than being a homosexual. That simple (or simplistic) valuation invites confusion between vocation and identity.

So far as 'being a Catholic' is a name for the most embracing divine call to me, it will be true by definition that 'being a Catholic' exceeds in comprehensiveness 'being a homosexual' or being any other particular sort of person.[20] But so far as 'being a Catholic' is only the name for an identity, for a particular interpretation of divine call as a mass identity, it need not be more embracing than 'being a homosexual'. For many of the lives I have been telling, I would want to argue that 'being a homosexual' may have contained more of Catholic living than 'being a Catholic' – understood, again, as a standardised and specifiable social identity.

It would be wiser to admit that the more embracing labels for vocation are also the most mysterious – uncertain, unspecifiable, changeable, elusive. A label that looks on its surface less embracing may actually suggest more of a vocation so far as it refuses to become an identity. 'Being homosexual' may look like a narrow and subordinate way of describing a vocation, but to the extent that it invites one to reject fixed identities, to participate in the creation of a more just society, or to become a witness for a holier Church – to that extent, it is in fact a more embracing label and so a better articulation for the mystery of vocation. Certainly 'being homosexual' may be a better example of an appropriately negative or apophatic theology of vocation than 'being Catholic' in many ordinary uses.

In theology, we are always at risk of being misled by false clarity. The risk may be greater in some fields of moral theology than in much of dogmatic or constructive theology. The risk is greater because it is concealed by the ruses of power. Bodily desires may lead us to discover those ruses, especially if they are desires that run counter to the violent certainties of sexual regulation. For all their historical transience and social pliability, our current versions of homosexuality offer an excellent introduction to how nature takes its revenge on false certainties that pretend to be grace. Some of us may now be called through the artefact 'homosexuality' to our encounters with God. All are called by the quarrel over 'homosexuality' to think again about the sovereign newness of divine calling.

Notes

1. This is the title of the fifth chapter in Vatican II's constitution on the Church, *Lumen Gentium* (21 November 1964). The best known of twentieth-century technical disputes over (clerical or religious) vocation is that between Lahitton and Branchereau, which was finally put to rest by Pius XII in the apostolic constitution *Sedes Sapientiae* (31 May 1956).

2. In what follows, I use 'queer' as a deliberately loose term for minority sexual identities involving same-sex desire in some manner or degree. I choose it because it carries less implicit ontology than the acronym 'LGBT' or any of its components.

3. George A. Hyde, letter of 6 June 2004, as on the website of the Eucharistic Catholic Church (Canadian Branch).

4. George A. Hyde, personal communication, 27 February 2005.

5. George A. Hyde, letter of 12 February 1977, to Raymond Broshears, GLBT Historical Society (San Francisco), Broshears papers, carton 4, 'Hyde' folder. Compare the block quotations attributed to Hyde by Helen Pappas, 'Happy Birthday, Jesus! Happy Anniversary, Beloved Church!', *SAGA Newsletter* (December 1976), pp. 8–10, at p. 9.

6. Pappas lists the forenames of the twelve protesters, of whom she was one. They include six women and six men, with four names appearing in couples. See Pappas, 'Happy Birthday, Jesus!', p. 8.

7. 'Sodom', reprinted from a 1947 issue of *VIA: Newsletter of the Church of the Holy Eucharist* in *SAGA Newsletter* (December 1976), p. 12.

8. For a sharply critical biography of Villatte and the churches descended from him, see Peter F. Anson, *Bishops at Large* (London: Faber & Faber, 1964), pp. 91–129 and 252–322.

9. Donald S. Lucas, undated survey letter (probably April 1964), as in GLBT Historical Society (San Francisco), Lucas Papers, box 7, folder 1.

10. I follow the printed summaries in Donald S. Lucas, *The Homosexual and the Church* (San Francisco: The Mattachine Society, 1966). I correct silently some errors in spelling or syntax. Some information about the respondents can be gathered from 'Background Material on Participants' pp. 5–8, but other facts are disclosed in the responses that make up the bulk of the booklet.

11. Lucas, *Homosexual*, p. 20, respondent no. 4.

12. Lucas, *Homosexual*, pp. 30–2, respondent no. 2.

13. Committee for Homosexual Freedom, broadside 'newsletter' of 5 June 1969.

14. These are listed in *Speaking Up* (MCC San Francisco) vol. 2, no. 7 (14 February 1971), p. 5.

15. I follow the chronology in Pat Roche, *Dignity/USA 25: A Chronology, 1969–1994* (Washington: Dignity/USA, 1995), especially pp. 1–13. I have supplemented that chronology with the recollections of some of the first members of the LA chapter, compiled by Armand Avila and Jim Kyger.

16. Complete statement inside the front covers of Jeannine Gramick, Robert Nugent and Thomas Oddo, *Homosexual Catholics: A Primer for Discussion* (4th printing, n.p.: Dignity, 1977), and Kathleen Leopold and Thomas Orians (eds), *Theological Pastoral Resources: A Collection of Articles on Homosexuality from a Pastoral Perspective*, 6th edn (Washington: Dignity, 1981).

17. Congregation for the Doctrine of the Faith, *Persona Humana* (*Declaration on Certain Question Pertaining to Sexual Ethics*, December 29, 1775), *Acta Apostolicae Sedis* 68 (1976), pp. 77–96.

18. Congregation for the Doctrine of the Faith, *Homosexualitatis Problema* (*Letter on the Pastoral Care of Homosexual Persons*, October 1, 1986), *Acta Apostolicae Sedis* 79 (1987), pp. 543–54.

19. Lucas, *Homosexual*, p. 31, respondent no. 2.

20. It should be clear that I use 'embracing' or 'comprehensive' to refer to aspects of a single person rather than to a number of persons being run together as if under a single species.

Chapter Eleven

Aftermath of Abuse

John Allan Loftus SJ

He had just finished presiding at the eleven o'clock Eucharist. It was a glorious fall day in small-town rural Ontario. Golden leaves swirled around the little town playground across the street from the tiny white church. Then he saw the little girl on the swing and playfully loped across the street to meet her. He tickled her briefly, enjoyed her squeals of laughter, and pushed her higher and higher into the blue sky.

A neighbour, not a parishioner, watched the scene with growing anxiety and consternation. She then phoned the police. They arrived in a matter of minutes with lights flashing, but mercifully without sirens. They promptly secured the priest and walked him to their waiting car. The little girl started crying but was soon joined by her mother who had just taken a moment to talk with a friend across the street.

The police said they had no choice but to drive the priest to head-quarters. They suggested the mother and little girl follow. Despite protests from the woman and her little girl, the police were firm. They had received a report of a priest molesting a child in the park. Even as the little girl kept crying out 'Daddy, Daddy', no misunderstanding was suspected.

The priest sharing a playful moment with the little girl was her father. He was a visiting Anglican priest from another diocese. But that possibility had not crossed anyone's mind that morning. Despite the painfulness of the mistake, no apologies were ever made and the priest was still sent by his bishop for a psychiatric evaluation – 'just to be on the safe side'. That's how we met.

This is a painful example of just one relatively small consequence of the sexual abuse scandals. It illustrates well one of the so-called secondary victims of the 'crisis', a father just playing with his daughter, but unfortunately also wearing his Roman collar. There are, and will continue to be, many other unintended consequences for society in the aftermath of this debacle. And the debate about its causes and remedy will occupy the Church for decades.

The broader picture

The fact that people do not always live up to their publicly avowed commitments is a story as old as Adam and Eve. It hardly surprises anyone any more. From divorce courts to corporate boardrooms, in London, New York, and just about everywhere else, copious examples flood modern sensitivities. We are almost saturated with stories of greed, selfishness and infidelity. But not quite saturated.

When the tale involves priests and sex, interest peaks. And it has indeed peaked over the past few years. Revelations of infidelity, at the very least, and of crass criminality, at the worst, have headlined newspapers around the world. To add insult to injury, the lurid stories of sexual misconduct with children and young people turn out to be only the tip of this proverbial iceberg. Church leadership, it is now clear, was in many cases knowingly complicit in this misconduct. And we are still waiting for the other shoe to drop: stories of sexual misconduct with age-appropriate partners are slowly making their own way into headlines. That will be a different story, but with sadly familiar features.[1]

The pain and suffering thus far has been enormous – not only for primary victims but also for what health professionals now call all the secondary victims. These include families, friends, whole parishes and church communities, and even other priests still working hard and faithfully. The immediate consequences, emotional, spiritual and economic, have been devastating all around the world. Certainly on some levels the Church will never be the same again.

But which of the consequences will have a longer lasting impact? Which have the staying power to effect change? Real change. That is much more difficult to discern. To be sure, there are voices – often strident and supremely confident – heralding one or another position. At one end of the spectrum are the voices of fidelity praying that this crisis will allow the Church universal to return to its former state of order, obedience and clarity. At the other end are voices that hear in this sad state of affairs a historic and unprecedented call to revamp the entire clerical and hierarchical structure itself.

Many of these ecclesiastical 'talking heads' have become the so-called experts. To paraphrase the oft-quoted slur used about Sigmund Freud and many fellow psychoanalysts: they are often wrong, but never uncertain.

As is often the case, both poles may have some truth to offer. Neither, however, has a crystal ball. And all the rest of us, we mere mortals, will either have to just live through the moment or decide to take an active part in shaping a new moment in the Church's life and history. This entire book is dedicated to and written for the latter group: those who are committed to continuing to 'open up' and grow in and for the future Church.

As is often the case, some reflection on how we came to this moment may help us move more peacefully into the next moment. How did the Church, in particular the Roman Catholic Church, ever get itself into this contemporary morass? Where did the sex abuse 'crisis' come from? And how could we have been so blind? Or were we?

Psychological explanations

The most obvious and even facile explanation for how so many priest sexual abusers could turn up seemingly all at once around the world leads some to label the obvious pathology, and then decry the equally obvious lax screening that allowed these men into priesthood in the first place. This is the 'few bad apples' theory. They are paedophiles, pure and simple. Indeed this simple explanation seems to work for some of the more notorious cases, the Paul Shanleys and John Geoghans in the United States, for example. A long-time serial rapist usually does have a clear, if not always simple, pathology. But this is not, for the most part, what has been revealed by the priests' misconduct story.

The vast majority of priests engaged in sexual misconduct crossed the line with post-pubescent young men. It is called technically, as I'm sure everyone knows by now, ephebophilia. Unfortunately, giving it a fancy-sounding name does not make anything clearer really. The professional community still does not know whether this proclivity actually exists as a distinguishable pathology. Nor do we know, even if it does exist, what treatment implications are indicated as a result. In a culture saturated by barely clothed teenaged models of both genders proudly 'strutting their stuff' on everything from candy packages to underwear, do we as a society really want to call our fascination with youth a psychosexual pathology? If so, the entire culture seems indictable.

My psychological colleagues and I have not, I'm afraid, been very helpful. Just look at the professional community's sad record on predicting recidivism in sex offenders. If the case is clear-cut and of significant duration to begin with, it can be fairly easy. But when the area is grey – as it was and is with most priest cases – the diagnostic horizon remains cloudy. Most of these men are not simply paedophiles.

The next most obvious psychological 'explanation' comes with the price tag of insulting a whole segment of the wider population. This is 'the gay explanation'. There are too many gay men in priesthood and the result is the age-inappropriate sexual acting out of most (all) of them.

Unfortunately, there are too many people who choose to remain blissfully unaware that there is not a shred of scientific evidence to suggest this correlation. Nor is there even much anecdotal evidence to substantiate it. In fact, it would appear the vast majority of gays in ministry live lives of integrity and are quite genuinely happy in their ministry – not withstanding the largely homophobic Church they serve. There is little but popular imagination – and largely erroneous imagination at that – that fuels the suspicion that gay clerics are less likely to honour their celibate commitments.

Perhaps few celibates of any sexual orientation live out their publicly avowed commitment with integrity. This is something that Richard Sipe,[2] for example, seems to have been suggesting for a long time now. But perhaps that conviction is also more wishful thinking just in order to make another point – about the desire for married priests, for example. The observation certainly is not based on anything approaching what the modern professional world would call real data. And a non-celibate clergy would in any case offer no guarantees against sexual misconduct. The record shows that the vast majority of current male sexual offenders are, in fact, already married.

Nonetheless, the 'gay scapegoat' manoeuvre remains very attractive to many in today's Church. It participates in the denial process so nicely by conflating two 'obvious' problems for the Church (homosexuality and sexual misconduct) and at the same time allows for neither issue to be explored carefully or independently. James Alison (another contributor to this book) has rather effectively exploded this dynamic in his eye-opening and marvellous book *Faith Beyond Resentment: Fragments Catholic and Gay*.[3] More recently, a pseudonymous priest illumines the same terrain in *Commonweal* magazine; his article is called 'A Gay Priest Speaks Out'.[4]

Cultural explanations

Donald Cozzens suggests in his latest book that the real explanation for the sex abuse crisis in the Church rests on the remnants of our feudal past that are still alive and operational in the Church.[5] All we have to do, presumably, is cast off those feudal vestiges and move into a new, democratised utopia run mostly by lay people now.

I do exaggerate a bit, but I continue to be amazed by the simplicity and optimism that would simply replace all clerics with laity and think most issues would resolve themselves. I get even more sceptical – and even a tad cynical at times – when I realise some of these voices are the same ones that only a few short decades ago told us to trust the clergy and hierarchy blindly.

This is a misplaced optimism, it seems to me. It may explain for some how cardinals and bishops could have turned such a blind eye. But it perpetuates a naive myth that the whole present crisis was created by some 'bad people' caught in a 'bad ecclesial situation'. This is not really truthful or hopeful to me. Worse yet, Cozzens concludes by telling us that unless we do move into this lay democratic Church, there is no hope at all. The Church will necessarily 'continue to practise denial, dissimulation, and deception'. I demur: reality – and the Church as part of that reality – is simply more complex than this.

The Catholic Church remains, no doubt, largely feudal in many significant ways. We should all encourage and applaud its updating. But as the ultimate explanation for the present scandal, it is a shamefully naive thesis.

Another more appealing cultural analysis is offered by Howard Bleichner in his new book *A View from the Altar*.[6] He begins by noting that 'by any measure, the sexual abuse scandals have struck the Catholic Church in the United States with the force of a tsunami, dealing the Catholic priesthood the worst blow in memory.' The analysis that follows offers a fascinating look at how the Vatican II reforms had already begun to reshape priesthood and the Church, particularly by the changes in the celebration of Eucharist and Penance.

These are the two sacraments in which specifically priestly power rested. In the post-Vatican II Church, both sacraments were dramatically altered, and both dramatically altered priestly identity. Then the changes in boundaries, both in moral theology and in daily lived experience for priests, arrived and were, Bleichner suggests, the fertile soil in which confusion, and especially sexual confusion, grew.

Most clinicians with experience in treating priest-offenders will testify that, while there were some with more or less clearly defined psychosexual disorders or other specific pathologies, the vast majority are more accurately described as confused men. They were confused in their professional identity; they were confused in their personal identity; they were confused sexually. Most often, they did not honestly know whether they were gay or straight. They were 'experimenting' as seemed to befit the times. Their behaviour was certainly still lamentable, and it was most often clearly illegal and demanded civil punishment. But their 'pathologies' are less demonstrable in simple diagnostic categories.

Speaking of 'lamentable', it is equally clear that the seminary structures that supposedly nourished these men and the social support systems their priesthood afforded them later, after ordination, both share a great deal of the blame. There is plenty of blame to go around. The problem itself, though, will not be easily explained away by recourse to such appeals. Nor perhaps will yet another seminary 'visitation' from Rome alter this psychic landscape much.

Ecclesial explanations

This diagnostic complexity helps explain why so many mental health professionals seemed shocked by the facile, so-called 'one-strike-you're-out' policy of the American bishops in Dallas. There is little doubt their decision was politically expedient. Bishops were being hounded by the media, some of whom were already demanding account-ability for the bishops' own role in all this. So they again deftly deflected attention back to the 'few bad apples', and lamented the lax and lascivious morals of American culture against which, they repeatedly reminded us, they had already been preaching for years. The minds of most intelligent Catholics, and most others on the planet, simply sighed: 'Nice try!'

Listening to 'official' explanations of the crisis from individual bishops, and sometimes from entire bishops' conferences, leads one to suspect that perhaps the only thing bishops have really learned in all this is a new 'spin' technique. Perhaps the current White House strategists have been tutoring them. Spin has risen to state-of-the-art perfection there. It is hard not to seem somewhat cynical.

One of the saddest consequences of official church attempts to explain the scandals has been the erosion of whatever little moral voice was left there. This emperor is now clearly naked for almost all to view in sadness. I say 'almost all in sadness' because there are those, of course, who delight in what seems to them to be this final embarrass-ment to the Church. Perhaps now, they reason, this meddlesome voice will finally remove itself from their lives, and especially from their bedrooms.

Others, though, lament the potential loss of a significant moral voice on the world stage, one that has initiated or aided innumerable efforts to bring greater justice and equity for the world's poor. There is a loss here, and there is long-lost lesson: this is not the first great human institution to stumble under the weight of a combination of arrogance and sex run amok.

Perhaps the saddest part of this pathetic debacle is that much of it could have been prevented. I speak now not so much of the aberrant sex-ual behaviour of some miscreant priests, but the profound disillusion-ment occasioned by the leadership vacuum.

The real issues raised by the scandal are not primarily sexual in nature. The credibility chasm that has been opened has more to do with the extraordinary inability of church leaders, at all levels from the local parish to the Vatican, to respond in truth and with alacrity to an obvious breakdown in their own moral compass and authority. The Church now seems to be devouring itself from the inside out (or at least from middle management on down). The dynamic is seen by many as genuinely very sad, but not totally unexpected. It is not really much less predictable, pathetic and paralysing than what Enron executives did to themselves.

Any institution whose very foundations are built on proclaiming truth as the ultimate path to freedom should be more careful and more humble. That seems impossible for us to remember – once again. In *Telling Truths in Church* Mark Jordan (also a contributor to the present book) provides a most lucid primer on the difficulties involved in remembering just how to tell the truth in a Church.[7]

What have we learned?

This is a difficult question to answer because many different people will claim to have learned different things. Some will contend that we might not have learned anything at all. Even though we are still in the immediate aftermath of the scandal, there are a few generalisations that seem to be true now and may enjoy some longevity.

I think we have learned, or at least are learning, that accountability must permeate all levels of even highly structured and hierarchical organisations. This does not necessarily mean the Church needs to become entirely democratic. It does mean no one person or group can stand beyond the judgement of fellow members of the body of Christ. It is an injunction as old as St Paul: bishops, too, must be accountable to the people of God. And it is the responsibility of the people of God to create the mechanisms for that accountability. It may require dragging bishops kicking and screaming to view their emptying coffers, but whatever it takes, there is a gospel mandate to demand greater accountability from all.

We have learned, or are learning, that respectful dialogue, which must include genuine attempts to really listen to each other, is an indispensable starting point. Something like the late Cardinal Bernadin's 'Common Ground Initiative' is more critical at this point in history than ever before. Bishops have a right and a duty to protect and defend orthodoxy, but they are losing (or have lost) the right to simply bluster anathemas at anyone with whom they disagree.

We have learned, or are learning, that at least a certain level of psychosexual maturity is a basic requirement for ministry in any church. This means that at least in seminaries and formation programmes, sex, in all its delightfully and frighteningly human variants, must finally be openly discussed. (Honest sex talk is, of course, also long overdue on

AFTERMATH OF ABUSE   143

everyone's Catholic plate.) In formation for ministry, we have learned so painfully that what you don't know can hurt you!

We have also learned, or are learning, that as an entire community of faith we are still far, far from living our cherished public ideals. We have not only scandalised the little ones (Matthew 18:6), we have harboured and encouraged by our silence an arrogant leadership recklessly bent on being served rather than serving in simplicity and honesty (Luke 22:26–27). And on all fronts, offenders, bishops and victims, we all still seem paralysed and incapable of the most basic understanding of the gospel mandate to forgive. Yet that is a hallmark of who we claim to be as Church; we pray it daily in the Lord's Prayer as we ask forgiveness for ourselves as we forgive others (Matthew 6:12). We know at a visceral level that if we cannot forgive, we cannot have life (Matthew 18:35).

Psychologists, of all people, know how long and how painful can be the road to forgiveness. And yet one of the saddest moments for me in the aftermath of yet another trial for scandal came at the closing sentencing hearing. The victim turned to the cameras and said coldly of his former-priest offender: 'I hope he dies in prison. And I hope it is a slow and very painful death.'

Even as I try to comprehend this pain, I am even more saddened to realise how little we can offer each other to promote forgiveness. We have all been damaged by the recent scandal; we are all diminished.

Challenge in the ashes

The Church has always loved high drama. In both the political arena and in its own liturgical arena, spectacle often dominates. Sometimes the spectacle serves the narrative; sometimes it obscures. Sometimes the spectacle unfortunately reveals only a little man in Kansas, hiding behind a curtain huffing and puffing with all his power to maintain the façade of a well-ordered Oz. In our case, it is lots of little men (and some big ones too) all trying, individually and sometimes in concert, to perpetuate and polish a similar myth.

The aftermath of the abuse scandal around the world offers another defining moment for the Church. This is not the first such moment, nor will it be the last. Only time will tell if it will be as spectacular a moment as some claim. I, for one, do not yet know, for example, if this moment rivals the Reformation for sheer potential to alter the ecclesial landscape, but I do believe that this moment does token another *kairos* in the life of the contemporary Church, a potentially graced moment of self-knowledge and self-acceptance. Whether or not anything lasting occurs because of this moment, will largely depend on what we make of it.

Joan Chittister has written powerfully about the experience of sitting in ashes and revisioning faith.[8] Hers is an apt image. Nothing short of a conflagration has erupted and remains smouldering deep within the hearts and minds of Catholics around the world. Contrary to some bishops' fondest hopes, this will not simply go away. It is naive and frankly stupid to just keep hoping it will. Business-as-usual attitudes created a large dimension of the problem in the first place. Ashes are just piled too high in many churchyards. And in some places, like Boston, their acrid fumes threaten to choke life itself out of the local Church. The anger and disillusionment are palpable. And yet there is hope in many hearts. There is a *kairos* expectation.

The hope, for many, lies in the invitation to own again the Church as a body of all believers. The painful insight that many, young and old, are again realising is that the Church does not 'belong' to any one group, not to priests, not even to bishops and cardinals, and certainly not to curial dicasteries in Rome.

Back to the future

'We' are Church! Together. We are multi-hued, we are female as well as male, we are gay and straight, we are all sinners and would-be saints. And we must learn again to listen to each other. More voices, and more educated and sophisticated voices from all sectors of the Church (lay voices, theological voices, scientific voices), are arising to shape the future. This is right, and feels right! This growing conviction is one of the greatest gifts in the aftermath of the scandals. Ironically, it is the very dream fashioned 40 years ago in Vatican II's *Dogmatic Constitution on the Church.*

Whether there will be massive structural change in the immediate future is quite unclear. I doubt it. There will certainly be death-defying attempts to derail any such hopes. Will there really be a massive strategic retreat to yesteryear? I doubt that too. These proverbial cows were let out of the barn 40 years ago. They're not going back – and they're not going backwards.

The worst-case scenario, it seems to me, would be to let so-called experts on either side of the great liberal–conservative divide of contemporary Catholicism keep polishing their crystal balls and setting the terms of engagement. Too many of them are crass lobbyists for pet projects – on both sides of the equation. Too many of them are still incapable of listening. They just talk.

Just because 'they' will not listen to me does not mean I cannot listen to them – whoever they are. The dream of a renewed Church was fashioned at Vatican II by Pope John XXIII's desire to listen carefully to the signs of the times. Listening is at the heart of whatever the Church was, is, and will become. We, too, now need to listen carefully to these signs. If history is at all predictive, what we hear will not be obvious. It will not enshrine either the liberal or the conservative agenda. Little in real life is that simple or that obvious.

Listening does demand, however, the patience and the courage also to speak. Opening up to honest dialogue is critical; that alone could have prevented much of what occasioned the sexual scandals in the first place. We cannot allow any party to simply close down behind self-erected barriers of ideology or ignorance. That would be the recurring and perhaps never-ending scandal.

The root meaning of the word scandal is connected with stumbling blocks. There are many in today's Church stumbling. The foundation on which the Church itself is built was also called a stumbling block by St Paul. In the contemporary Church, we are, it seems, in good company. The aftermath can become prologue. It has before. It can again. There is always hope.

Notes

1. See Jane Anderson, *Priests in Love: Roman Catholic Clergy and Their Intimate Friendships* (New York: Continuum, 2005).
2. *A Secret World: Sexuality and the Search for Intimacy* (New York: Brunner/Mazel, 1990).
3. London: Darton, Longman & Todd and New York: Crossroad, 2001.
4. Gerard Thomas, 28 January 2005.
5. *Faith That Dares to Speak* (Collegeville, MN: Liturgical Press, 2004).
6. New York: Crossroad, 2004.
7. Boston, MA: Beacon Press, 2003.
8. *Fire in These Ashes: A Spirituality of Contemporary Religious Life* (Kansas City, MO: Sheed & Ward, 1995).

PART THREE
A WORLD IN CRISIS

Chapter Twelve

When the Paradigm Shifts, Even the Church Has to Change

Diarmuid O'Murchu MSC

The concept of a paradigm shift has been in vogue for the past forty years.[1] It denotes a quality of fundamental change that really only makes sense with hindsight. From a Catholic perspective we think of the Second Vatican Council of the 1960s as the instigator of major change. Indeed, it was, and still is in many spheres of Catholic life. The response to Vatican II on the part of clergy and people varied enormously, and still does. Whereas some feel frustration at an apparent entrenchment in recent years, there are still those who feel that the Catholic Church embraces change too rapidly and readily.

Among Catholics, and humans in general, there is a widespread assumption that we control change and that basically change only happens as we decide. A little reflection will show how naive and un-realistic this assumption is. That is the challenge posed by the notion of paradigm shifts. At a conscious level, we can activate change. I make a decision to buy a new coat. Yet even this simple piece of behaviour is not as free as we often assume. Advertising, fashions, comparisons we make with what others wear, all influence my choice.

Paradigm shifts address the issue of change from a cultural and evolutionary perspective, postulating that change is essential to growth and that 'life' continuously activates change at the service of growth. This frequently happens through the paradoxical cycle of birth–death–rebirth. It happens continuously within our human bodies, but also at every level of cosmic and planetary creation. Frequently, we cannot identify particular causes for the change happening around us, nor can we control the direction such change will take. In every paradigm shift, the new catches up with us more quickly than we think. Not surprising-ly, therefore, faced with a paradigm shift, many people and organisations simply revert to denial. It is just too much to take in. Better carry on and pretend that all is well.

As a Christian social scientist, I am enthralled by the paradigm shifts affecting religions and Churches in the contemporary world. I want to begin these reflections by highlighting some paradigmatic features of contemporary Catholicism before reviewing two major catalysts for such shifts, namely the new cosmology and the Christian concept of the Kingdom of God.

Three dynamic features

Undoubtedly, Vatican II was a major turning point in the recent history of the Catholic Church. One could argue, however, that Vatican II merely brought to the fore what the Holy Spirit was already activating in the world generally. A new creative freedom was unfolding; in 1960 alone 17 African nations declared independence. People became aware of other cultures and began to celebrate diversity. Mutual empowerment began to flourish as hierarchies softened. Words like consultation, delegation and collaboration entered the vocabulary. And significantly for all the Christian Churches, lay people began to read and study theology.

Cumulatively, these trends contributed to a new paradigm within Catholicism, one that is still not widely recognised although it continues to grow rapidly. Three dimensions are of particular significance.

First, in 1960, two-thirds of the Catholic population of the world lived in the northern hemisphere. Today, 75 per cent lives in the South. The demographic constitution of the Catholic Church – for the first time in history – has changed dramatically in the past forty years. The heart-centre of modern Catholicism is no longer in the North – symbolically signified by Rome and the papacy of Benedict XVI. It has shifted to the South. To keep the focus on the North, and to keep talking about what is coming out of Rome, as the Church tries to do, is a classic example of seeking the living among the dead (cf. Luke 24:5) – or at least among the dying.

Second, male clerical priesthood, the linchpin of Catholicism, particularly since the sixteenth century, is in terminal decline and is unlikely to survive. This is obvious in the West, and a similar trend can be detected in countries like the Philippines and Brazil. Catholic priesthood in Africa is likely to implode because of its rigid adherence to patriarchal values. In my opinion, we will not see a revitalisation of clericalised priesthood. One cannot resuscitate an old paradigm. The responsible thing for our time is to face the terminal decline and learn how to 'bury the dead'. Only then will we become truly free to embrace the radically new paradigm to which the creative Spirit is inviting us.

Third, in the 1960s, lay people began studying theology, thus breaking the clerical monopoly affirmed by the Council of Trent. The official Church did not instigate this movement; presumably – it was the subversive Holy Spirit, doing what the Spirit is good at doing. Today, lay theologians outnumber priest theologians by at least four to one. Theology no longer belongs to the clericalised 'teaching' Church; it is now in the hands of the laity and that will be the pattern of the future.

Lay people bring a different consciousness to theology: they theologise from the context of the urgent questions facing the world rather than from the basis of ecclesiastical tradition. In scholastic philosophy we are told that action follows thought. When we change the level of our awareness, we start attracting a different reality. The Catholic Church today is at a new theological threshold, engaging a new theological paradigm. The implications are far more formidable than most people realise.

The Catholic Church is gone global, and the more global it becomes the more the institution will desperately try to put things back in the closet of the previous paradigm. And this is where the people's Church and the guardians of the institution begin to part company. This is the confusion many lay people allude to in contemporary discourse. In truth, more lay people today tread lightly on the periphery of the institutional Church, rather than commit deeply to its inner reality. Catholics are rapidly growing up and becoming adult in their faith – another paradigm shift. Assuredly, they look to leadership for inspiration but no longer will they collude with codependent control.

Pedagogically, many of us (laity and priests) have not been prepared for this new adult-based culture of faith, and therefore huge numbers drop out, not knowing how to handle the new levels of adult responsibility.

To abandon or to outgrow?

As a social scientist, most of my ministry and pastoral experience has been with non-Catholics, often folks of other religious persuasions. Consequently, my perspective for the remainder of this essay will be on the Church in general rather than merely the Catholic Church. For many years now, I have encountered people who speak of having outgrown the need for the Church, as distinct from having abandoned it. This is a crucial distinction rarely recognised or named in its true significance. Many people who give up on the Church are doing so for seriously conscientious reasons, but often there is no forum where their voice can be heard or honoured.

All the religions are bedevilled by dualistic distinctions, philosophically neat, but often meaningless in the real world. According to the dualistic world-view, one is either in or out; fine for an organisation like the army, but not for a living organism like a faith community. In negotiating faith today, we encounter many liminal spaces, new and inviting horizons, where the living Spirit of God ploughs radically new furrows.

Some of us choose to be there; more of us know deep in our hearts that we have no choice but to be there, no matter what price we pay.

New cosmology

The horizon I wish to explore is the world as understood by contemporary science and by the new cosmology. I begin with a disturbing statement by the renowned world scientist, Stephen Hawking, made during a radio interview many years ago. Acknowledging that religion and mysticism would play a central role in future science, yet sticking to his stance as a non-religious believer, Hawking answered the interviewer's question 'Why do you find it so hard to believe in God?' with 'Because your God is not big enough for me.'

Implicitly, Hawking is asserting that through his scientific research he is aware of mystery and depth in creation. Intuitively he knows something of the reality of God, more – dare we suggest? – than many overt religious believers. But he gets stuck precisely as many religious people do: he over-identifies God with religion, and without religion feels he cannot have God.

This is strangely disturbing for a person of such brilliant mind. Why can't Hawking just trust his intuitions and flow with them? If his God is bigger than that of religion, why doesn't he honour that sense of God? If religion can't cope with his big picture of God, then that is religion's problem, but sadly Hawking seems to be making it his problem too.

This is a widespread pastoral and pedagogical problem. Overtly, ours seems to be a godless culture, but as several researchers indicate, there is widespread curiosity about religious matters, in fact a type of mystical fascination. While the outward world is addicted to making money and accruing power, people in the inner realm search for solutions that do not rely on, nor require, yesterday's religions. Perhaps, unknown to us humans, consciousness is changing – rapidly and massively.

The information explosion is part of the explanation, and evolution itself is obviously up to something significant. Whatever the precise explanation – and I suspect a precise one does not exist – all of us are forced to think and perceive in a bigger and deeper way than in previous times. And this is exactly how paradigm shifts work.

A new way of seeing the world

A paradigm shift undermines conventional models of reality precisely by plunging our understanding into a deeper level. Therefore, that which looks radically new is in effect quite ancient; the newness is in its relevance to the new evolutionary breakthroughs of the current times.

The new cosmology[2] is a view of global reality long known to our ancient ancestors and cherished by mystics of all the great religious traditions. These are its chief tenets:

1. All creation is alive, endowed with a life-form far more resilient, sophisticated and enduring than human life; everything, including the human species, is begotten from the primordial womb of cosmic creation.
2. The life-stuff of creation, which scientists call energy, spirituality calls living spirit. Holy Spirit has been fully at work in creation since the dawn of time, long before the notion was ever conceived by religion.
3. Energy, or living spirit, functions through a relational matrix, not through a set of atomistic building blocks. Relational interaction is the clue to understanding the dynamic flow of everything in creation.
4. Creation evolves and grows through the principles of holism: the whole is greater than the sum of its constituent parts, yet the whole is contained in each part. Quantum physics unravels the ensuing challenges for human understanding.
5. And holism includes destruction as well as creation. Paradox thrives at every level of creation; it cannot be understood through the rational mind, nor can it be resolved by the patriarchal strategy of domination and control.
6. While externally creation seems to exhibit layers as in a hierarchy, on closer examination holarchy is the governing principle. So-called 'nested hierarchies' are in effect holons within greater wholes from which they receive meaning and purpose.
7. Evolution evolves as an open-ended story, not as a set of rational facts. And evolution thrives on cooperation, not on competition. However, for cooperation to function effectively legitimate self-interest must be safeguarded.
8. Humans are a relatively recent addition to the great story of creation. We seem to have the most highly developed capacity for self-reflexive consciousness (the ability to think about the fact that we can think), but through our arrogant and anthropocentric use of this gift we are now posing a serious threat to the rest of planetary life and consequently reaping our own self-destruction.
9. Evolution thrives on paradox and chaos, yet when viewed on the grand scale, elegance and creativity and a preferred sense of direction are abundantly manifest. And the eternal nature of cosmic creation (world without end) is no longer taboo for growing numbers of scientists.

10. God's creativity in this paradigm is understood to be within creation rather than something initiated or activated from without. Some scholars call it *panentheism*. Advocates of the new cosmology refrain from saying much about God or God's revelation. For them creation abounds with divine energy; we need to befriend creation in a much more enlightened way and then God will no longer be a problem which humans tried to sort out by inventing religion.

Today, the world is invading the Church, indeed invading all religions, through the new consciousness begotten from the new cosmology. Religion's patriarchal desire for control has been unmasked; the patriarchal, father-like, ruling God is seen as an anthropocentric projection to validate human rule; the fundamental flaw (original sin) is a means of distracting humans from the fundamental paradox on which all creation thrives: the first revelation of the divine is in creation itself, and not in religion; humans have engaged with holy mystery for thousands, probably millions, of years before religion was ever instituted.

Regrounding the Jesus story

For Christians, this inevitably forces us to ask: 'And where does that leave our faith in Jesus?' Elsewhere, I explore this question in greater length.[3] Our faith in Jesus has been couched in a co-dependent paradigm, inculcating in many people a rather immature sense of faith. In several cases, people seem to have taken into adult life the understanding of faith they inherited as children. Little wonder so many people flock into sects and cults that provide a childlike certainty and simplicity, while others veer in the opposite direction and abandon faith completely.

The Christian churches themselves have also kept Jesus safe and respectable within the codependent world of patriarchal governance. Jesus is depicted as the childlike, suffering servant, ever faithful to the Father-God. And the Jesus story is couched in the restrictive norms of the Judaeo-Roman world. Jesus has been reduced to a human imperial artefact, which on closer examination can be seen as an ideological abomination, rapidly losing credibility for contemporary Christians.

The Jesus Seminar[4] is one group of contemporary scholars striving to rescue Jesus from this cultural minimalism. What needs to be rescued more than anything else is the primordial vision on which Jesus staked his mission as an ambassador of God for the world. The gospels describe this mission in terms of the Kingdom of God, a biblical concept the fuller meaning of which has eluded Christians for much of the 2000 years of Christendom.

Using this paradoxical rubric of 'the Kingdom of God' Jesus laid out the ingredients of his prophetic mission. Amid much exploration and debate,[5] contemporary scholarship considers the following to be some of the key elements of this new vision:

1. By adopting the language and concepts of earthly kingship, Jesus subverted that vision and replaced it with a radical egalitarian way of living.
2. Power from on high became empowerment from the base up; therefore the poor and marginalised inherit the Kingdom first.
3. While kingly regimes differentiate between who is in and who is out, for Jesus everybody is in, especially those excluded because of their 'unworthiness'.
4. According to royal patronage, power is invested primarily in people at the top; for Jesus it is invested in the rank and file and in strategies of mutual empowerment.
5. According to royal protocol you earn your way up the ladder of status and power, and conditions are laid down on how you make progress; for Jesus there are no conditions, other than that of unconditional love through which everything is offered as pure gift.
6. In the time of Jesus earthly kings were assumed to be God's primary representatives on earth. For Jesus God works primarily through all who seek right relationships in bringing about a reign of love and justice.
7. Royal patronage adopts a rational rhetoric heavily protected by law; Jesus released the new Reign of God through storytelling and often broke the rules of his own religion – as in healing and table-fellowship.
8. Kingly rule is territorial; Jesus stretches all conventional paradigms in the direction of new global horizons.

This vision of Jesus was so original, radical and profound, it seems to me that it has taken Christians 2000 years to catch up with him. We are still a long way from coming to terms with what Jesus initiated for us. What seems most elusive to us is the world vision out of which Jesus operated. Jesus was light years ahead of the culture of his day – and of ours as well.

We stand a much better chance of discerning the mind of Jesus by situating him in the context of the new cosmology as outlined above. I don't think we will ever grasp the breadth and depth of the new Reign of God until we see it in the context of the new cosmology. It was this enlarged world-view that made Jesus such an enigma to his own people;

it is still the central feature that eludes people in our time.

Jesus, the world and the Church

Most Christians identify Jesus primarily with the Church because that is what the Church has always promulgated. But is that what Jesus actually wanted? If we truly honour the primacy of the new Reign of God, it seems to me that two corollaries are inescapable. First, Jesus was committed to a whole new way of being in the world and relating to it in terms of justice, love, liberation and compassion. Consequently, Jesus embraced a vision bigger and more inclusive than any religion or cultural process. And second, it is highly unlikely that Jesus wanted a denominational ecclesiastical institution to be established in his name. I guess he is disgusted and shocked that we now have fourteen hundred denominations in his name.

If Jesus did not want a denominational religion or church, how did he envisage his dream unfolding over time in the human family? In other words what would Church look like if it were to honour the primacy of the new Reign of God? Many theologians ask this question, but few answer it doing full justice to the radical call of the Kingdom. The following seem to be basic requirements for a church faithful to Kingdom values:

1. A faith vision that can embrace the whole of God's creation beyond the dualistic division of the sacred versus the secular, and embracing the governing principle of holarchy rather than hierarchy.
2. A quality of community in which people know each other intimately and challenge each other to engage more deeply in the life of faith, the model known as Basic Christian Communities.
3. A body that proclaims the living word of God through storytelling that liberates enduring truth.
4. A faith that fosters deep love by seeking justice in all things.
5. A justice that discerns and promotes the right relationships that enable life to thrive at every level: cosmic, planetary, social and personal.
6. A commitment to building up right relationships through networking with a wide range of agencies: political, social, economic and cultural.
7. An inculturation of faith in creative rituals around key life experiences; this includes formal sacraments, but more than this.
8. A radical commitment to the open table from which no one is ever excluded. This is not just about eucharistic inclusion; it is much more about being proactive to make sure that every person has daily food to eat and water to drink.

9. A pastoral strategy based primarily on healing and liberation, and not just on preaching and teaching.

10. A diversity of ministries, shared in partnership, to serve the building up of authentic community and justice-making in the world.

For me the theologian Peter Hodgson captivates something of this model of Church when he writes: 'Ecclesial community is the human community, transfigured in the direction of liberation, actualizing in the world a universal reconciling love, that liberates from sin and death, alienation and oppression.'[6]

Set my people free

Can this new way of being Church – serving the Kingdom afresh in the contemporary world – be activated within the current ecclesiastical paradigm? Probably not. In the words of the gospels, we can't pour new wine into an old wineskin, though we acknowledge that many are trying to do that, and with a measured degree of success. The agenda of the Kingdom, as I understand it, favours revolution rather than reformation. Jesus was a cultural, mystical subversive who was not too worried about his inherited religion. He often seems to have broken the rules quite blatantly in order to inaugurate the new paradigm for which he gave his life and death.

Beyond the Jesus story is the subversive role of God's living and sustaining energy, which in Christian language we call the Holy Spirit. Christians claim that we receive the Holy Spirit in Baptism and a greater fullness in Confirmation. According to that understanding, the Holy Spirit belongs largely if not exclusively to human beings. The Australian theologian Denis Edwards tries to face this issue with admirable transparency: 'What is required is a holistic theology of the Spirit, that begins not with Pentecost but with the origin of the universe 14 billion years ago.'[7] The theologian Mark Wallace[8] illuminates this vision in an even more compelling way.

At the end of the day the Church, like all embodiments of living faith, is in the hands of God's creative Spirit who blows where she wills. She will set us all free, probably in ways we only vaguely envisage, at this or any other time. I believe it is that same Spirit at work in Catholicism that has shifted the demographic focus from the northern to the southern hemisphere, that is plunging patriarchal clerical priesthood into terminal decline, thus challenging us all to become more fully the people of God; that is awakening theological wisdom (*sophia*) right across the Christian community and not just in a selective clerical subgroup.

The Spirit is doing what I suspect the Spirit is always good at: stretching horizons beyond even our wildest imaginings. But in that process, she is also recalling us to where she primarily operates: not in any one church or religion, but throughout the length and breadth of God's amazing creation.

On that note, I end these reflections with what must surely rank as a perennial parable for both the Church and world of our time. I wrote this essay as the world stood aghast at the appalling loss of life and the destruction caused by the tsunami in the Indian Ocean in late December 2004. For all of us, it was not easy to stand in solidarity with such pain and devastation. Understandably, many people were asking: 'Where is God in all this? What is God up to?'

Perhaps part of the answer rests in this parabolic story: on 26 December a group of gypsy-fishermen near Bangkok, in Thailand, noticed that the sea waters had receded far beyond their usual limit; consequently fishes were popping in and out of the shallow waters with greater frequency. These fishermen knew their sea waters well; they lived in a type of convivial relationship with the living spirit of the seas. Both their collective folklore and intuitive wisdom told them that the receding of the waters indicated that massive waves would crash upon their shoreline later that day. They gathered their few possessions and took refuge in nearby hills. Nobody in their tribe was killed, and they were able to save most of their meagre possessions.

Is this what reading the signs of the times is all about? Is this how the Spirit of wisdom works? Is this not the kind of wisdom we all need, not just to survive, but to be truly responsive to the Spirit who blows where she wills, calling forth the new in our turbulent and stormy times? With this quality of wisdom, we can reach towards the larger horizons I have briefly explored in these pages, and hopefully we can respond not just with caution but, more importantly, with the deep wisdom of the gypsy-fishermen. After all, the Kingdom of God was founded on the lives of gypsy-fishermen, and I guess a church faithful to the Kingdom will always need a good supply of them.

Notes

1. There are several useful web pages on this topic. I find the following particularly helpful: www.enformy.com/ions.newparadigm.html;
   www.paradigmshifts.iwarp.com/customs3.html.
2. For me, the classic work on this subject is Brian Swimme and Thomas Berry, *The Universe Story* (San Francisco: Harper, 1992). For a Catholic readership, I recommend Terence L. Nichols, *The Sacred Cosmos* (Grand Rapids, MI: Brazos Press, 2003).
3. Diarmuid O'Murchu, *Catching Up with Jesus* (New York: Crossroad, 2005).

4. For further information see web pages: www.westarinstitute.org/JesusSeminar; www.religion.rutgers.edu/Seminar.

5. On the topic of the Kingdom of God I recommend the following sources: John Fullenbach, *The Kingdom of God* (Maryknoll, NY: Orbis Books, 1995); M. M. Quatro, *At the Side of the Multitudes* (Quezon City, Philippines: Claretian Publications, 2000).

6. Peter G. Hodgson, *Winds of the Spirit* (London: SCM Press, 1994), pp. 297–8.

7. Denis Edwards, *Breath of Life: A Theology of the Creator Spirit* (Maryknoll, NY: Orbis Books, 2004), p. 1.

8. Mark I. Wallace, *Fragments of the Spirit* (Harrisburg, PA: Trinity Press International, 2002).

Chapter Thirteen

The Poor Come First

Julian Filochowski

The papacy of Benedict XVI has begun in the year in which we celebrate the fortieth anniversary of *Gaudium et Spes*, the jewel in the crown of the Second Vatican Council. *Gaudium et Spes* was the council fathers' pastoral and doctrinal constitution on *The Church in the Modern World*, and the gateway to a new way of being Church. We were to be the People of God engaged in the transformation of the world, 'eloquent proof of its solidarity with the entire human family'.[1]

The frequently quoted opening lines set the direction: 'The joys and the hopes, the griefs and the anxieties of the men and women of this age, especially those who are poor or in any way afflicted, these too are the joys and hopes, the griefs and anxieties of the followers of Christ.'[2] It moved the focus from an all-powerful God and Church to an all-loving God and a Church of loving service in the quest for justice and peace. It opened the way to Paul VI's 1967 encyclical on human development, *Populorum Progressio*, to the Medellín Conference of Latin American Bishops in 1968, and to the subsequent formulation of the preferential option for the poor. *Gaudium et Spes* remains today a beautiful and highly relevant epistle to the universal Church and to this globalised and globalising world.

The Jesuits – faith and justice

It was ten years after *Gaudium et Spes* that the Society of Jesus, at its 32nd General Congregation, proclaimed a preferential option for the poor. In the documents from that landmark global gathering, the Jesuit mission was rearticulated as the service of faith and the promotion of justice.[3] The two, they said, would in future be inseparable.

> The injustice which racks our world ... where millions of men and women, specific people with names and faces, suffer from poverty and hunger, from the unjust distribution of wealth and resources ... is, in fact, a denial of God in practice, for it denies the dignity of the human person, the brother or sister of Christ. The cult of money, progress, prestige and power has as its fruit the sin of

institutional injustice ... and it leads to the enslavement not only of the oppressed, but of the oppressor as well, and to death.[4]

They went on:

We have to overcome the fear ... which blocks us from truly comprehending the social, economic and political problems which exist in our countries and on the international scene ... We cannot be excused from making the most rigorous possible political and social analysis of our situation ... From analysis and discernment will come committed action; from the experience of action will come insight into how to proceed further.

And then they sounded a prescient warning:

If we have the patience and the humility and the courage to walk with the poor, we will learn from what they have to teach us what we can do to help them. But without this arduous journey our efforts for the poor will have an effect just the opposite from what we intend; we will only hinder them from getting a hearing for their real wants and from acquiring the means of taking charge of their own destinies, personal and collective.[5]

In a later decree[6] there came a further valuable elaboration.

Full human liberation for the poor and for us all lies in the development of communities of solidarity at the grass roots level and the NGO level, as well as at the political level, where we can all work together towards total human development.

They are powerful and inspiring words – and together they provide a route map for the contemporary follower of Jesus seeking to take *Gaudium et Spes* seriously and to make that option for the poor real in their own lives. The Church's social teaching is full of fine words and powerful exhortations which all too often are published and then ignored – left to gather dust on the bookshelf. This has earned it the title 'the Church's Best Kept Secret'.[7]

But the Society of Jesus determined that it would actively seek to implement this commitment. And as Pedro Arrupe, the Jesuit Father General, had forewarned, it brought troubles aplenty around the world in those places where the Jesuits acted with steadfast resolution. Central America was one hotspot, and in particular their Central American University José Simeón Cañas in San Salvador, the UCA, which I know especially well.

El Salvador

This last 30 years the UCA has strived, in a society of grotesque social division, conflict and civil war, to be a centre of educational excellence which nevertheless remained connected to all the diverse realities of El Salvador and its people. It analysed with great precision the reality of institutionalised injustice in El Salvador and spoke and published that truth fearlessly. It actively promoted social and economic reform, human rights, dialogue and peace. It provided support and accompaniment to popular movements and Christian base communities, publicising and celebrating their struggles.

In 1977 a rural parish priest, the Jesuit Father Rutilio Grande, was assassinated. Then the whole Society of Jesus in El Salvador was collectively and publicly threatened with execution by a death squad, calling itself the White Warriors' Union. Those in the UCA were accused of being the intellectual support of the guerrilla organisations. The university rector received his own death threats.

Calumnies and attacks in the press were commonplace. Some Jesuits were expelled from the country; others prevented from returning. On 16 November 1989 at the height of the civil war, a military patrol entered the Jesuit community house on the campus in the middle of the night and slaughtered six priests – Ignacio Ellacuría (rector, philosopher, theologian, political analyst and peace broker); Segundo Montes (sociologist and human rights analyst); Ignacio Martín-Baró (director of research and psychologist); Amando López (philosopher and theologian); Joaquín López (community education promoter); Juan Ramón Moreno (theologian and librarian); plus their housekeeper, Julia Elba, and her daughter, Celina Ramos.

In one way or another, these Jesuit martyrs were all immersed in that prophetic enterprise of the witness to faith and the promotion of justice. They were truly at the epicentre of interlocking 'communities of solidarity' functioning locally, regionally and globally. They were emblems of a Church of the poor and heralds of 'a new catholicity' for our time. Like Archbishop Oscar Romero of San Salvador in 1980, they were murdered because they were dynamic and authentic followers of Jesus of Nazareth. They were 'good news' to the poor, real joy and hope.

They were therefore 'bad news' to the rich and powerful caught up in the idolatry of wealth and national security. But the rich and powerful could kill the individuals, and indeed celebrate the killings, but they could never destroy the truth the men they had killed spoke and the inspiration they gave. Today, in 2005 at the beginning of a new pontificate, these Jesuit martyrs remain incredibly important models for us, as we revisit *Gaudium et Spes* and as we struggle with our ecclesial identity and even with our Christian faith commitment.

Ecclesial identity and the poor

The Church identity which many of us in the Justice and Peace movement embrace has its origins in that Second Vatican Council description of the 'People of God'. Our Church identity has been moulded through the lived and shared experience of bread-breaking, justice-seeking ecclesial communities and networks in Europe, Africa, Asia and the Americas, all of them committed to transforming the misery and cruelty of their world. They possess a visible bond of unity which has been a stark countersign to a dominant culture of individualism, consumerism and all too often amnesic indifference to the plight of the poorest and most vulnerable in every society.

But the broader development of Catholic social thinking together with the unfolding of liberation theology in Latin America and beyond has been crucially important to the fixing of that identity, in particular the articulation of the preferential option for the poor. We make up a single human family on this planet, all sons and daughters of the same God, brothers and sisters of Jesus Christ. But the poor come first.

The poor come first. That is the radical and seminal contribution of the Latin American Church to Catholic social teaching now freely, indeed routinely, invoked in theological reflection, cited in episcopal and even papal discourse.[8] The living out faithfully of that preferential option, even to the point of martyrdom, means that it cannot be dismissed simply as the contextual rhetoric of the late twentieth century. On the contrary, the preferential option for the poor is now part of the genetic code of the post-Vatican II Church.

In the traditional formulation set out in the Nicene Creed, the Church has four characteristics. It is one, holy, catholic and apostolic. It would seem at the dawn of the new papacy of Benedict XVI that we should add a fifth. The true Church of Christ will be recognised by its unity, its sanctity, its universality, its apostolicity *and* its option for the poor.

A succinct and eloquent expression of our ecclesial identity, which I cherish, drawing from both *Gaudium et Spes* and the work of Mary E. Hunt, is that as a Church we are 'a global people united in sacrament and solidarity striving to follow the Lord in this broken and divided world'.

Gaudium et Spes sets our task as 'to stand as the sign and safeguard of the transcendent dignity of the human person'. In consequence whatever threatens that dignity – whether it be state-sponsored torture or abject and dehumanising poverty – becomes the business of the People of God. So, looking at the lives and deaths of Archbishop Romero and the Salvadorean Jesuits, the challenge to us, through 'communities of solidarity', is to discern carefully what is happening in this broken and divided globalised world; then to speak that truth loudly and to unmask all those structures and policies that bear down on the poor; to look simultaneously for a constructive and critical engagement with processes of transformation that will bring tangible renewal of the world and rescue the inalienable rights of the poor from the waste-bin of history; and, above all, to put ourselves alongside the most vulnerable and the very poorest. From that locus we must give and receive hope and encouragement from those communities that are struggling for their rights and for survival.

Broken and divided world

Every year the United Nations Human Development Report tells us, table by table, the condition of our globalised and globalising world. It is an invaluable encyclopedia of the state of creation. The 2003 and 2004 reports both make challenging reading.

At the start of the third millennium, in this world of superabundance, 830 million people go to bed hungry every night. Each day 24,000 people die from hunger, most of them before their fifth birthday; 1.2 billion people have no access to safe water; 2.4 billion have inadequate sanitation; 104 million school-age children are not in primary school. Over 40 million people are living with HIV/AIDS, 90 per cent of them in the Third World. Statistics can send us to sleep, but as Paul Brodeur once wrote, 'statistics are human beings with the tears wiped off'.

A fifth of humanity, 1.2 billion people, exist in absolute poverty on less than $1 a day, the most minimal level of subsistence. Half the world's population, three billion people, live on less than $2 a day. They are in poverty and manage only with great difficulty. At the same time calculations made by CAFOD demonstrate that the average European cow currently receives $2.50 per day in finance provided to European farmers by their governments; in the USA it is nearly $3 per day; and in Japan over $7 per day. This is the cow fact. The brutal reality is that three billion people in the South would be better off as cows in the North. We might call this 'the preferential option for the cow'.

According to OECD figures, Europe spends some $50 billion dollars per year in agricultural support and subsidies through its Common Agricultural Policy. The US figures are similar. This scandalous misallocation of resources creates massive surpluses. But it becomes a crime against humanity when dumping the subsidised produce on the market destroys the livelihoods and survival prospects of some of the poorest people on earth, creating destitution, marginalisation and indeed death.

At the 2003 World Trade Organisation meeting in Cancún, Mexico, four of the least developed, cotton-producing countries in Africa – Benin, Burkina Faso, Mali and Chad, respectively 159th, 173rd, 172nd and 165th in the human development league – presented the case for abolition of cotton subsidies. These four developing countries depend for two-thirds of their export earnings on cotton.

Ten million African farmers and rural workers absolutely depend for their livelihoods on cotton. They have modernised and invested at the behest of the World Bank, but the price of cotton dropped by half between 1997 and 2002. The USA subsidises 25,000 cotton farmers to a total of $3.3 billion dollars every year. The European Union provides $1 billion to cotton farmers in Spain and Greece. The end result is that cotton is sold at prices lower than the production costs in Africa.

The four African supplicants came away from Cancún empty-handed. It is an economic and human catastrophe for these four countries.

The inequalities, between nations and within nations, are staggering. The richest 5 per cent of the world's people receive 114 times the income of the poorest 5 per cent. The richest 1 per cent receives as much as the poorest 57 per cent.[9]

The chasm has been widening for 40 years, and in the 1990s, the first decade of the new globalisation, it got still worse. In Africa, where more than half the population is living below that minimal $1-dollar-a-day income threshold, 19 countries had negative growth rates in the 1990s. At the beginning of that decade children under five in sub-Saharan Africa were 19 times more likely to die than in the rich countries. Today it is 26 times more likely. Poverty, without doubt, is the most potent weapon of mass destruction today.

Globalisation and poverty

Talk to any shanty-town dweller, small farmer or market trader in any developing country about the source of their problems and they will be far more likely to mention their government whether it is of the right or the left, corrupt local politicians, the police, middlemen of all sorts, money lenders, unscrupulous land grabbers, rather than globalisation or its agents. The heavy responsibility of the rich and powerful in the South for many of the problems that beset the peoples of their countries cannot be ignored.

But the deleterious effects of globalisation have a mighty impact too, even in countries such as Mexico and Brazil, relatively powerful players on the world stage, but much more so in the least developed countries of Africa, as the cotton example illustrated. Their power in international negotiations is minimal or non-existent. Yet they must comply with trade agreements which can pauperise their people. On top of that their budgetary resources, with or without the corruption and misgovernment that are endemic, are utterly inadequate to provide minimal safety nets, let alone to finance the ambitious UN millennium development goals.

Globalisation is the overall result of global interdependence in the economic, political, social, cultural and technological spheres. It brings connectedness and homogeneity but also fragmentation and contradiction. Economic globalisation is the driving force of rapid change bringing economic integration, the universal spread of the market, and the omnipresence and enhanced power of transnational corporations. The necessary global economic frameworks are in place in the World Trade Organisation and the Bretton Woods institutions to manage the process in line with the so-called Washington Consensus.

It is not a global consensus of the great majorities of the peoples of the world, or even of the governments of our world. It is the 'consensus' of the G8 group of major industrial powers, together with the transnational business and financial players. Its principal pillars are indiscriminate liberalisation and wholesale deregulation and privatisation. The goal is to prise open the global market and hence maximise trade, maximise economic transactions, and maximise profits with no regard to the human consequences. Some nuances are creeping in now, nearly 15 years after the Washington Consensus was first formulated, but it is clear that most politicians in the rich countries of the North share the end goal of trade liberalisation and open markets.

In contrast, the global political institutions have been weakened since 9/11. Even with the International Criminal Court established, we are a very long way from the globalisation of the protection and fulfilment of human rights – civil, political, economic, social and cultural rights.

Alongside the wealth and prosperity which the North has enjoyed and the unprecedented global advances in information and communications, economic globalisation has also had its 'winners' within Southern countries – when jobs and livelihoods have come on the back of international investment and growth – and it would be wrong to ignore them. During the 1990s the number of people living in extreme poverty in East Asia and the Pacific was halved. That is a significant achievement.

Decade of despair

But for others it was 'the decade of despair'. As we have seen, Africa went backwards in the 1990s. No change in the percentage of people living on less than a dollar a day in the 1990s actually meant in absolute terms that some 60 million people more were living on less than a dollar a day by the year 2000 than there were in 1990.

The simple fact is globalisation has a logic but it has no ethic. In the globalised market there is no distinction between a 40th coat for a man who already has 39 and a coat for a shivering man who has nothing. The economy and trade are not ends in themselves simply to be maximised. They are the means to an end, and that end is the flourishing of the whole human community. There was no fiercer or more consistent critic of the pernicious effects of globalisation and the idolatry of the market than Pope John Paul II. One of the principal challenges for his successor, Benedict XVI, is to maintain and even amplify that witness on the international stage.

Fundamentally absent from globalisation is a global ethic which keeps rights and responsibilities in balance. Human rights, the right to development (and, as we might expect, the option for the poor), are totally missing. The primordial task then is to embed a proclamation and commitment to the global common good inside the silicon chip of the globalisation machine (in its software and operating system; not in an unplugged peripheral device). A code of ethical globalisation might then finally emerge in which human rights, civil and political, social, economic and cultural, enjoyed without discrimination, become part of the rules of the game.

I am reminded of the words of the Prophet Ezekiel in the Hebrew Scriptures, spoken in the name of God:

> From all your idols I will cleanse you. A new heart I will give you and a new spirit I will put within you. I will remove from your body the heart of stone and give you a heart of flesh. I will put my spirit within you ... Then you shall live in the land I gave to your ancestors; and you shall be my people, and I will be your God.[10]

A new catholicity of engagement

Because globalisation is not a given like the weather, it can be shaped. It is imperative that we seek to do so. Theologian Robert Schreiter describes a 'new catholicity' that must be present at the boundaries of those who profit and enjoy the fruits of globalisation and those who are excluded and oppressed by it. His exhortation is worth quoting:[11]

> We must seek ways of engaging globalization, so that we do not engage in ineffective resistance, we do not succumb to its enticement, and we do not resign ourselves to its inevitability. We must not simply repeat the formulae that have served us in the past. We must rather reflect on them in a way that will allow us to draw from them what will help us most. We must also analyze the situation and not simply remain content to denounce it.

Denunciation may give us the comfort of feeling prophetic but it may not in itself change much in such an all-pervasive and complex situation.

And tangible change is what marginalised communities desperately seek and what we should strive for in pro-poor policies, which offer the prospect of sustainable lives lifting people out of destitution. As Ignacio Ellacuría would say: the crucified people, the victims of globalisation, must be taken down from the cross and we must ensure that others are not put up in their place.

It is important that the 'communities of solidarity' that we establish, as Church – whether it be through Caritas or through 'We Are Church', in Christians for Human Rights or in the National Board of Catholic Women – are networked together, North–South, South–South, and North–North. Then we will be in a position, first, to challenge (and it is crucial that we do) the guardians of the governance of the current globalisation project, not only in Washington and Geneva, but through the UN system, and in all the G8 capitals.

Second, we must insist, promote and demand an ethic of globalisation, an explicit, wholehearted, binding commitment to total human development. That involves resisting those economic and trade policies which bring immiserising economic growth and create excluded and discarded peoples.

'Another World is Possible' is the banner of hope and the cry of determination from the World Social Forum, which brings together tens of thousands of grass-roots movements and organisations around the globe. Even the World Economic Forum in Davos, which is managed by the drivers of economic globalisation, and with whom critical dialogue is both possible and necessary, has responded with its own slogan 'A Better World is Possible'. A 'new catholicity' is the ability to hold those two together in tension – those concerned largely with protecting the logic of globalisation and those concerned with the human consequences of globalisation – fostering communication and dialogue, asserting the global common good, seeking convergence and reconciliation.

Human rights agenda

Sadly the global human rights agenda has been eclipsed by the war-on-terror agenda. There has been massive erosion in civil and political liberties since 9/11. There is an intimate association between the notion of the rule of law and its exercise internationally and the credibility within the UN and the international community of the human rights frameworks. Any action that tends to confirm the view that governments rule by power and in their own interest, rather than by law and in obedience to agreed international standards, weakens the notion and appeal of human rights which depend on principles of unbiased justice.[12]

In the wake of the war against Iraq led by the US and Britain, which, without UN sanction, was almost certainly illegal under article 2 of the UN Charter, and in the wake of the physical abuse and sexual humiliation of prisoners in Abu Gharaib[13] and Guantanamo,[14] political cynicism is today more widespread than ever before. There is very little public confidence that powerful states will respect the rule of law or human rights principles when it is not in their interest to do so. It is vital, therefore, to rebuild sound and effective international institutions, reinvigorated with renewed purpose, and ensure that they operate in an honest manner.

The strength and authority and scope of international political institutions are still today inadequate to co-govern the globalisation process. Kofi Annan, Mary Robinson and Sadako Ogata have led processes to mainstream human rights in the UN system, to foster the concept of a 'human security' agenda with the principles of empowerment and protection of those who are vulnerable or at risk. But these relate largely to civil and political rights which have mechanisms of enforceability written into the conventions. They are part of rehabilitating the multilateral rights-driven international regime threatened by the new 'security paradigm' which responds more directly to narrow security concerns in a polarised political climate much less sympathetic to rights. It is a mammoth task.

Guantanamo and the Iraq debacle, because of the human rights violations and the associated issues of compliance with international conventions and standards, have provoked frenzied debate, intense publicity and worldwide anger and anxiety. As a result there has been immense political and diplomatic pressure on the principal protagonists and legal recourse even to the Supreme Court in the United States to restore rights that have been infringed. That is to be welcomed, even if the outcome, as in the case of the post-Belmarsh arrangements in Britain, is still very far from satisfactory.

Poverty and rights

But the big question is why there has been no similar frenzied activity in regard to the manifestly more widespread suffering and greater death toll that comes from the constant and long-standing failure to protect and secure the rights to food, social security, education and basic health care as set out in the Universal Declaration of Human Rights of 1948. The right to life has as much to do with providing the means to stay alive

as with protecting against violent death. The guarantee of the right to
security cannot really be said to exist if an individual is starving.[15]
Human rights are indivisible. Economic, social and cultural are equal
rights alongside political and civil rights, but too often have been arbi-
trarily defined or rationalised as secondary.

A human rights approach to poverty is about the empowerment of
poor people and the most fundamental way in which empowerment
occurs is through the introduction of the concept of rights itself. Once
this concept is introduced into the context of national and international
policy-making, the rationale of tackling poverty no longer derives merely
from the fact that the poor have needs, but from the fact that they have
rights. The presence of illiteracy, homelessness or poor health is a violation of human rights. Indeed poverty itself, defined in Amartya Sen's
terms[16] of low levels of basic capabilities, can be seen as a violation of
human rights. Human rights empower individuals and communities by
granting them entitlements that give rise to obligations on others. A
rights-based approach treats people as subjects rather than objects or
instruments of policy.

Rights are most relevant to the weakest and most vulnerable, who in
participatory or consultation processes are frequently the least articulate,
the least organised and most remote and therefore too often go unheard.

But if there are rights or claims, then there are duty-bearers who must
be obliged to respond to or respect those claims. National states are
expected to respect, protect and deliver the human rights of those within their jurisdiction, but attention is also being given in recent analyses
to the responsibilities of private sector actors.

Economic, social and cultural rights are codified in a separate UN
Covenant and are often described as aspirational because in many
societies it would be prohibitively expensive to implement them. Indeed
their protection in international law is on the basis that a state will implement them progressively, over time, and in recognition that a state cannot
do more than available resources permit. This is a major flaw because it
means that in the end states are not liable to trial in a court of justice for
failing to deliver economic and social rights. Perpetual procrastination is
possible. These rights have not simply been invented by those who claim
them but have been solemnly agreed by governments in international
meetings such as the 1989 International Convention on the Rights of the
Child or the 1995 World Summit for Social Development. They are
therefore officially sanctioned aspirations to which governments can be
held accountable – not necessarily for their violation, as there may be no
perpetrator, but for their non-fulfilment.

For Africa, especially, the resource gap is real and critical. Without international development aid, in many least-developed countries it will be impossible to see the realisation of the rights to food, education, basic health care and social security. The duty-bearers must be wider than the national governments of these poor countries. With the twin principles of 'the universal destiny of the goods of the earth' and 'the preferential option for the poor', Catholic social teaching points unambiguously to the governments of rich countries and international business corporations as duty-bearers and the transfer of resources from North to South to finance development as an urgent imperative. In its reference to international cooperation, article 22 of the universal declaration does recognise implicitly that richer countries are duty-holders.

Such transnational obligations to fulfil social and economic rights are still opaque and the process of definition will certainly be difficult when the question of assuming an international responsibility hits the issue of national sovereignty. That is precisely because many of the military and political interventions and the economic conditionalities imposed in Southern countries during the last decade are viewed as infringements of national sovereignty.

Transnational obligations to protect social and economic rights could be critically important in the whole economic globalisation jamboree. Once it was recognised that particular obligations on poor countries – for example, the removal of tariff protection to peasant farmers, or the repayment of international debt through cutting expenditure on hospitals – would inevitably lead to new impoverishment and the violation of rights to food and basic health care, then it would be incumbent on the WTO, the IMF or the rich country governments concerned to desist from those policy demands so as to protect the human rights of the affected people.

But there is no court existing or legal mechanism established through which a poor country or a poor community in that country could enforce these rights and transnational duties. Certainly 'rights' in regard to poverty and development are under construction but the building is far from complete.

Millennium development goals

As we read the signs of our times there is one window of hope for a global response to the never-ending *via crucis* of the poorest communities and poorest peoples, which offers an opportunity to us and to our 'communities of solidarity' around the globe. It is the UN Millennium Declaration which was signed and proclaimed at an extraordinary gathering of heads of state in September 2000. It was a compact in which together, North and South, winners and losers in the globalisation casino, first recognised that globalisation was not working for the poor, then reaffirmed together their commitments to human rights, good governance, the protection of the environment, fostering peace and disarmament, promoting development and eradicating poverty.

But they also set eight millennium development goals (MDGs) regarding poverty and hunger, child and maternal mortality, education, HIV-AIDS, water and the environment, with 18 specific targets and, even more astonishingly, a fixed timeline of 2015 to achieve them. It could not be shrugged off as empty millennial rhetoric to be forgotten as soon as the ink had dried on their illustrious signatures – even though some might have liked to do so. It was a solemn jubilee manifesto.

The key target is, by 2015, to halve the proportion of people living on less than a dollar a day. The most difficult and challenging is to tackle debt and trade issues within a global partnership for development. The rich countries have willed the ends; they must also will the financial means. In Monterrey at the UN Conference on Finance for Development in 2002 the costs were calculated and it was agreed that $50 billion per annum would be required in additional financial flows.

The 2015 deadline attached to the MDGs, together with the firm moral commitment to substantially more development aid and debt relief to make them possible, plus the continued insistence that the current trade round negotiations will produce a pro-development outcome, provide us with a series of levers to begin to convert those long-standing declarations of social and economic rights from mere timeless aspirations to reality. Equally if the goals are continuously anchored within a human rights framework it will help ensure that they are achieved through empowerment in an inclusive and sustainable manner.

The goals and associated targets will probably be met globally because of the massive economic growth and development taking place in China and India. They will not be met in Africa unless very great resource transfers come into play. At the present rate of progress the targets on hunger and absolute poverty will be achieved in Africa in 2147! They have to be met everywhere, country by country, El Salvador as much as Ethiopia, Belarus alongside Burma.

The goals are far from perfect. We cannot imagine reciting Mary's Magnificat prayer. 'He filled half the hungry with good things ... He raised two thirds of the lowly.' In that sense they may be minimum development goals, but nevertheless they provide a valuable tool, a lever or ratchet in advocacy and campaigning to shame backsliding governments.

The agenda set by the Millennium Declaration has been reinforced by two major reports – *Investing in Development: A Practical Plan to*

Achieve the Millennium Development Goals[17] and *Our Common Interest – Report of the Commission for Africa.*[18] Both reports acknowledge that the poorest countries have multiple problems and that their own governments have a heavy responsibility to tackle issues such as corruption and bad or weak governance, but they are also emphatic that these problems should not be used as excuses by donor governments to withhold the dramatic increases in aid that are a prerequisite for sustainable development. Happily, the G8 in Gleneagles brought useful renewed momentum in pursuit of the MDG agenda.

The task ahead

With a rights-based approach alongside the MDGs there is an agenda which will enable us first to tackle every government to deliver on every goal and every target and to be accountable for the results (and no excuses); second, to press the global financial institutions to include the Millennium Declaration at the front of all their plans as a clear statement of commitment to total human development and the right to development; third, to demand substantial international aid transfers for human development programmes especially to the least developed and near bankrupt countries of Africa; and fourth, to unite 'communities of solidarity' across the globe around a common achievable focus.

If, when 2015 arrives, the principal goal on poverty is actually achieved, it will still leave behind some 900 million people hungry and in absolute poverty. It will not be a lottery: we already have a good idea who they will be. They will be the 'chronically poor' – those whose destitution is for extended duration; those who could not work even if a decent job opportunity appeared; the elderly; the disabled; the permanently sick; those living with AIDS; remote tribal people; those for whom development programmes are not designed; those whose human rights are most easily ignored.[19] The vast majority will be in Africa. Our option for the poor surely points us in their direction to form with them new 'communities of solidarity', to analyse with them their plight, to help them establish their rights. An option for the 'chronically poor'; an option for Africa; an option for the elderly; an option for people living with AIDS.

God without neighbour?

A few years ago, Pedro Casaldáliga, the recently retired bishop of São Félix do Araguaia in Brazil, said: 'In the Third Millennium Christians will either be poor or friends of the poor or they will not be Christians at all.'

These are shocking words for those Christians who would have 'God' without 'neighbour', sacrament without solidarity. As a culture of consumption and possessions increasingly displaces the human instinct for community and communion, the option for the poor may seem to many to be an uncomfortable straitjacket rather than the radar guiding us home to Jesus Christ present today in our globalised world in the chronically poor and destitute.

The fortieth anniversary of *Gaudium et Spes*, at the very beginning of this new papacy, is another moment for the People of God to stand back and take stock of our world. The countdown to 2015 is under way and there will be no shortage of analyses of the structures of sin which are still held in place by the idolatry of wealth and the greed and self-interest of the rich nations. Remembering Archbishop Romero in the jubilee year of his martyrdom may also inspire us at this cardinal moment of discernment and fill us with a new passion for the option for the poor, so that it does not remain just more words, words, words but rather a renewed and systematic engagement in prayer and in action to build another world, a more just world, in witness to our faith and to the Gospel.

Notes

1. *Gaudium et Spes* 3.
2. *Gaudium et Spes* 1.
3. Decree 4: 'Our Mission Today. The Service of Faith and the Promotion of Justice'.
4. 'Our Mission Today' 20, 29.
5. 'Our Mission Today 43, 44, 50.
6. The 34th General Congregation (5 December 1994 to 22 March 1995), Decree 3: 'Our Mission and Justice'.
7. The title of a 1985 monograph from the Centre of Concern in Washington. Fourth edition (2003) from www.coc.org.
8. See *Sollicitudo Rei Socialis* (1987); *Tertio Millennio Adveniente* (1994).
9. UNDP Human Development Report 2003, p. 39.
10. Ezekiel 36:25–28.
11. Robert Schreiter, *Mission in the Third Millennium* (New York: Orbis Books, 2001), p. 120.
12. I am indebted to Robert Archer, International Council on Human Rights Policy, Geneva, for insights and documentation which informed this and subsequent sections.
13. On 27 October 2004 Amnesty International issued a report which condemned the US administration for violating human rights in the name of national security or so-called military 'necessity', creating in the wake of 9/11 'its own iconography of torture, cruelty and degradation'.
14. For much of the world it has replaced the Statue of Liberty as the symbol of the United States' welcome to strangers.
15. *Duties Sans Frontières* (International Council on Human Rights Policy, 2003).

See www.ichrp.org.

16. Amartya Sen, *Development as Freedom* (Oxford: OUP, 1999).

17. *Investing in Development: A Practical Plan to Achieve the Millennium Development Goals* (UNDP 2005) published in London by Earthscan.

18. *Our Common Interest – Report of the Commission for Africa* (London: Commission for Africa, March 2005). The Commission for Africa was set up in 2004 by the British Government. Its recommendations have been endorsed by Tony Blair, Gordon Brown and Hilary Benn (Secretary of State for International Development) and now constitute official UK policy.

19. See www.chronicpoverty.org.

Chapter Fourteen

Can a Catholic Be a Good Democrat?
Aidan O'Neill QC

Strangers in a strange land

The historian Linda Colley puts forward the thesis in *Britons: The Forging of a Nation*[1] that the creation of the United Kingdom of Great Britain, following the 1707 Parliamentary Union between England and Scotland, was cemented by a new patriotism. This patriotism, she argues, was consciously built on several key elements: the new nation's island status; the Protestantism of its peoples; and its parliamentary heritage, which betokened such fundamental principles as popular sovereignty, limited monarchy, separation of powers and respect for the fundamental rights and liberties of the individual subject. In all these things Britain was to be contrasted with the regimes of other rival powers on continental Europe, notably the French, whose constitution was seen as embodying everything that was unBritish, namely: popery, despotism and servility.

To be Catholic was, from the perspective of a patriotic eighteenth-century Briton, to be untrustworthy and constitutionally suspect. Papists had no appreciation for, or understanding of, individual liberty. Their Church was founded upon priestcraft and a requirement of unthinking obedience to their bishops. Their religion infantilised its followers. It prevented them from exercising individual judgement. It did not recognise freedom of conscience. It encouraged duplicity. And it made absolute claims on their loyalty.

Accordingly, the loyalty of individual Catholics to the British State could not be guaranteed. Catholics could not be trusted to hold positions of power and influence within the State. Thus, the British State – in order to preserve itself and its ancient constitution and liberties – passed laws which sought to exclude Catholics from public life. The Test Act of 1678 required individuals seeking to take up civil or military offices within the State and all those sitting in – or voting for – the United Kingdom Parliament to take an oath by which they publicly and expressly repudiated as 'superstitious and idolatrous' the doctrines of transubstantiation, the sacrifice of the Mass, and the invocation of Mary and the other saints. And article two of the Acts of Union of 1707 – which ratified the Parliamentary Union of England and Scotland – provided (and still provides) 'that all Papists and persons marrying Papists, shall be excluded from and forever incapable to inherit possess or enjoy the Imperial Crown of Great Britain and the Dominions thereunto belonging or any part thereof'.

But that was then, and this is now. Apart from the provision that an individual royal will lose any claim to the throne on becoming or marrying a Catholic, the laws against Catholics participating within the British State have been repealed in the course of the nineteenth and twentieth centuries. The country's vestigial anti-Catholicism grows ever weaker.

Catholics now take a prominent and leading role in the public life of the British State. In 2005 we have Catholic peers, Catholic MPs, a Catholic as Speaker of the House of Commons, Catholic members of the Cabinet, Catholics elected as leaders of the major political parties, Catholic judges, Catholic QCs, Catholic EU Commissioners, Catholic university professors, and a Catholic heading the BBC. Even the Prime Minister (whose wife and children are Catholic) regularly attends Mass with his family and, if press reports are to be believed, has himself given serious thought to converting to Catholicism once he leaves office.[2]

Much, then, has changed in the 300 years of the existence of the British State both as regards its attitudes to its subjects generally and to its Catholic subjects in particular. Most importantly, the British constitution has in this period effectively transformed itself from a constitutional monarchy to a parliamentary representative democracy. But what has changed in Catholicism's attitude to the State in that period?

Things were perhaps easier and more straightforward when Catholics were explicitly marginalised or could claim to be oppressed by the State. Then the moral imperative was simply to hold on to the 'faith of our fathers ... in spite of dungeon, fire and sword'. In such a situation the position of the Church could simply be one of separation from the workings of the State, and opposition to its more oppressive elements. The problem is, now, as we have seen, that those who hold the keys to the dungeon and the hilt of the sword, who wield executive, legislative and judicial power in the British State are themselves, often, members of the Catholic Church.

The question I wish to address is whether Catholics can indeed fully, unreservedly, and conscientiously carry out the duties of their various public offices in accordance with the laws and constitution of the democratic and pluralist State in which they live. Or does the fact of being Catholic mean that their ultimate loyalty, even in the performance of their public office, lies elsewhere? Put crudely, are Catholics committed by their religion to being the Pope's 'Fifth Columnists', supporting the structures and laws of the State only in so far as permitted to do so by the institutional Church. Or can one instead be both a faithful Catholic and a loyal citizen and servant of the State?

My concern arises from the fact that, in the past few years, the authorities in Rome have purported to issue instructions to lay Catholics as to how they should exercise public offices held by them within the State – whether as judges or lawyers,[3] or as politicians and legislators.[4] Some of the language used, the images chosen, the metaphors adopted in these recent church documents seem to me to place real difficulties in one's being able to say with absolute confidence that one can be a loyal subject of both God and the King, or of both the Church and Parliament. And if those two loyalties cannot, in fact, be reconciled, then the issue arises as to whether Catholics can properly accept, or be appointed to, public office in the State. Does the Church require, in effect, the withdrawal (or rejection) of Catholics from public life?

The Pope and democracy

In a series of personal reflections collated in 1993 but only published in 2005, as the book *Memory & Identity*, John Paul II made the following observations among others: 'Catholic social ethics favour the democratic solution in principle because it corresponds more closely to the rational and social nature of man. Yet it is important to add that we are still a long way from canonizing this system.' He went on:

> This moral code [set out in the Ten Commandments], coming from God ... is the intangible basis for all human legislation in any system, particularly a democratic system. The law established by man, by parliaments, and by every other human legislator must not contradict the natural law, that is to say, the eternal law of God ... As a 'rational ordering' law rests on the truth of being: the truth of God, the truth of man, the truth of all created reality. The truth is the basis of natural law. To this the legislator adds the act of promulgation. For God's law this happened on [Mount] Sinai, and for modern legislation it happens in parliaments.

Later he wrote:

> We must question certain legislative choices made by parliaments of today's democratic regimes. The most immediate example concerns abortion laws. When a parliament authorizes the termination of pregnancy, agreeing to the elimination of the unborn child, it commits a grave abuse against an innocent human being, utterly

unable to defend itself. Parliaments which approve and promulgate such laws must be aware that they are exceeding their proper competence and placing themselves in open conflict with God's law and the law of nature.

And he further stated:

Nor are other grave violations of God's law lacking. I am thinking, for example, of the strong pressure from the European Parliament to recognize homosexual unions as an alternative type of family, with the right to adopt children. It is legitimate and even necessary to ask whether this is not the work of another ideology of evil, more subtle and hidden, perhaps [than Nazism and Marxism], intent upon exploiting human rights themselves against man and against the family.[5]

These are, of course, personal reflections by the late Pope and do not necessarily accurately represent church teaching, any more than did the musings of the fourteenth-century Avignon Pope, John XXII, that the saints' vision of God would occur only after the Last Judgement, thereby putting into question the efficacy of any invocation of the saints. But his remarks do deserve to be taken seriously, at least for the purposes of discussion, since they might be seen to presage and set the tone for subsequent official church documents, emanating both directly from the Vatican and from a few of the more enthusiastically ultramontane diocesan bishops.

The late Pope's remarks above seem to indicate a certain dissatisfaction with the democratic process. He seemed to think that the role of parliaments is simply to promulgate a pre-existing moral code, and that democracies were legitimate only in so far as their legislation accorded with (his views as to) God's law. He appeared to be of the view that legislation is to reflect the will of God, rather than the (potentially misguided) will of the people. He considered that the language of human rights was potentially subversive, and might be used to further what he regarded as evil rather than the good.

In *Evangelium Vitae*, Pope John Paul II went so far as to claim: 'The doctrine on the necessary conformity of civil law with the moral law is in continuity with the whole tradition of the Church.'[6]

By contrast, however, St Thomas Aquinas – whom Pope John Paul otherwise sought to pray in aid for his views – held that it was *not* the business of human law either to restrain all moral vices, or to require all virtuous acts. Immorality, on his view, did *not* directly map on to illegality.[7]

As Aquinas notes:

Laws should be appointed to men according to their condition; St Isidore remarks how law 'should be possible both according to nature and the custom of the country' ... Law is laid down for a great number of people, of which the majority have no higher standard of morality. Therefore it does not forbid all the vices, from which upright men can keep away. But only those grave ones which the average man can avoid, and chiefly those which do harm to others and which have to be stopped if human society is to be maintained, such as murder and theft and so forth.[8]

But Pope John Paul seemed to be impatient with such legalistic considerations and nice distinctions. While admitting that the issue of human freedom is fundamental, he tended to the view that 'freedom is properly so called to the extent that it implements the truth regarding the good', anything else being deemed a 'corruption of freedom' which leads to dangerous moral consequences.[9] On his analysis it would seem that one is free only to do what the pope says. None of this is particularly promising for the idea of how individual Catholics should participate and exercise public office within pluralist liberal democracies.

Perhaps consistent with the late Pope's approach to freedom,[10] in the course of the 2003 US presidential election some American bishops threatened the canonical sanction of exclusion from communion against individual Catholic candidates for election whose prior voting records when in office or public pronouncements when running for office were deemed by those bishops to be not sufficiently 'pro-life' or 'pro-family'.[11] And in July 2005 a Canadian Catholic MP, Charlie Angus, was publicly barred from communion by his parish priest (apparently acting with the support of the diocesan bishop) for voting in favour of a Parliamentary Bill which extended throughout Canada equal access to marriage to same-sex couples. The threat to refuse communion was also extended even to those individual Catholics who exercised their democratic rights by voting for such candidates deemed by their bishop to be unacceptable.

Voting in this way was said to be sinning, and this sin could be purged only by repentance and acceptance of due penance as determined by the ordinary of the diocese[12] – or presumably by moving house and taking up residence in another diocese on the basis that the US bishops' conference stated that, on this matter, 'bishops can legitimately make different judgments on the most prudent course of pastoral action.'[13]

Although the point was not specifically raised, the logic of the rigorist bishops' position – at least within the US constitutional context – should have also led them to direct their threats of ecclesiastical sanctions against those Catholic judges who failed to favour the appropriate 'pro-life/pro-family position' in cases that came before their courts. In particular, three (Justices Scalia, Thomas and Kennedy) of the nine current justices of the US Supreme Court are Catholic and, with the resignation of the moderate Episcopalian Sandra Day O'Connor, a vacancy has arisen on that court to which, at the time of writing, President Bush has nominated another Catholic, Judge John Roberts. Should the bishops not also be threatening to withhold communion to those justices who are Catholic on the basis of how they vote and reason in particular cases before them?

In particular, the Supreme Court Justices' failure or delay in overturning the 1972 case of *Roe v. Wade*[14] – which declared that access to abortion was a right covered by the implicit right (read into the US Constitution) to respect for an individual's private life, and that therefore federal or state laws which, on the court's estimate, unduly restricted access to abortion would be struck down as unconstitutional – directly impacts upon the availability of abortion in the United States far more than, say, John Kerry's voting record in the US Senate, which was the subject of the bishops' particular ire. Just five individuals' votes in the US Supreme Court could result in the de-constitutionalisation of abortion and the restoration of its regulation to the legislatures of the individual states.

If the votes of the Supreme Court Justices are determined not by law or the terms of the US Constitution, but by the requirements of their religion (as told to them by their bishops) is there not a problem about separation of powers and of Church and State? The First Amendment to the US Constitution states that 'Congress shall make no law establishing a religion.' Any perceived attempt by church authorities to influence the votes of individual Catholic judges on the issues that come before their courts might well be interpreted as an attempt by the Church to establish Catholicism within the US Constitution.

In order to defend the Constitution consistently with the requirement of the First Amendment, one could conceive of legislation being passed – or Congress acting in a manner such as – to prohibit the appointment of Catholics to the bench. One suspects that any episcopal attempt to dictate to Catholic judges (whether in the United States or the United Kingdom) would result in a backlash against religious interference in the affairs of the State. But it is unclear why – for other than prudential reasons – these bishops should not be seeking to assert their ecclesiastical authority over those of their flock who hold judicial office, just as they have sought to assert it over those who hold or seek executive or legislative office, and over those citizens who might vote them into such office.

The legislature (and courts) within a democratic society in which

Catholic voters voted for the political candidate favoured by the bishops, and where Catholic citizens, legislators (and judges) voted in accordance with the bishops' moral instructions – might be expected to push through a radical legal programme. This specifically 'Catholic agenda' might include such issues as:

1. the domestic re-criminalisation of abortion and the banning of IUDs and the morning-after pill;
2. the outlawing of human embryonic stem cell research and any therapeutic or reproductive cloning of human embryos;
3. strict regulatory control on the use of human *in vitro* fertilisation with a view to avoiding the creation of 'excess embryos' and the prohibition of surrogacy and donor arrangements in relation to assisted pregnancy;
4. strengthening the laws against euthanasia or any physician-assisted suicide;
5. the improvement of prison conditions and the abolition (except, perhaps, in the most extreme circumstances) of the death penalty;
6. limitation on the availability of contraceptives and the positive promotion of a sex education curriculum directed against the fostering of a 'contraceptive mentality';
7. withdrawing legal recognition from unmarried de facto family relationships;
8. making divorce more difficult, and – conceivably – also prohibiting remarriage after divorce;
9. supporting measures aimed at allowing women to participate equally and without suffering discrimination in the workplace;
10. promoting measures aimed at the integration of people with disabilities within society, and particularly to ensure their non-discrimination within the workplace;
11. withdrawal of the protection of any anti-discrimination legislation covering sexual orientation and a veto over any possible legal recognition of same-sex unions; and
12. the licensing and encouragement of (beneficial) bio-technological innovations (including genetic modification) in the area of plant and (non-human) animal life.

The passing and enforcement of such a legislative programme would not depend on there being a general consensus among the electorate, or even a majority opinion in their favour, since legislation of this nature would be intended to instantiate the natural law, reflecting the world as God intended it to be. The model assumes, as we have seen, that the civil law of the State should mirror and enforce these moral norms of natural law because they are said to be standards which everyone, regardless of religious belief or culture, can properly be expected to recognise and affirm.

The failings of democracy

The late Pope's apparent failure or unwillingness to recognise the independent dignity and integrity of the system of the positive law of civil society as itself creating a normative order of binding obligations – regardless of its supposed consistency or congruence with the moral order – seems to have arisen from a profound lack of sympathy on the part of the Vatican with legal developments, particularly occurring in western democratic societies in the areas of sexuality, family and life issues. Seeking to justify this apparent disdain for these results of contemporary democracies, Pope John Paul observed on a number of occasions in *Memory & Identity* that the democratic system could be abused, noting that 'those who came to power in the Third Reich' did so 'by democratic means' and commenting:

> It was a regularly elected Parliament that consented to Hitler's rise to power in Germany in the 1930s. And the same Reichstag by delegating full powers to Hitler (*Ermächtigungsgesetz*) paved the way for his policy of invading Europe, for the establishment of concentration camps and for the implementation of the so-called final solution to the Jewish question, that is to say the elimination of millions of the sons and daughters of Israel.

What Pope John Paul failed to mention in this passage was that the Enabling Act 1933 (the *Ermächtigungsgesetz*) – which granted sweeping dictatorial powers to the Nazi Chancellor, Adolf Hitler, to modify the 1919 Weimar Republican settlement and thereby transform the German constitution into one of totalitarian dictatorship – was only given the necessary two-thirds majority to pass through the German Parliament, the Reichstag, with the support of the Catholic-based Centre Party (*Zentrumspartei*). This political support by the Catholic party's parliamentarians was given with the knowledge and backing of the Vatican authorities, anxious to conclude with the Nazi State a concordat, the terms of which still govern relations between the Catholic Church and the State in Germany.

The Enabling Act was passed on 23 March 1933. Three weeks beforehand, on 28 February 1933, the German government had promulgated the Reichstag Fire Decree (*Reichstagsbrandverordnung*) as their immediate response to the previous day's (Nazi-engineered) terrorist attack on the German Parliament building. The Reichstag Fire Decree suspended

most of the human rights which the 1919 German Constitution had protected. It abolished the German equivalent of *habeas corpus*, that is to
say the principle of no imprisonment without trial. It empowered the
authorities to carry out searches and confiscations of individuals'
property. It authorised government interception of letters, parcels and
telegraphs and the tapping of telephones. It placed severe restrictions on
freedom of speech (including the freedom of the press) and on the
freedom to organise and assemble.

The measure was immediately used by the Nazi authorities to arrest
and imprison Communist Party deputies who had been elected to
Parliament, thereby preventing them from voting against the measures,
subsequently introduced before the Reichstag to entrench Nazi power.

Surely, if any lessons are to be learnt from history, it is not – as Pope
John Paul's remarks seem to imply – that democracies are not to be trusted, but rather that proper democratic processes are essential if we are to
avoid falling into tyranny and, even more pertinently, that the church
authorities should not seek to interfere in those parliamentary processes
for their own apparent sectional gain. It is respect – for the law's procedures; for the messiness of parliamentary debate, opposition, discussion,
amendment and compromise; for an independent and impartial judiciary
able and willing to proclaim and protect the substance of each individual's
fundamental rights even in the face of duly promulgated laws – that is our
safeguard against totalitarianism or despotism, however enlightened.

And it is simply not enough to get to the 'right result', whether that
be defined (by a pope) as the outlawing of abortion, or (by the Prime
Minister in the context of the rushed debates on the bill which became
the Prevention of Terrorism Act, 2005) the revocation of *habeas corpus*
and the introduction of internment without trial as a 'control measure'
against possible terrorist attacks.[15] What is of fundamental importance
is the following of due parliamentary means to achieve that end and
respect for individuals' rights in pursuance of that result. Without that,
there is no legitimacy. To criticise parliamentary opposition to one's
desired result as 'irresponsible', or to characterise judicial reversals of
oppressive laws as 'exploitative of human rights' is to undermine – in the
hot flush of Messianic zeal – the very rule of law.

The late Pope's reflections – and arguably the Prime Minister's
remarks on the parliamentary and judicial opposition to the 2005 Act
and similar measures – show an impatience with, and lack of sympathy
for, the institutions and democratic processes of the law. There is an
unwillingness to accept that it is these structures which are in place precisely to prevent power being abused in the name of the requirements of
the good.

Moral vision of a democratic state

Despite what Pope John Paul II may have thought and claimed, democracies do have values. The values that western democratic states proclaim (and seek to instantiate) are those of liberty, equality, tolerance, pluralism, and – following the post-war trials of the Nazi war criminals at Nuremberg – explicit respect for human rights and the structures of the rule of law. Civil democratic society does not – it would appear – differ radically from the institutional Church on the question of the substantive fundamental values which it seeks to promote: human rights discourse is common to both communities. And in both cases it is also recognised that one of the purposes of reference to human rights is precisely to protect minorities against the possible tyranny of the majority.

The difference between civil democratic society and the Church lies rather in two aspects. Defined negatively, it might be said that in comparison to the Church, civil democratic society shows a lack of certainty or finality in the judgements made on how those substantive values are to be realised, and on the requirements of the common good. Defined positively, civil democratic society differs from the Church in its openness to the possibility of other views of the good than those which currently hold sway, and in its procedures for general consideration and popular participation in the process of deliberation and decision on how we might achieve the common good.

Civil society – in contrast, it would seem, to the Church – admits its fallibility in getting the right answer, but it has procedures and institutions to allow for continued debate, and for the possibility of change in the rules and the law in this search for the right answer. Such an admission of fallibility does not mean, as is sometimes charged, that a democratic society is therefore committed to 'ethical relativism' as is so often claimed in church documents, critical of moral and legal developments in civil society.[16]

Ethical relativism is an assertion that there is no right answer. The structures of a democratic civil society are precisely to allow for the continued search for the right answer.

The values which the post-Nuremberg democratic State has sought to incorporate, and bind its institutions (public authorities) to, are based on the inestimable worth of the individual as being an end in himself or herself and never merely a means. We are, then, now as a matter of (positive) law, heirs to the Christian tradition, to the Enlightenment and to Kant. Legal positivism – the claim that the law is no more and no less than the command of the powerful no matter its content – has been routed. We are all natural lawyers now.

What the democratic State brings into the realisation of those values (which the Church does not, and hence the apparent mismatch in rhetoric and practice between the two discourses) is the idea of due process, of the rule of law, the procedural rights of the defence and the like.

A civil democratic society is one which allows that where a decision has to be taken on such issues, the decision is taken on the basis of the vote of the majority of the people (or their representatives). A civil democratic society will also be a pluralist society: that is to say one which allows for the possibility of individuals holding different views of questions of political and moral importance and having the right and opportunity to express, publicise and proselytise for those views – whether it be fox hunting or abortion regulation. A civil democratic society will also be a liberal society, that is to say one which aspires or seeks to allow individuals the greatest degree of freedom to express those views, consistent with due respect for others who express opposing views.

An essential part of what it is to hold public office in a democracy is a quality or disposition of 'open-mindedness'. That is to not to say that one has to be committed to a form of relativism – that there are no objective truths – but that one is open to persuasion that the truths one holds and perceives may not be the definitive or last word. This is most clearly an essential quality for those acting as judges within civil society – without a capacity for detachment from one's initial views, an ability to suspend one's immediate judgement on an issue and be willing to listen to argument – there can be no true act of judging impartially.

But even among members of the legislature and the executive – although sometimes obscured by the party whip system – the ideal is that they too should be independently-minded, willing to hear other voices and, having heard them, to deliberate and come to their decision on the requirements of the common good.

Human rights within civil democratic society are based on the recognition of the value of the individual human being and on the value of democratic process and the maintenance of dialogue and free expression as the only means toward the resolution of moral and political disputes. From the viewpoint of civil democratic society, it makes no sense to seek to disentangle ideas of substantive 'human rights' from the deliberative and procedural matrix in which they have been engendered.

If it is going to use the language of human rights, the Church is – from the point of view of civil society – in fact committing itself to a particular moral and political vision: one which speaks of the value of the individual but which also speaks of the value and fundamental importance of democratic processes. Dialogue within a liberal pluralist democracy involves a willingness to listen as well as a readiness to speak and an acceptance of the existence of different and dissenting voices. It involves, too, an acknowledgement of the value of the procedures existing within society for the resolution of differences on questions touching on the common good – whether this be by legislation or litigation. It necessitates respect for the 'rule of law'.

Any church teaching on the proper relationship between the civil law and the 'moral law' needs to take account of the fact that in the context of the democratic State, the legitimacy of each individual law comes not from the end which it achieves, but from the fact that it has passed through the democratic process and has been found, by the institutions of the State duly charged with this task, to be in conformity with respect for the fundamental rights of those falling within the care of the State.

Laws in the democratic State are not fixed and final, and its governments are not eternal. Precisely because the ideal which democracy represents is that the law continues to be responsive to and reflective of the community, there is provision for lawful change. Lawful change is brought about by using the mechanisms of a democratic society which allow for campaigns to be mounted; petitions gathered; public discussions initiated in the press and the broadcasting media; parliamentary debates sponsored; and ministers lobbied, all with a view to bringing change in the law, the better for it to reflect the common good and to instantiate justice. All of these are activities in which the Church may legitimately take part.

In a democracy, the approach taken is that those who object to particular laws should campaign for their amendment or repeal by the democratic legislature in accordance with the values of the constitution. Simply to claim that there is always and everywhere a right immediately to disobey the laws which the Church considers to contravene 'natural law' is to threaten the integrity of the whole legal system which sustains the democratic State, and to seek to bring it down in anarchy and with it the very institutions which exist within a democracy to facilitate dialogue and change.

It is just not good enough for comparison to be made between the legal and political systems which currently exist within western democracies with that which existed in Nazi Germany. The case of the German legal system from 1933 to 1945 is one of a system which was systematically corrupted in its subordination to the Nazi tyranny such that all those who participated within it (and more generally in public life) were tainted by its failings. It became truly a system of, and only of, state oppression, such that it became no longer worthy of the name of a 'legal system' because in no sense could it be said to embody or seek any vision of the common good. The only moral response in relation to such wholesale corruption was for the just to withdraw from any participation in it and indeed to seek to overthrow the regime – by 'unlawful' revolutionary means if need be – which sustained it.

It does not seem to me that that is a situation which, on any view, could be said currently to hold within the legal systems of western democracies. But if that is indeed the Church's assessment of those legal systems which make provision for the possibility of procured abortion, then the only option would be for the Church to instruct its members to withdraw wholly from participation in the public lives of these societies. Yet the overall tenor of at least John Paul II's remarks seems to be more that while he accepted that some – indeed the majority – of the laws within western democratic systems were indeed aimed at the common good, others – notably in relation to abortion and other issues associated with respect for human life – failed to achieve this ideal.

The proper response of the Church which continues to accept the overall legitimacy of the legal systems of western democracies cannot be to call for revolt against the system as a whole, but instead to call for change in specific aspects and laws thereof. And if such change is indeed to be legitimate within the terms of the legal system it has to be one mandated by the accepted democratic and constitutional process. Accordingly, in order to promote such change it is necessary to engage in debate within the market place of ideas.

As one Jesuit commentator has put it:

> The willingness to subject the civil law and public policy to moral critique within ecumenical political dialogue must constitute the heart of the doctrine of the necessary conformity of the moral law and the civil law in a pluralistic society. That doctrine can be most fruitfully understood as a call for critical moral reflection on contemporary standards of civil law, rather than as a dogmatic insistence on the imposition of Christian morality on a religiously pluralistic society.[17]

The beginning of dialogue

The Congregation for the Doctrine of the Faith (led at the time by Cardinal Joseph Ratzinger, now Pope Benedict XVI) in its 2003 communication attacking proposals for the legal recognition of same-sex unions, acknowledges the primary importance of individual conscience by alluding to the existence of a right (or, indeed in certain circumstances a duty) of 'conscientious objection' over the demands of the law.[18] Of necessity, that same right of informed conscientious objection has to be conceded within the institutional Church if the baptised are to remain moral agents.

As the then (1969) Father Joseph Ratzinger observed in his commentary on article 16 of *Gaudium et Spes*:

> For [the Venerable Cardinal] Newman, conscience represents the inner complement and limit of Church principle. Over the Pope as the expression of the binding claim of ecclesiastical authority, there still stands one's own conscience, which must be obeyed before all else, even if necessary against the requirements of ecclesiastical authority. This emphasis on the individual, whose conscience confronts him with a supreme and ultimate tribunal, and one in which the last resort is beyond the claim of external social groups, even of the official Church, also establishes a principle in opposition to increasing totalitarianism.

He went on:

> Conscience is made the principle of objectivity, in the conviction that careful attention to its claim discloses the fundamental common values of human existence ... Above all, however, conscience is presented as the meeting point and common ground of Christians and non-Christians and consequently as the real hinge on which dialogue turns. Fidelity to conscience unites Christians and non-Christians and permits them to work together to solve the moral tasks of mankind, just as it compels them both to humble and open inquiry into the truth.[19]

On this analysis, the pronouncements of the Congregation for the Doctrine of the Faith, then, may be relevant to, but are certainly not determinative on, questions as to how the individual may live a moral life, faithful to Christian values. If the bishops are to take seriously this traditional Catholic teaching on the primacy of individual conscience and of the universal discernibility of natural law, then they are going to have to learn to:

1. allow that individuals may, in conscience, differ as to what moral action demands of them in any particular circumstance;
2. allow that questions regarding how best to legislate in or regulate areas of moral dispute or controversy – where people of good will in fact reach contrary positions – are ones for the prudential judgement of the elected legislators rather than for *ex cathedra* pronouncements of the higher clergy;

3. be willing to listen and to engage in dialogue within civil society and within the Church, without resorting to the use of anathema or ecclesiastical sanctions;
4. seek to persuade by the authority of their reasoning rather than to command obedience to their views by reason of their authority; and
5. be willing to accept that they may themselves get it wrong.

In sum, the bishops have to listen to and trust the people (of God). As the Irish moral theologian Father Seán Fagan has put it:

> The Church is not made up of two separate sections, one teaching and the other learning. In fact, the whole Church is a learning Church (including Pope and bishops), a community of believers in which we must listen to each and learn from each other. At the same time the whole Church is a teaching Church in so far as every mature Christian has, at some time or other, to play the role of teacher, *magister*.[20]

Such an approach, if adopted, would also mean that there was no longer the radical incompatibility between the principles embodied in the institutional Church and those proclaimed by western democracies, in that both would seek to protect individual liberty of conscience, freedom of speech, equality of treatment, tolerance and pluralism. Tolerance and pluralism are not to be equated with ethical or cultural 'relativism'.

Instead a society characterised by tolerance and pluralism is one in which it is accepted that sometimes – in areas of particular moral complexity or controversy – the right answer may not be immediately evident or clear and that individuals may, in good faith, reach different answers on these issues. It is a society which places value on the process of dialogue and discussion among differing views; one which sees that process of debate as being the right way – indeed, the only way – to seek to discern the common good for all.

As was stated in *Gaudium et Spes*:

> The laity should not imagine that their pastors are always experts, that to every problem which arises, however complicated, they can readily give a concrete solution, or even that such is their mission. Rather, enlightened by Christian wisdom and giving close attention to the teaching authority of the Church, the laity need take on their own distinctive role. Often enough the Christian view of things will itself suggest some specific solution in certain circumstances. Yet it happens rather frequently, and legitimately so, that with equal sincerity some of the faithful will disagree with others on a given matter. Even against the intentions of their proponents,

however, solutions proposed on one side or another may be easily confused by many people with the Gospel message. Hence it is necessary for people to remember that no one is allowed in the aforementioned situations to appropriate the Church's authority for his opinion. They should always try to enlighten one another through honest discussion, preserving mutual charity and caring above all for the common good.[21]

The model for Church–State (and lay–cleric) relations which such a tolerant and pluralist society entails would be one in which neither side – Church or State – claims to be in a relationship of hierarchy or superiority over the other. Instead, each is engaged with the other in a dialogue, a conversation in a relationship of mutual respect.

Such a conversation presupposes an ability and willingness to listen and a readiness to at least consider that the other may have something useful to say. It requires that neither side believe themselves to have a monopoly on the truth, because to claim such a monopoly would be to render the whole dialogue a sham and is simply a disguised reintroduction of the superiority/inferiority relationship which the model disavows from the outset.

It is a model which allows members of the Church to participate fully within the public life of civil society. Crucially, in so far as members of the Church do so participate, it also involves the institutional Church imposing on itself a self-denying ordinance – out of respect for the web of obligations involved in civil society and the duties of public office – to refrain from instructing its members as to how specifically they are to carry out their duties as public office-holders within civil society. The bishops (and all members of the Church exercising the office of teacher) may seek to articulate the principles of ethics and justice, but it would be illicit for those holding office within the Church to purport to *direct* those holding office within civil society on how to do their jobs.

The duty of public office-holders is to uphold the constitution under which they hold office, not to undermine that office by seeking to further the agenda of another body or to promote values which are not compatible with the civil society in which they hold office. All that the Church can properly expect from its members participating in the public life of the polity is that they will carry out their duties in accordance with their conscience and with the civil law.

Such an approach would appear to require a change of heart, a conversion experience, a *metanoia*, on the part of some of the hierarchy, certain of whose pronouncements in areas of particular sensitivity and complexity have perhaps not been marked out by the language of charity and humility which one might hope to see under the new model.

We may note in this regard, not only the late Pope's musings in *Memory & Identity* when he lumps within the one category of 'the ideology of evil' the Nazi extermination of the Jews with proposals by the European Parliament to 'recognize homosexual unions as an alternative type of family', but also the more subtle intimations set out in the Congregation for the Doctrine of the Faith's 2003 communication on legal recognition for same-sex partnerships. This appears to have been issued from the offices of the Congregation for the Doctrine of the Faith on 3 June 2003, the Memorial of St Charles Lwanga and his Companions, Martyrs. St Charles Lwanga and his Companions were executed – by being put to the fire and the sword – on the orders of King Mwanga of Uganda after their conversion to Christianity and, apparently, because of their refusal to submit to the King's homosexual advances. The very dating of the document then carries with it potent images of burning, martyrdom, tyranny, homosexual desire and denial. Is it intended to give a subliminal warning of the dangers which the Holy Office, at least, sees as being inherent in any further social acceptance of homosexuality? It seems that for the then Cardinal Ratzinger – inverting St Paul's dictum to the Corinthians on matrimony[22] – it would be better for homosexuals to burn than to marry.

But as the document itself notes at the outset:

> The present considerations do not contain new doctrinal elements; they seek rather to reiterate the essential points on this question and provide arguments drawn from reason ... Since this question relates to the natural moral law, the arguments that follow are addressed not only to those who believe in Christ, but to all persons committed to promoting and defending the common good of society.

The document is, then, suggesting that its arguments be assessed and judged, not in the light of doctrine, but in the light of reason. As such it is not, and cannot be, the last word on the subject. Rome may well have spoken, but the particular cause (the legal recognition and regulation of same-sex partnerships) is not finished, precisely because we do live in a democracy. Rather than ending discussion of the matter, the document may be seen to mark an invitation to open debate and to begin a dialogue. Let us hope that this dialogue – both within and outside the Church – may be allowed to proceed in good faith and with good will on all sides.[23] The Catholic Church claims, as an expression of its universality, its true Catholicity, to found its moral teaching on universal truths accessible by reason. As a member of this religious body, I believe that one not only has the right to engage in such a dialogue, but that it is indeed one's responsibility as a committed (and still faithful) member of the Church to bear such witness.

Notes

1. See Linda Colley, *Britons: Forging the Nation 1707–1837* (New York and London, 1992).
2. See: Francis Beckett, 'God's conviction politician', *The Tablet* (9 October 2004); and *The Daily Telegraph* (15 October 2004).
3. See John Paul II, Papal Address to the Roman Rota on 'Divorce and the duties of canon lawyers and of Catholic civil lawyers and judges' (28 January 2002, the Feast Day of St Thomas Aquinas).
4. Congregation for the Doctrine of the Faith, *Doctrinal Note on Some Questions regarding the Participation of Catholics in Political Life* (24 November 2002, Solemnity of Christ the King); and Congregation for the Doctrine of the Faith, *Considerations regarding Proposals to Give Legal Recognition to Unions between Homosexual Persons* (3 June 2003, the Memorial of St Charles Lwanga and his Companions, Martyrs).
5. John Paul II, *Memory & Identity* (London, 2005), at pp. 147, 151, 152 and 12–13.
6. John Paul II, *Evangelium Vitae* (25 March 1995), para. 72.
7. *Summa Theologiae* IaIIae q.95 aa.4, 5.
8. *Summa Theologiae* IaIIae q.96 a.2.
9. John Paul II, *Memory & Identity*, at p. 47.
10. See the Memorandum from (then) Cardinal Ratzinger to Cardinal Theodore McCarrick, 'Worthiness to receive Holy Communion: general principles', published in *The Tablet* (10 July 2004) at p. 36 and online at http://213.92.16.98/ESW_articolo/0,2393,42196,00.html.
11. Archbishop Raymond Burke of St Louis, Missouri, USA, *On Our Civic Responsibility for the Common Good* (1 October 2004, the Memorial of St Thérèse of Lisieux).
12. Bishop Michael Sheridan, Pastoral letter on *The Duties of Catholic Politicians and Voters* (1 May 2004, the Feast of St Joseph the Worker).
13. United States Conference of Catholic Bishops, *Catholics in Political Life*, published at www.nccbuscc.org/bishops/catholicsinpoliticallife.htm.
14. *Roe v. Wade*, 410 US 113 (1973).
15. See, now, the Prevention of Terrorism Act 2005.
16. See John Paul II, *Evangelium Vitae*, at paras 69–70.
17. Gregory Kalscheur SJ, 'John Paul II, John Courtney Murray and the relationship between civil law and moral law: a constructive proposal for contemporary American pluralism', *Journal of Catholic Social Thought* (Summer 2004), pp. 231ff. at 268.
18. Congregation for the Doctrine of the Faith, *Considerations* (June 2003) at para. 5.
19. Fr Joseph Ratzinger on 'The Dignity of the Human Person' in Herbert Vorgrimler (ed.), *Commentary on the Doctrine of Vatican II* vol. V (London, 1969) – concerning *The Pastoral Constitution on the Church in the Modern World* – Part I Chapter 1 at pp. 134–6.

20. Seán Fagan SM, *Does Morality Change?* (Dublin, 2003), at p. 18.

21. *Gaudium et Spes* (7 December 1965), at para. 43.

22. 1 Corinthians 7:9: 'It is better to marry than to burn.'

23. See, for an example of the beginning of just such debate, Gareth Moore OP, *A Question of Truth: Christianity and Homosexuality* (London, 2003).

Chapter Fifteen

Peace, Conflict and the Future of the Church

Valerie Flessati and Bruce Kent

'Peace' is a word which gets frequent mention in the Liturgy of the Church. Immediately before the reception of Holy Communion, for instance, we are reminded that Jesus promised peace to his apostles, and we ask for the peace and unity of God's Kingdom. It is, we are told in the Gospel, a 'peace such as the world cannot give'.

Well, what sort of peace is on offer? Not simply the peace of regular order and discipline. Prisons and detention centres pride themselves on order and discipline. Nor is it the peace of tranquillity. Graveyards and museums are places of tranquillity. Again, it is not the peace imposed by superior power as a way of maintaining sinful structures of injustice.

Pope Paul VI in *Populorum Progressio* described Christian peace as 'the fruit of anxious daily care to see that everyone lives in the justice that God intends' (#76). Peace is not then a matter of enduring injustice or of pretending that conflict does not exist. Conflict is part of the human condition. One person's perception of what is just will not always be the same as the next person's. Living together in love despite our different perceptions, while doing all we can to remove the structures of injustice and to improve the mechanisms of non-violent resolution of conflict, is part of the peace promised in our Liturgy.

By contrast, peace in secular terms is frequently defined exclusively as a military matter. Supporters of nuclear deterrence, conveniently forgetting the numerous proxy wars fought by East and West, still claim that nuclear weapons gave us peace for forty years. A stalemate based on threats of mass murder has nothing to do with Christian peace. The term 'security' is constantly used as if it means freedom from military threat. Real human security means much more: freedom from the perils of disease, starvation, pollution, competition for vital resources such as even water, and from persecution and fear. 'Integrity will bring peace, justice give everlasting security' (Isaiah 32:17).

We cannot call 'peace' an unjust economic order which, despite all the resources which the world has been given, involves the death, every day, of thirty thousand people, mostly children, from poverty, disease and malnutrition. This ongoing silent slaughter has its open, inescapable, bloody side in the wars which disfigure our human community. Some, like the war on Iraq, are expensive and high profile. Some, like the ongoing Rwanda/Congo conflict, involve even more casualties but escape the same level of media coverage.

The scope and scale of war today is far wider than many imagine. The last century alone claimed about 100 million deaths in warfare. Global military expenditure is currently creeping up again to nearly $1000 billion a year, half of which is spent by the one remaining superpower. Over twenty wars are in progress, many of them within, rather than between, states. There are now at least eight countries armed with nuclear weapons, and over twenty thousand such weapons available for use, some on instant alert. Nuclear war resulting from an accident or misperception is a constant and real danger. The arms trade remains a profitable business for the companies involved, granted that, thanks to government subsidies and credit guarantees, they could hardly fail to make a profit.

Military planners think in terms that are incomprehensible to most of us. Those working for the United States Space Command are not at all shy about the purpose of their work. It is all set out in their illustrated brochure, *Vision for 2020*. The aim is to dominate 'the space dimension of military operations to protect US interests and investment'. The cover picture on the brochure shows an orbiting satellite equipped with a laser ray capable of striking any point on the earth's surface. That is supposed to enhance US 'security'.

Living on permanent alert in the current 'war on terror', almost any sacrifice seems to be required by the elusive god of security. In fact the appetite of this god is insatiable, demanding countless young lives, infinite natural resources, the best scientific research, an enormous budget, the distortion of democracy and law, religion and culture.

The contribution which the Christian churches could make to the removal of the cancer of militarism from the body of humanity is substantial. The International Synod of Catholic Bishops, which met in Rome in 1971 to discuss the theme of justice, reminded us that the Gospel is there to free us from what sin has done to our society. Behind war lies greed, pride, ignorance, fear and lack of hope: all evident signs of precisely such sin.

Many have been led to believe that wars are somehow inevitable, or even 'natural'. That war has been a significant feature of human life far back into our history is perfectly true. The rule of law has taken a long time to evolve. Relics of war – ranging from castles to war memorials – are all around us in Britain, but our world has moved on. Castles have turned into museums. Private militias have been abolished. Even to possess a deadly weapon requires some form of licence.

Murders do happen, but they are a rare event, condemned by all. Even though individuals may feel the urge to take violent personal revenge if they are wronged, they do not usually do so, because we have an effective police force, and courts of law that pass judgement on criminal behaviour and adjudicate in civil disputes. A whole range of people and organisations – from Neighbourhood Watch groups to social workers and probation officers – help the community to deal with conflict in nonviolent ways. Collectively they ensure that nonviolence is the norm and violence the aberration on the local and national level.

Making international nonviolence moral

'The world is soaked with mutual blood. When individuals commit homicide it is a crime; it is called a virtue when it is done in the name of the state. Impunity is acquired for crimes not by reason of innocence but by the magnitude of the cruelty' (St Cyprian of Carthage, *To Donatus* 6).

The evidence is all around us that the circle of non-violent conflict resolution can be, and has been, extended. Political and economic interdependence mean that Germany and France will never fight another war with each other. Nor will Norway and Sweden; or Canada and the USA. This interdependence has resulted from initiatives to strengthen connections between states for their mutual benefit.

The Church has much to offer in fostering an outlook where other people are seen as neighbours. People of the Gospel should be people of hope and of empowerment. Too often a sense of impotence breeds apathy. Christians know that in their hands is the power for positive change. We have been given talents and we are expected to use them.

In the construction of a world where we settle international disputes nonviolently there is still much to be done. It is easy enough to list the mechanisms that we lack. The International Criminal Court is now up and running, thanks to the persistent vision of a few, but it does not have universal jurisdiction and the United States administration is doing its best to undermine its competence.

We still lack a trained international policing body immediately available to the United Nations Security Council. Collective security does not exclude international UN military action if all other ways of resolving a dispute have failed. Indeed, governments cannot hide behind exaggerated claims of national sovereignty if they are guilty of criminal violations of human rights. But policing and war are different animals. War aims at destruction of enemies, policing at the apprehension and detention of criminals. Murders resulting from terrorism are crimes to be dealt with as crimes, not acts of war. At the same time we have to find out why people are so determined that they are even willing to sacrifice their own lives in pursuit of their cause.

'Any serious campaign against terrorism also needs to address the social, economic and political conditions that nurture the emergence of terrorism, violence and conflict.' So said Archbishop Renato Martino, the Pope's envoy at the UN in 2001.

There is no UN agency charged with not just controlling but eliminating the trade in weapons. The gap between rich and poor, between and within countries, grows wider, but the economic organs of the world are not under the control of the United Nations. Many oppressed minorities within existing states feel that the only way to assert their rights is to take up arms. We need a body like the Trusteeship Council to be responsible for the human rights of minorities and to give such groupings a representative voice.

All this will mean a challenge to old notions of exclusive state sovereignty and to the extreme nationalism which is the source of so much conflict today. Respect for the obligations arising from agreed international treaties is a cornerstone of peace. In addition, the Secretary General of the UN needs to have at his disposal an agency charged with advance warning and mediation so that conflicts do not remain ignored until it is already too late to prevent violence.

Finally we need in every country programmes of peace education, and not least about the UN itself. In Britain most people know more about the Highway Code than they do about the UN Charter. There is much the Church could contribute by way of support for the United Nations and its various agencies, and work for its renewal and reform. Of criticism there is an endless supply. Of credit for the amazing achievements of the World Health Organisation, the Food and Agriculture Organization, the UN High Commission for Refugees, and UNICEF, to name but a few of them, little is ever said. The history of the International Court of Justice or its regular, year-in-year-out, patient resolution of inter-state conflict is little known.

An end to 'just wars'?
As we gathered in Hyde Park recently for another demonstration against the war in Iraq, a friend arrived wearing a T-shirt with the slogan: 'Peace – just do it'. That is exactly what ought to be said in answer to the question 'How can the Church help to abolish war?' No more statements, no more agonising over phrases and theoretical positions. Just get on with the job: the innumerable small, but practical tasks which are part of making peace.

Not that the theological debate which has exercised Christians for centuries is not valid and important. How do we reconcile the demands of justice, and the protection of human rights, with the demands of peace: thou shalt not kill? Or the right to self-defence with loving our enemies?

Too often we indulge in the intellectual satisfaction of having a watertight argument and being able to classify people as 'pacifists' or exponents of the 'just war'. However, the time has come when this polarised debate is holding us back from seeing things as they really are and from moving purposefully towards our goal of making war a thing of the past. At a recent conference, to the surprise of his elders, 14-year-old William put it in a nutshell: 'War is so-o-oh twentieth century.'

Gaudium et Spes asked us to 'evaluate war with an entirely new attitude' (#80). That attitude has to be informed by the realities of war as it is waged in our day, and many now conclude that the criteria set out by the 'just war' theory can never actually be met. They cite criteria relating both to the decision to go to war (*ad bellum*) and to the actual conduct of war (*in bello*).

In relation to the decision to go to war there is a global authority (the UN) to which member states have assigned the responsibility for resolving conflict and deciding whether military action is necessary.

In relation to the conduct of war, modern weapons certainly do cause excessive suffering and, despite the hype about precision weapons guided to military targets, we know that countless civilians are also certain to be killed. War has an inbuilt dynamic towards excess, and as the struggle intensifies, every weapon, however monstrous, will be used. Despite the legal and moral prohibitions, war is not in practice limited.

Most compelling of all, it is practically impossible to calculate that any beneficial outcome of a war will outweigh the destruction it causes. Common observation tells us that most wars end in a disastrous mess, with refugees surviving in misery: landmined fields, ruined villages, a shattered infrastructure, disrupted livelihoods, wrecked mental and physical health, and the seeds of future conflicts buried only for a generation or two before they will once again spring up. Another twist in the spiral of violence. War begets war. The 'just war' criteria of discrimination and proportionality, in particular, lead to the conclusion that modern war is unjustifiable.

Rather than suggest that the 'just war' theory is outdated and should be abandoned, this actually proves how useful it still is. As a tool it has not been bettered. It has provided the skeleton on which our international laws of war have been constructed and its terms seem to have entered common parlance. The 'just war' criteria were widely debated in the secular media before the Iraq war.

Letting go of war

The just war theory is like a mirror through which the Church can reveal why 'in this age which boasts of its atomic power, it no longer makes sense to maintain that war is a fit instrument with which to repair the violation of justice' (*Pacem in Terris* #127). Judging by the reaction to the long-planned war against Iraq, many people are now deeply cynical about excuses for war, very reluctant and uneasy about resorting to war, yet unable to let go of war because they are unconvinced that there are viable alternatives. Even those who support such wars in their political rhetoric are not prepared to see their own soldiers killed.

For those who protested against the Iraq war, many for the first time, there is bitter disillusionment that widespread opposition – and a million-strong march in London represents many more sympathisers at home – made no difference to the government's decision. Among Christian peace activists there is disappointment that our local church leaders spoke up boldly before the war but fell silent as soon as British troops went into action. Peace and nonviolence are not just for the times between wars. Advocating peace between wars is like vegetarianism between meals.

Many now think the Church should take a much more unequivocal stand against war and revert to the radical pacifism and nonviolence of early Christianity. It is the only logical way to go. In fact, this is the direction in which church teaching has been moving, though few have noticed.

Even if it is desirable, the Church is not going to arrive at such an unequivocal position overnight. We've got to teach the teaching and practise the preaching. Peace – just do it. It is in the process of actually doing the job that our thinking will change and we can collectively achieve greater clarity.

Catholic social teaching is not static. There has been a rapid evolution in Catholic teaching on war in just the last half-century, never mind the two millennia that went before. The older generation will remember being told that 'Catholics cannot be conscientious objectors'. Before the Second World War, when a small group of Catholics formed the PAX society because they already judged that modern weapons and warfare were incompatible with the traditional 'just war' principles, they were told by the authorities of Westminster Diocese that 'the conscientious objector has an erroneous conscience ... he is entitled to respect and sympathy such as would be given to any misguided person ... but error remains error and no Catholic organisation may make it one of their purposes to support an attitude of conscientious objection which is at variance with Catholic teaching' (Letter from the Archbishop of Westminster's Private Secretary to PAX, 1936).

Correspondence in diocesan archives shows that individuals seeking guidance from their bishops during the Second World War were given much the same advice – as also were German Catholics. In England PAX could only find a handful of priests willing to appear at tribunals and testify that a Catholic could have a legitimate moral objection to joining the armed forces.

In the 1960s a few young Catholics in Italy, Spain and Portugal bravely refused conscription and went to prison instead. In this context the right to conscientious objection was first recognised by the Second Vatican Council: 'It seems fair that laws should make humane provision for conscientious objectors, so long as they accept another form of service to the human community' (*Gaudium et Spes* #79).

It also gave qualified support to nonviolence: 'We cannot but praise those who renounce violence in defending their rights and use means of defence which are available to the weakest, so long as this can be done without harm to the rights and duties of others or of the community' (*Gaudium et Spes* #78)

The assumption was that these were attitudes for rather exceptional individuals; military participation was normal. Since then, Pope John Paul II set the Church more resolutely in the direction of abolishing war as a means of resolving conflict. He started doing this when he visited Hiroshima in 1981. 'The waging of war is not inevitable and unchangeable,' he said when there. 'Clashes of ideologies, aspirations and needs can and must be settled and resolved by means other than war and violence.'

Taking this further, John Paul went on later to present nonviolence as a realistic and collective means of working for justice and not simply a valid option for extraordinary individuals.

> It seemed that the European order resulting from World War II and sanctioned by the Yalta agreements could only be overturned by another war. Instead, it has been overcome by the nonviolent commitment of people who, while always refusing to yield to the force of power, succeeded time after time in finding effective ways of bearing witness to the truth … Many people learn to fight for justice without violence, renouncing class struggle in their internal disputes and war in international ones. (*Centesimus Annus* #23)

His 1991 encyclical letter continued:

> No, never again war … Just as the time has finally come when in individual states a system of private vendetta and reprisal has

given way to the rule of law, so too a similar step forward is now urgently needed in the international community. (*Centesimus Annus* #52)

The Church is now travelling on a different track from that of 'just wars', and has firmly set about detailing some of the weapons in the nonviolent arsenal. 'Effective non-violent means to settle disputes exist,' stated the Pontifical Council for Justice and Peace in 1994. 'Dialogue, negotiations, mediation, arbitration, or popular pressure have long proved their worth in re-establishing or obtaining justice' (*The International Arms Trade: An Ethical Reflection* #4/11).

In the last twenty-five years there has been significant movement beyond simply rejecting war and advocating peace. Pope John Paul's output on peace issues was absolutely astonishing. Not only did his annual messages for the World Day of Peace explore peace from every angle, but also he used every opportunity to witness to reconciliation in places associated with the worst atrocities committed by human beings, apologising for slavery, persecution and anti-Semitism, and inviting religious leaders of other world faiths to join him in the common cause of peacemaking.

From words to deeds

If only all of these wise exhortations had been acted upon. We need no more statements to move the Church towards the abolition of war. We just need to put into effect the ones we already have. The issue is no longer between pacifism and just wars. We must unite around a 'preferential option for nonviolence'. How can this be done in practice?

The first task is one of spiritual formation. Catholics need to be equipped to embody the peace of Christ and to take a resolute stand against many of the widely accepted values and goals which are offered by the contemporary political version of peace and security. Catholics need enhanced training in hope, solidarity, nonviolence and service if they are to challenge the fear, greed, violence and power-seeking by which that version is nourished.

Questions about war and peace are questions of life and death, and as such have a place in all our teaching about reverence for life, and the formation of consciences to make the right personal as well as political judgements.

It should be axiomatic that Christians will challenge the concept of absolute state sovereignty. To involve others in wars demands a culture of obedience and authority, a stress on outside threats, and above all a summons to national patriotism. The Christian has no problem with love of country as long as love of family and love of humanity come first.

God has no favourites, St Peter finally realised, but much of world conflict is built on the notion that my country or tribe or culture is more important than any other.

'The great task ahead for the twenty-first century is to move the world from a culture of violence and war to a culture of peace,' Archbishop Martino told the United Nations in 1998. 'UNESCO has already taken a lead in promoting a culture of peace. This consists in promoting values, attitudes and behaviours reflecting and inspiring social interaction and sharing, based on the principles of freedom, justice and democracy, human rights, tolerance and solidarity.'

The Church is in a privileged and influential position – with countless opportunities for developing this sensitivity to peace. Many years ago, the Dutch bishops challenged the Church to turn aspirations into practical reality: 'Looking for peace means giving peace work a real place, not just as a pious wish in our hearts and on our lips, but in our thoughts, in our interests, in our educational work, in our political convictions, in our faith, in our prayer, and in our budgets' (*To Banish War*, 1969). It is in this spirit that we offer a checklist at the end of this essay of just some of the ways in which peacemaking could be given a 'real place' in the life of our Church. It is by no means comprehensive, and many of the suggestions could apply under more than one heading.

Sacramental life

- Penance: repentance for the conflicts which divide us but perhaps also identification of some new sins (selling weapons for example?).
- Reconciliation: with the wider world as part of our personal reconciliation with God.
- The sign of peace: a symbolic expression of unity and reconciliation with God's whole family before approaching the altar.
- Eucharist: receiving the body of Christ prohibits our violation of his body in other people, by subtle exploitation or by overt violence.
- Confirmation: the occasion when young people opt for non-violent resistance, a lifestyle committed to peacemaking.

Liturgy and devotion

- Friday penance: directed at prayer, fasting and almsgiving for peace.
- Dedication: of a peace chapel or altar to prayer for peace.
- The parish calendar: relating feasts and other events to aspects of the peace of Christ – Peace Sunday, Fairtrade Fortnight, Ash Wednesday, Hiroshima and Nagasaki commemorations, Racial Justice Sunday, Black History month, UN Day, Remembrance Sunday, Human Rights Day, and so on.

- Bidding prayers, children's liturgical activities, decorations and exhibitions, special events, to bring this calendar to life.
- Seasonal perspectives: such as 'giving up' violence for Lent (an initiative of the World Council of Churches' Overcoming Violence programme).
- May devotions: to Our Lady Queen of Peace, saying the rosary for peace.
- Honouring the saints who model virtues of peacemaking: canonisation of Franz Jägerstätter and Dorothy Day.

Catholic schools
- Stories which introduce the heroes and heroines of peacemaking.
- Foundation skills of communication and cooperation to tackle problems.
- Peer mediation training for resolving conflicts and bullying.
- Science and technology: exploring exciting solutions to human needs and discussing moral implications of research.
- Citizenship with a global perspective: information about international structures and especially the United Nations.
- Real-life experience of democracy: by participation in a school council.
- Careers advice: promoting job satisfaction based on service, and careers that further world peace.
- Work experience and 'gap year' projects: with organisations working for social justice.
- Resisting the inducements offered by links with arms companies: which anyway undermine the stated values of Catholic schools.
- Creating a peace garden: using symbols, stones and plants that represent unity and peace.

Adult education
- Discussion: about the culture of violence, influence of TV and video, music, toys, games and magazines which promote war as entertainment (and profit from it).
- Parental guidance and sharing of experience about Christian values and discipline, methods for conflict resolution at home, explaining world news to children.
- Catholic press: ensuring a substantial proportion of world news alongside the parochial and national stories.
- Regular preaching and educational programmes about moral issues of war and peace, impact of the arms race, nonviolent options in an interdependent world.
- Training in seminaries about the power and relevance of the Church's moral influence in the political arena.

- Professional support groups: where moral responsibility can be sensitively discussed by those working in scientific research, the media, politics, defence industries, military forces.
- Providing information and opportunities for parishioners to get involved in action for peace.

Military personnel
- Courses: (like those for marriage preparation) about church teaching on war, the laws of war, the role of personal conscience and human rights, prohibition on use of torture, ill-treatment of prisoners etc.
- Promote transformation of the military into international police force.
- Support for soldiers and families: dealing with dehumanising and traumatic effects of war.

Military chaplains
- In-service training: on how to advise soldiers on limits to military obedience, especially in time of war, and on the emotional and moral impact of military training and fighting experience.
- Ensure that chaplains are familiar with application procedures for conscientious objectors.
- Start a dialogue with other denominations and armed forces about revising the chaplains' role: set a date by which they would be 'disestablished' – paid as civilian priests rather than by the Ministry of Defence.

Conscientious objectors and whistle-blowers
- Support at diocesan level: counselling advice, job opportunities, accommodation and emergency financial help for those wanting to leave on grounds of conscience.
- Use of parish network to find alternative jobs when necessary.
- Guidance for parishes: on relationship with arms firms providing jobs in locality.

Conflict prevention and resolution (including conflict within the Church)
- Develop theology of peace: in particular contribute to thinking out new criteria to guide humanitarian intervention and policing operations.
- Recruit and train for civilian peace forces: especially those going to work for the Church in conflict areas.
- Start an international peace research institute: (for example in Rome) to train the Church's own specialists and mediators.
- Vatican representatives at UN institutions to meet Christian NGOs

(non-governmental organisations) on regular basis.
- World Day of Peace ('Peace Sunday') to become an international armistice day.
- Send some parishioners for mediation training (e.g. courses run by the Mennonites).
- Develop links across the neighbourhood with other local organisations working for unity.
- Get to know other faith communities in the area: use the Westminster inter-faith peace walk as a model.

Structures for peace
- Reassess priorities: in light of 1971 Synod to give justice and peace greater prominence.
- Make Peace Sunday ecumenical.
- Promote and support Pax Christi, the international Catholic peace movement, which individuals can join.
- Provide proper funding and resources for Justice and Peace workers at national and diocesan level.
- Demonstrate explicit link between personal generosity of charity and support for policies and reforms required by social justice.
- Make full use of Church's international network to strengthen solidarity with Church in conflict zones: visits, messages, twinning, web links, political action.

Lead by example
- Look at Church investments: switch from arms companies, or anything indirectly supporting conflict.
- Audit church buildings: on energy conservation, recycling, use of resources, purchasing policy in support of Fair Trade etc.
- Check that Church is inclusive and welcoming to every section of community, with proper representation of gender and race in liturgical, educational, management and social functions.
- Open and just employment policy: making use of professional expertise present in every parish.
- Dialogue with those alienated or wronged by the Church and develop models and mechanisms for reconciliation.
- Examine whether the language of prayers and hymns might convey approval for militarism and exclusiveness.

The future of the Church

After the bloodiest century in history, can the world advance into the twenty-first century by abolishing war? We believe that human ingenuity and determination to overcome remaining obstacles could make war redundant, unnecessary and outmoded.

In the past the Church had military orders, crusades and papal armies, and thought them essential to spreading the Gospel. Today we see things differently. Rigorous application of 'just war' criteria excludes modern war as a moral choice. Can the Church extricate itself from any further complicity with the barbarism of war?

We believe that by putting its own words into action, applying energy and resources to creating a culture of peace, and demonstrating a 'preferential option for nonviolence', the Church could forge as distinctive a contribution to peace as it has on the other issues where human life is at stake.

Chapter Sixteen

The Spirit of Reconciliation: Mission in a World of Many Faiths, Identities and Conflicts

Robert Kaggwa MAfr

The world in which we live is a world of many violent conflicts. It is crying out for peace and stability. But as we know, there can be no peace, no harmony, without forgiveness and reconciliation.

It is important to recognise that the work of reconciliation is first and foremost God's work. The enormity of the misdeeds that we experience today is so great that it overwhelms the human imagination to consider how they can be overcome. Who can undo the consequences of war, of genocide or of centuries of oppression? Who can bring back the dead? It is only the God of life.

Reconciliation is about new creation. Only God can begin that. This does not mean that humans have to sit back and wait until God restores understanding, peace and harmony among peoples. If reconciliation is God's work, it is also our task. But the starting point has to be found in God.

There is a story about a young man apprenticed to a master artist, who produced the most beautiful stained-glass windows anywhere. The apprentice could not approach the master's genius, so he borrowed the master's tools, thinking that was the answer. After several weeks, the young man said to his teacher, 'I am not doing any better with your tools than I did with mine.' The teacher replied, 'It's not the tools of the master you need but the spirit of the master.'

In a pluralistic world often marked by conflicts of all sorts we may recognise more than ever before that Jesus did not leave us clear guidelines and tools to handle all the problems that we are facing. We need to be creative. I would like to propose a rediscovery of the 'spirit' of reconciliation. By this I do not only refer to the attitude we should have, but first and foremost to God, the Spirit who renews the face of the earth by including us in the mission of reconciliation in our world of many conflicts.

In her address to the World Council of Churches' Conference in

Canberra in 1991, the Korean theologian Chung Hyung Kyung prayed in these words:

> Dear sisters and brothers, with the energy of the Holy Spirit let us tear apart all walls of division and the culture of death that separates us. And let us participate in the Holy Spirit's economy of life, fighting for our life on this earth in solidarity with all living beings and building communities for justice, peace and the integrity of creation. Wild wind of the Holy Spirit, blow to us. Let us welcome Her, letting ourselves go in Her wild rhythm of life. Come, Holy Spirit, renew the whole creation. Amen![1]

Her words caused outrage to many conservative members of the assembly and she is even reported to have received death threats.

A world of conflicting spirits

Today we realise that finding solutions to many problems is harder than anything comparable in the past. Books on theology, which had a high reputation fifty years ago, will now strike us as being generally simplistic. As Christians we need to admit that we do not know the consequences and answers to many of today's questions. We do not have special knowledge. Our contribution can only be part of the whole of humanity's search for meaning.

Yet in all this we can see movements or trajectories of the Spirit, possibilities for reimagining a new future. The Spirit works in all times and places and, in this time of uncertainty, we will discover both blessings and demonic elements. It is a world of conflicting spirits. The discernment of the movements of the Spirit in the midst of all these spirits belongs to the Church's mission, a process of exploring the significance of the Good News in history.

The last century may be remembered as one of the most destructive periods in history. A new sense of evil and collective human sin was demonstrated in the two World Wars, the Holocaust, Hiroshima, Chernobyl, as well as in the genocide in Rwanda, and in numerous other violent ethnic and religious conflicts all over the globe. But our world has also been transformed from a set of self-contained tribes and nations into a global reality. Centuries ago, the unity of humanity was an idea in the minds of a few visionary intellectuals. Today it is a concrete reality.

This world gives us a new perspective for building a meaningful human community. However, it can also not be denied that despite this unique chance of coming closer that is set before us, we still tend to live by outdated divisive patterns. Human beings have never been so close to each other as they are today, and yet never have they also been so divided. Yet God has created a world full of vitality and variety. It is not uniform. How can we acknowledge others in their otherness? How can we be enriched by religious and cultural differences? Dialogue becomes even more important today. I would like to argue that for Christians the rediscovery of the Holy Spirit ought to lead to a rethink of right relations.

One of the main causes of conflict today has to do with the multi-faith world in which we live. We must admit that there has been a tremendous development in people's understanding of otherness, encounter and dialogue not least with other faith traditions. But what does it mean to confess faith in the Spirit of God in a pluralistic, fragmented and uncertain world, a world of many faiths, identities and conflicts?

As I see it, in earlier treatments of the question of dialogue with other faiths, too much stress had been put on the Church and on Christ, sometimes neglecting the role of the Holy Spirit.

The impasse

Much can be said about numerous texts in the New Testament that point to Jesus Christ as being the only way to salvation. The Gospel of John (14:6) says that 'He is the way, the truth and the life', while 1 Timothy 2:5 affirms that He is the 'one mediator between God and human beings'. And Peter declares in Acts 4:12 that 'there is salvation in no one else; for there is no other name under heaven given among humans by which we must be saved.' What are we to make of all this?

Generations of Christians have regarded the above texts as proving that Jesus and no one else provides the way to salvation, and that by extension there is no salvation outside his Church. Some have argued that Jesus Christ is the way for all, as the above texts refer only to Jesus and not to the Church: people of other faiths are also included in God's plan of salvation. Others affirm that Jesus Christ is the way for Christians, while their respective faith traditions constitute the way of salvation for others.

The problem is that all these views lead to an impasse in which inter-faith dialogue becomes almost impossible. It may be that the exclusion of a theology of the Holy Spirit is responsible for this. Indeed the reality of religious pluralism should lead to a rediscovery of the Holy Spirit as a remedy to this impasse.

Rediscovering mystery

The Holy Spirit has often been described as 'the mysterious One' of the three in the Godhead. Some have referred to the Spirit as 'the Cinderella of theology', 'the unknown', 'the faceless', 'the half-known' or 'the shadowy'. These designations need not be taken negatively. A spirit of reconciliation needs to rediscover the importance of mystery.

In popular language a mystery is something beyond our understanding, something inexplicable. Very often mystery also means something that we do not yet know – a mystery story that will be solved at the end of a book, a film or a puzzle in nature that scientists are working to answer. In the Christian and Jewish tradition, however, there is a strong abiding sense that God will always exceed our comprehension. Mystery is reality that is so rich that our understanding can never exhaust it.

Mystery may be defined as a known unknown. It is 'a mixture of certitudes and uncertainties; of probabilities, hypotheses, realities that surpass us, and fundamental questions to which we have no answers ... It is one of those words that is indefinable, but that can in the final analysis be part of any definition.'[2]

This explanation of the word mystery is indeed paradoxical. But mystery itself is about paradox in life. In his book, *The Courage to Teach*, Parker Palmer describes how we have become masters of 'thinking the world apart'.[3] We live in a polarising culture. We are trained neither to voice both sides of an issue nor to listen with both ears. Most of us are trained in becoming experts of polarisation. 'Tell me something and I will find any way, fair or foul, to argue the contrary!'

We look at the world through analytical lenses. We see everything as this or that; either ... or; on or off; positive or negative; in or out; black or white. We fragment reality in an endless series of 'either ... or'. In short, we think the world apart. Of course, this has given human beings a great power over nature, a lot of success, many gifts of modern science and technology. But we can say that we have also lost the sense of mystery.

This dualism of 'either ... or' thinking has also given us a fragmented sense of reality that destroys the wholeness and wonder of life. It misleads and betrays us when applied to the perennial problems of being human in this world. Therefore, we need to move away from an 'either ... or' attitude to a 'both ... and' attitude. In certain circumstances, truth is a paradoxical joining of apparent opposites, and if we want to know that truth we must learn to embrace those opposites as one. Obviously in the empirical world there are choices to be made: an apple tree cannot be both an oak tree and an apple tree. But there is another realm of knowing and here binary logic ('either ... or') misleads us.

This is the realm of profound truth – where, if we want to know what is essential, we must stop thinking the world into pieces and start thinking it together again. In terms of Christian mission, for example, there are significant paradoxes to note: dialogue and proclamation, openness and responsiveness, sensitivity and activity, humility and boldness. Feminist scholars have also rejected the binary, hierarchical, misogynistic and dualistic anthropology that has characterised philosophy, theology and church praxis and have pointed to 'a diversity of ways of being human'.[4]

Profound truth rather than empirical fact is the stuff of which paradoxes are made and this is common in our daily life, even if we are not often aware of it. We are ourselves paradoxes that breathe. We are mystery. Indeed breathing itself is a form of paradox – requiring inhaling and exhaling to be whole. The poles of paradox are like the poles of a battery: hold them together and they generate electricity, pull them apart and the current stops flowing.

Consider other paradoxes, for example our need for both solitude and community. Human beings were made for relationships. Without a rich and nourishing network of connections, we wither and die. It is a clinical fact that people who lack relationships get sick more often and recover more slowly than people surrounded by family and friends. But at the same time we are also made for solitude. Our lives may be rich in relationships, but the human self remains a mystery of enfolded inwardness that no other person can possibly enter or know. If we fail to embrace our ultimate aloneness and seek meaning only in communion with others, we wither and die. The farther we travel towards the great mystery, the more at home we must be with our essential aloneness in order to stay healthy and whole.

We need to embrace all these apparent opposites. This means entering into mystery. The result is a world more complex and confusing than the one made simple by 'either/or' thought – but as simplicity is merely the dullness of death, entering into mystery is characterised by a creative synthesis of 'both … and'.

To speak about God who is infinite is another way of entering into mystery. For Christians, the invisible, infinite God is made visible in Jesus of Nazareth. And yet God who is revealed in this particular, historical, limited individual remains nonetheless concealed, hidden, veiled. It also means that God is 'personal'. As humans we speak of a person revealing herself/himself to us. By that we do not mean knowing facts about that person's life, but seeing with the 'eyes of the heart' who that person is, grasping through love their ineffable and inexhaustible mystery. The more intimate our knowledge of another, the more we are drawn to that person's unique mystery and the deeper that mystery becomes.

Knowing the unknown

The Spirit may be described as the point of contact between God and ourselves in history. The Spirit reminds us that God remains mystery and will always remain mystery. How then should we come to the knowledge of the 'Unknown'? The Spirit is not directly knowable but the experience of the Spirit can be known.

From the very beginning of creation, the Spirit is present like 'a mighty wind that hovers over the waters' (Genesis 1:2). The Spirit is present in the long journey of Israel and of the nations, as giver of life (Genesis 2:7), and speaking through the prophets (Ezekiel 2:2). The Bible uses a rich variety of images and symbols such as water, wind or breath and fire to signify this life-giving function of the Spirit of God. Wherever there is life, the Spirit of God is present. Not only Christianity but also other faith traditions throughout the world have been bearers of this life.

This is particularly important in the so-called indigenous religions (which have often been written off as 'animism' by western imperialism). African traditional religions, for example, portray a strong awareness of life in creation and of the spirit world. Christian theology will certainly need to discern the Spirit of God in the spirit world of indigenous religions. Recent thinking that addresses contemporary environmental issues is a welcome direction in recognising the presence of the Holy Spirit in other faiths. What we can learn is that the Spirit is this creative and life-giving person animating all creation.

The Spirit was present in the conception of Jesus (Luke 1:35) and was poured upon Jesus from his baptism and his ministry right through his passion, death and resurrection. The same Spirit was then promised and given to Jesus' disciples to teach them and lead them to the truth (John 14:26; 15:26). Thus we can say that the Spirit preceded the coming of Jesus, was active throughout his life, death and resurrection, and is also sent as the Paraclete by Jesus to all humans and all creation.

The action of the Spirit is thus present before and after the coming of Jesus. The Spirit is not only the giver of life but also the giver of faith. Religious traditions that have nurtured the faith of millions of peoples and cultures throughout history cannot be excluded from the action of the Spirit of God.

The New Testament describes Jesus as a Spirit-filled person. The Spirit empowers Jesus and sends him but Jesus also sends the Spirit (Luke 4:1; John 16:7). But there is no Spirit independent of Christ. Life in Christ and life in the Spirit are mutually interdependent (Romans 8:9). An ancient Church Father, Irenaeus of Lyons, referred to Christ and the

Spirit as 'the two hands of the Father'. They go forth hand in hand, but in history it is the Spirit who comes first. Indeed coming before does not mean that one is more important than the other but it may have profound implications for dialogue.

First, this shows that God acts even before the coming of Jesus. By insisting on the role of the Spirit even before the coming of Jesus, we are trying to point to God's activity that has animated faith communities in different times and places. Second, we could not even recognise Christ if it were not in the power of the Spirit. Paul writes (1 Corinthians 12:3) that no one can say that Jesus is Lord except in the power of the Spirit. Thus being in Christ and living in the Spirit are two sides of the same coin. The Spirit is the sole possibility of any knowledge of the Father and the Son.

The Spirit is the point of contact where the Father and the Son touch history. Maybe we can say that the Spirit is the 'how' and Christ is the 'what'. In other words, we cannot get to that centre without the power of the Spirit. This view opens the way to the understanding of God's action outside the Church and also to the realisation that God can always surprise us in many and different ways. Other faiths with their traditions and sacred texts, other cultures, other peoples, are also bearers of the Spirit (something that the absolutism of imperial Christianity denied). This has always to be discerned and in that way we can never say that all religions and religious experiences are equal. That would amount to vague pluralism, which helps no one.

The insistence on the presence of the Holy Spirit in Christianity and other faiths, cultures and traditions always needs discernment. The Spirit is elusive and unpredictable. The Spirit blows where she/he wills and only discernment can lead to the recognition of the Spirit's presence. But this involves distinguishing between the many spirits at work in this world and the Spirit of God.

Discernment is necessary, proceeding on a case-by-case basis – but this does require Christians to embrace the reconciling work of the Spirit. Each particular religious experience should not be denied (Joel 2:28–32). Each experience can be seen to give particular testimony to the nature of humankind and of humanity's relationship to God in anticipation of the full reconciliation to be accomplished in the reign of God.

The Spirit of reconciliation points to the experience of community and to creativity in order to reinvent our responses to the Spirit who renews the face of the earth.

Knowing in community

All knowing begins in experience. If, as I have suggested, the Spirit is the contact point between God and history, our experiences reveal the presence or absence of the Spirit. For the early Christians the experience of the Spirit was a social experience and the basis of community. It was a shared experience of the Spirit. The Spirit brings about both unity and diversity in those who share in the Spirit's experience. Not only glory but also sufferings. In this sense, the Spirit is the energy of connectedness that unites all.

Community is essential to all reality. It is the matrix of all being and we know reality only by being in community with it ourselves. Modern scientists have rediscovered this way of relational knowing. Knower cannot be separated from the known and nuclear physicists cannot study subatomic particles without altering them in the act of knowing. It is thus impossible to maintain an objectivist gap between reality 'out there' and the detached observer 'in here'.

How can a historian or a literary critic study a text of the past without leaving the mark of his or her personal experience? This relational knowing is a strength that connects us. Today we can celebrate being part of a cosmic community precisely because of this rediscovery of relational knowing. The question is, do we draw appropriate conclusions from this experience?

Openness to the Spirit is what saves us from both absolutism and relativism. In relational knowing we are empowered by the Spirit to discover the 'other', who has often been suppressed. We learn to embrace diversity. In absolutism we claim to know the intentions of the Spirit, so there is no need to dialogue with the 'other'. We possess the truth and have only to transmit it. With relativism, we claim that knowledge depends on where one is. Once again there is no need to continue dialogue because everyone has their truth and the difference is not important.[5]

The unpredictable and hidden Spirit is this energy that binds and connects, leading into the unknown, overturning our categories and boundaries. But knowing in community also requires boldness and creativity.

Trajectories of the Spirit

A theology of the Spirit requires a lot of imagination. It requires us to abandon old certainties. As John Taylor writes, 'To think deeply about the Holy Spirit is a bewildering, tearing exercise, for whatever [the Spirit] touches [the Spirit] turns it inside out.'[6] It is really about new creation and looking towards the future. Anyone writing on the Holy Spirit 'is hardly burdened by the past and finds little guidance there'.[7]

Just as in the story of the young man who was not helped by the tools of the master, today we too need the Spirit to reimagine our future. Prophetic imagination is a gift that we will always need. The Spirit, who speaks through the prophets, gives the freedom to dream and create metaphors of connection. Elizabeth Johnson describes the Spirit as one who 'hovers like a great mother bird over her egg, to hatch the living order of the world out of primordial chaos'.[8]

> If the Spirit is associated with bringing to birth ('Fill the earth, and bring it to birth' as the old hymn put it), then the imagery of the cosmic egg is timely. The Spirit is watchful for the moment where the cracks in the discourses of violence appear, where humanity at last admits vulnerability in having no answers, and commits itself at last to a different kind of listening.[9]

It may be that in our culture, so full of cracks and uncertainties, we need a different kind of listening: listening to the experiences of the 'other', the marginalised, listening to the 'eccentric' (were the prophets not often declared eccentric?), listening to secular movements of liberation, listening to the aspirations of so many young people who have been disillusioned by the institutional Church, listening to their apathy, listening to the resistance coming from the underside of history, listening to gay and lesbian people, listening to women and to the contribution of feminist spirituality, listening to the immigrants and asylum-seekers who come with their own spiritualities.

Of course, discernment will be necessary. But let us not be cautious of this in such a way that we stifle the Spirit of God. The prophecy of Joel (2:28–32), repeated in Peter's sermon at Pentecost, refers to a multiplicity of experiences and testimonies of the Spirit (Acts 2:17–18). It is an all-inclusive vision.

> I will pour out my Spirit on all flesh;
> your sons and daughters shall prophesy,
> your old people shall dream dreams,
> and your young people shall see visions.
> Even on the male and female slaves,
> in those days, I will pour out my Spirit.
>   (Joel 2:28f.)

Many identities

The Holy Spirit in our world of many faiths, identities and conflicts is a theme that needs all our attention. This points to two important conclusions. First and foremost, we need to take pluralism as a cultural and religious fact, a gift of the Spirit who creates diversity. It is an expression of the human quest for meaning and an occasion for our own self-discovery. Our world of many identities is evidence of God's historical and unpredictable engagement with humankind.

Second, we need to recognise the 'spiritual and moral goods' found in otherness. Religious and cultural otherness has to be seen as a value in itself and an opportunity for mutual cross-fertilisation. To recognise this is also a gift of the Spirit who blows where she/he wills. The Holy Spirit is not 'incarnate' and therefore not limited, but transcends the limits of our world, history, faiths, cultures and traditions.

Reflecting on the Spirit of reconciliation points to continuing the career and praxis of Jesus who was anointed with the Spirit (Luke 4:14–30) to proclaim the Good News of liberation to all those who are excluded, 'faceless' and forgotten, 'the others'. The Spirit is the inclusive God; the God of the periphery and of the underside of history; the God of risks, the God of surprises, empowering us to explore new avenues in our midst. The mission of the Spirit then forbids us to think of one tradition, theology or culture as the centre into which all others can be drawn.

It is the exploration and discovery of the 'other', who is different and valuable but excluded or suppressed by universal assumptions. It is a Spirit of diversity, a Spirit of dialogue, unity and reconciliation with the whole of creation.

Notes

1. Quoted by S. McFague, 'Holy Spirit' in L. Russell and S. Clarkson (eds), *Dictionary of Feminist Theologies* (Louisville, KY: Westminster John Knox Press, 1996), p. 147.
2. I. Gebara, *Longing for Running Water* (Minneapolis: Fortress, 1999), p. 133.
3. P. Palmer, *The Courage to Teach* (San Francisco: Jossey Bass, 1998), pp. 61–6.
4. E. Johnson, *She Who Is: The Mystery of God in Feminist Theological Discourse* (New York: Crossroad, 1992), p. 155; D. McEwan, Editorial, *Feminist Theology* 14 (1997), p. 7.
5. Is this not the dilemma of absolutism and relativism which cohabit in today's world? The Vatican document, *Dominus Iesus* (5 September 2000), is legitimately worried about modern forms of relativism in what concerns salvation in Jesus Christ but unfortunately its response only accentuates the absolutist dimension. The Spirit is rarely mentioned in this document.

6. J. V. Taylor, *The Go-Between God* (London: SCM Press, 1979), p. 179.

7. K. McDonnel, 'A trinitarian theology of the Holy Spirit', *Theological Studies* 46 (1985), p. 191.

8. Johnson, *She Who Is*, p. 134.

9. M. Grey, *The Outrageous Pursuit of Hope* (London: Darton, Longman & Todd, 2000), p. 72.

PART FOUR

THE OPPORTUNITIES FOR BENEDICT XVI

Chapter Seventeen

An Ecumenical Pilgrimage: Stepping Out from Security

Wilfrid McGreal OCarm

Pilgrimage – the journey to a holy place or shrine – is something all the religions have in common: Rome, Jerusalem or Mecca. But pilgrimage is not just the journey to a place. It is also the inner journey where a pilgrim discovers something about themselves.

Pilgrimage is an important element in my life as I have been part of the Carmelite community that cares for the shrine at Aylesford in Kent. It is a place that welcomes every year people of every race, language and way of life. I know from conversations with pilgrims that their experience is life-giving and often challenging.

However, as I help care for others, I have to ask what about my own journey, do I ever step out of my context? Do I take the risk of being challenged, of being open to a new perspective? I realise that two events in my life's journey have a deeper meaning and involve a challenge. The first was a chance visit to Ephesus, the other a pilgrimage from Rome and back to Kent.

Whenever I read the Letter to the Ephesians, I have in my mind's eye an image of Ephesus itself. I came to Ephesus one cold March afternoon in 1987 and saw an immense expanse of Graeco-Roman ruins that stretched into the distance, magnificent fragments of what had been a huge, prosperous bustling port. It was in that exciting city that Paul nurtured a group of Christians for whom he had a special love.

His Letter to the Ephesians contains a prayer that eloquently yet economically celebrates what God can do in our lives. The prayer speaks of the fullness of God that can fill us and the power working within us that can do infinitely more than we could ever imagine. The vision is of a growing strong in our inner self, open to and giving God freedom. 'In the abundance of his glory may he, through his Spirit, enable you to grow firm in power with regard to your inner self ... Glory be to him whose power, working in us, can do infinitely more than we can ask or imagine' (Ephesians 3:16, 20; for the whole prayer see 3:14–21).

That passage stands out in my mind alongside verses from John's gospel where the writer in chapter 15 reminds us that it is God who chooses us, who wants our friendship and who wants our love for one another to be the sign that we abide in Christ. 'You are my friends ... I call you friends ...You did not choose me, no, I chose you ... My command to you is to love one another' (see John 15:8–17).

These two passages say something radical about our relationship with God in Jesus Christ but also give us a sense of how we could live together in the Christian community, as disciples who befriend and are befriended.

In the autumn of 2004 I took part in a pilgrimage that shook me out of security and set me searching for an understanding of where I was in my journey as a Christian. I was taking part in a pilgrimage from Rome to Rochester that commemorated St Justus journeying to England with Augustine and being called to found the diocese of Rochester in 604. The pilgrims were, in the main, Anglicans; the Catholics were just five in all. However, while on one level the journey was in a familiar context – the Italian countryside – on another there was a difference: the challenge of the Anglican majority.

While we were in Rome we were greeted by Cardinal Walter Kaspar who is President of the Council for Christian Unity. The cardinal said something to us that was provocative and significantly hopeful: the journey to truth is by the way of love and friendship, not just the hammering out of agreements or of refinements and qualifications. In that statement that highlighted love and friendship, there was a reminder that Jesus, whom we confess as Lord and Saviour, is the love and friendship of God and, in the acknowledgement of that reality, we are bonded in our Christian faith.

As I travelled through Italy on that pilgrimage – and since returning to England – I have found that I am being challenged to a new perspective and even being asked to throw away the map, taking risks rather than sticking to familiar territory. What are the implications of giving God freedom in our lives and, if we are called to friendship, why do we seem to be so anxious about how we live out that friendship in the community of the disciples?

A friend is someone with whom we experience freedom and mutuality. Friendship does not grow with wanting to please. Rather there is an acceptance and an openness to something that is ever richer. Our entry into this friendship is through baptism or, rather, when life helps us to open up to the implications of that event. It is when we realise that we are being called that our new life in Christ becomes real and the formal nature of our relationship comes alive. We are transformed from being church members into disciples, called like the disciples 2000 years ago for a mission to continue Christ's work of proclaiming and living the Kingdom of God.

Travelling light

Like those early disciples we need to travel light. Perhaps we might be encouraged in this by the cut-price airlines that tell us to pare down our luggage to a small bag that will fit in the overhead locker. The first disciples were sent out without even a rucksack. They carried nothing superfluous. We also need to travel light, shedding customs, ways and practices that could be an obstacle to proclaiming the Kingdom. It should be borne in mind that the first proclamation of the Kingdom was accompanied by works of healing and of reconciliation.

Could this mean that there is a need for all of us to address the work of inner personal, spiritual healing? First, be reconciled in yourself and before God so that then you can be involved in the work of healing for the sake of the Kingdom. This healing often includes the healing of memories and should inspire an attitude that enables us to allow enemies to become friends. Personal healing allows us to move away from atavistic stances and is crucial in any work that includes moving away from tribalism, disunity or conflict in general. Hurtful memories can be scars on the psyche. If these scars are aggravated, they can erupt with negative consequences.

So much that went wrong in the former Yugoslavia was caused by a reawakening of past hurts. The present situation in Northern Ireland cries out for healing at every level so that the climate of fear and mistrust can change and people feel free to accept and acknowledge each other. The common bond of baptism does not figure as a positive already realised state. Instead the communities at an official level seem anxious to endorse difference.

However, if we return to Jesus' words in John's gospel, they show we are called by God to friendship. That means God likes us and asks us in turn to like and love each other. We need, more than ever at this moment, to move from fragmentation to friendship. The call is for communities to seek healing and realise that reconciliation will enable the future. There is a need to move into a world of dialogue and hospitality. The stranger needs to become our guest, someone with whom we listen and share. Then dialogue becomes possible.

If we want a model for hospitality then Abraham stands out. While Abraham was a stranger in Canaan, he was there waiting to welcome the stranger and he welcomed angels. Rublev's icon, the hospitality at Mamre, symbolises that moment of hospitality which is seminal for

Christians, Jews and Muslims. Abraham risked sharing what little he had and was enriched beyond any dreams.

Hospitality is the invitation to enter another person's space and, once there, the possibility of listening to the other initiates dialogue. In a world of sound bites and simplification, it is all too easy to categorise the other before we know them. Dialogue is essential if we want to avoid fundamentalism, literalism or the populist. It enables diversity to be recognised and welcomed and reminds us that difference is enriching.

Again we have a ready model – Jesus' encounter with the Samaritan woman in John's gospel and, even more forcefully, his willingness to change his stance as he listens to the Syro-Phoenician woman. Jesus goes to the person and is willing to have a real encounter with them. There is no complacency in his dealing either with those close to him or strangers. He wants to find the real person and in the encounter he shows respect. Dialogue overturns exclusivity and reminds us that the joy is not having the answer but being challenged by new questions to journey deeper into the heart of reality, to discover the newness of God. The truth will set you free, as John's gospel declares. That truth is the Word of God incarnate in Jesus Christ.

The richness and the surprising newness of God as revealed in Jesus Christ reminds us that our Christian life is not about having the answer to everything but about our openness to transformation. If we have entered into the spirit of dialogue we realise that listening is of the essence and that respectful conversation where we are willing to learn is the creative way forward. Perhaps the greatest hurdle to Christians finding a common life in Christ together has been the tendency by those invested with authority to imply that they know what we should be believing rather than realising that the whole community of disciples has to be a learning community. Only with that knowledge can those entrusted with the ministry of teaching and leading articulate how we live in a way that is faithful to the Gospel.

However, sometimes it can seem that roles of leadership promote styles of teaching that can be deaf to the needs and experience of the community of believers. At the beginning of the twenty-first century there is a definite need for church leaders to be at the forefront of communities that work for reconciliation and transformation. The individual Christian can do much to address their own personal need for healing and openness to other Christians and society in general. At a local level Christians are finding they have more in common than they have that divides them. Groups that pray together, share the Scriptures or work for justice find bonds of faith and friendship drawing them close together.

Shared Eucharist

The one activity that is impossible is to share Eucharist, to celebrate in holy communion the life of Christ present in each one in baptism. The obstacles come from questions about the faith and the practice of our churches. Eucharistic sharing, it is held, will only be possible when we have full and final agreement and, while some dispensations from the norm are possible, it does seem that there is a long journey still to be completed. In this case is the best going to prevent the good from happening?

The reality at the local level is one of sadness and confusion. It would seem that there is something like the Greek myth of Sisyphus, where the stone almost reaches the top of the hill only to roll time after time back to the bottom. The work for Christian unity is acknowledged to be the prayer of Christ, but our human frailties and inability to come to that perfect moment constantly inhibit Christ's desire.

Liturgical reform in the Catholic Church and in the reformed tradition has taken us back to the early Church. The eucharistic prayers used by Catholics, Anglicans and other reformed traditions have a similar shape. At their heart are the words of institution and the invocation of the Holy Spirit (epiclesis). The actions of the celebrants and the devotion of the people all indicate an awareness of Jesus Risen present in the worshipping communities. Those who worship today are seeking God's grace so that they can live the Gospel and its mission in the twenty-first century, not living out an agenda of the sixteenth century.

However, the response at the official level is that we need greater clarification and qualification before we can go forward. Moreover differing attitudes to women's ordination can appear an insuperable obstacle, while divisions in the Anglican Church on moral issues lead to questions such as who is speaking for that communion. Yet the paradox remains the Eucharist. Its sharing is meant to be a sign that binds and heals all baptised believers. The question should be asked: would eucharistic sharing, understood as reconciling and healing, help in a progressive conversion of the churches to one another? Thérèse of Lisieux once exclaimed 'All is grace', so cannot the saving action of Christ on the cross now be freely shared as a gift, so that communities divided by the sin of disunity can be healed by sharing in the one perfect sacrifice of the cross of Christ?

The fullness of unity and the fulfilment of the churches' mission will only come with end time, the *eschaton*. In the meanwhile the Church is a pilgrim people. Yet, as Enda McDonagh (another contributor to this book) has said elsewhere, 'God's pilgrim people do not enjoy a detailed route map. The call of God ... is a call of loving creativity.'[1]

How can that call of loving creativity be achieved? What is needed is a sensitive listening to the needs of the people. If the Church is to be the light of the world it must, in the spirit of Vatican II's *Gaudium et Spes*, answer the cries of the people. Faith involves risk. If on our pilgrimage to the *eschaton* we take risks by loving, surely the God who loves us will guide us with the wisdom of the Spirit.

I believe the time is ripe for a deep discernment about how we go forward as Christians. Is our sharing in a belief that Christ is Saviour and our common baptism basis enough to allow eucharistic sharing? A sharing that will help undo the shackles of history and heal. We need to be able to move away from the past – otherwise we will always let the shadow of polemics affect our attempts to build a present and future unity.

Another aspect of our willingness or not to share the Eucharist touches our rules for those we include and exclude. Kevin Kelly (another contributor to these pages) has recently written about the Eucharist and violence.[2] He sees the exclusion from Eucharist as violence in this sense: if people come to Eucharist as baptised Christians and are welcomed to the celebration but not allowed to receive communion, that exclusion could be construed as violence. Kelly not only has Anglicans and other Christians in mind, but also those excluded by second marriages or because they are gay.

Again we face the problem that the sacrament which is meant to signify healing now becomes a threshold that is impossible to negotiate. It would seem our living as a community appears to be so different from the hospitality that Jesus proclaimed. He came to bring healing to the one who needed the physician. He sat down with those society classified as outcasts and was unperturbed by criticism. Are we like the scribes and Pharisees, so intent on wearing the cloak of correctness that we abandon the risk of compassion?

The current discipline, while logical, does seem to be over-restrictive. Sacraments are meant for people. They are the moments where the divine life is communicated, where we can meet the risen Saviour. Is it right to limit access to Christ? Can we prevent encounters that could enable the healing that would signify the Kingdom breaking out among us?

On the level of the work for Christian unity, does the present situation help when dialogue is now dialogue with other faiths as well as Christians of differing traditions? If the work of reconciliation among Christians is so fraught with difficulty, what chance has an outreach to bring understanding with other faith traditions? The adage that peace among religions is a prerequisite for peace on earth remains true.

Authority in the Church

The remaining question in all this remains that of authority and its exercise in the Church. For Catholics authority seems above all to mean the Pope, now Benedict XVI, the Roman Curia or, in popular parlance, the Vatican. My pilgrimage from Rome to Rochester included an audience with Benedict's predecessor. Despite his illness Pope John Paul II came to the Sala Clementina to accept the greetings of the Anglican Bishop of Rochester, Michael Nazir-Ali. During the audience the Pope gave Bishop Michael a pectoral cross, indicating his esteem for the Anglican Communion but also expressing the reality of hospitality given at great personal cost because of his ill health. This loving gesture reminded me of 1982 when the Pope was in England. At the end of a long day he showed amazing sensitivity to a young woman. On both occasions the Pope was as Peter, pastoral and reaching out in generosity.

The journey of a pilgrim Christian over the last 25 years has not been easy. At times it has seemed that both the spirit and the letter of Vatican II have been relegated and a process of restoration has taken over. Commentators have observed that the reforms of the Council of Trent were carried out with greater energy than those of Vatican II. Sometimes the cry has been that Catholic identity is being lost or authority undermined. Perhaps we need to ask the question: is the issue one of difference or diversity?

In the case of authority, its role is strengthened when the community feels able to receive a particular teaching. Reception of doctrine does not only go one way. The whole Church is a learning Church. The teacher gains respect and is heard when dialogue has taken place that enables mutual understanding to flourish.

In the years since Vatican II, there has been a tension between the centre and the local Church. Such tensions have centred round Christian unity, ethical issues, styles of church government and liturgy. The impression given is that the centre fears it cannot hold and that there is therefore a need to control. The role of individual bishops and of episcopal conferences has come to resemble that of branch managers rather than that of successors of the apostles. Complaints made to Rome can result in groups or individuals coming under a scrutiny that leaves little room for hearing the other side of the argument. The perception is that the investigator is also judge and often that the person under scrutiny is not sure of the issue under judgement. The result is that the Church loses its sense of being a community of friends bonded by love.

However, Pope John Paul II issued in 1995 an encyclical letter to all Christians entitled *Ut Unum Sint* (*That They May Be One*). It was his commitment to ecumenism, a significant document and set out a challenging, hopeful and creative position. It was also revolutionary as the Pope calls for reform of the papacy as integral to the work for unity. He wrote on the threshold of the twenty-first century about seeing this work for unity as essential to the mission of the Church. Division among Christians disabled the preaching of the Gospel. Humanity was riven by so many divisions that continuing disunity among Christians only aided sinful structures in our world.

From the very first lines of the letter, the Pope expressed the irrevocable commitment of the Church to unity, something that Pope Benedict XVI himself has now stressed soon after his election. John Paul's prayer in the letter was that God in his mercy would help Christians to come to the point of full unity. What came over, in a way that was new, was John Paul's attitude to the present situation. The work was so important that he could only engage in it if he could sense that as a fellow pilgrim he was supported in prayer by fellow Christians.

He also showed the paradox that if we share a common belief in Christ by baptism, how could we allow disunity? John Paul went on to acknowledge that the Spirit was at work in all the churches, endowing them with gifts and bringing an existing union that we can too easily overlook. The work of ecumenism, of Christian unity, was to bring that partial communion to the point where we could reach full communion.

However, at the heart of any genuine commitment to unity was conversion, a deep change of heart that comes from prayer and dialogue. There was a need for each individual to seek conversion and then the community would have a new impetus, stemming from this personal chnage, to move forward in love, freed from the burdens of the past. This new mentality also would allow a fresh look at the language we use in expressing our beliefs.

John Paul II, echoing his immediate predecessors, was clear that truth was something given, but its expression, its language, could change. The content of faith has to be translated into cultural contexts so that people can receive it in every time and place. For him, prayer and pilgrimage were interlinked. His journeys to all parts of the world gave him the chance to be alongside Christians of different traditions and to join in prayer with the people and their church leaders. For those who live in Britain his pilgrimage to Canterbury enabled him to pray at the site of the martyrdom of St Thomas à Becket along with Archbishop Robert Runcie, leader of the Anglican Communion. The image of the Pope and the Archbishop at prayer together remains a powerful icon of unity. Again in his encyclical John Paul reminded us that the Christian martyrs of the twentieth century were a sign of a shared commitment to the meaning of the cross of Christ.

The love that comes from common prayer and a desire to shape our lives more and more to the Gospel enabled dialogue to flourish. Dialogue grew from mutual respect, prayerful listening and a willingness to understand the roots of disputed issues. John Paul noted that dialogue between Catholics and Lutherans had enabled substantial agreement to be reached on one of the key disputes of the sixteenth-century Reformation – the whole question of justification by faith. However, above all, dialogue and agreements could be achieved when we realised that we are brothers and sisters in Christ. It was good to recall John XXIII's words 'what unites us is greater than what divides us'.

Over and beyond issues that come from the past, the churches have found unity in their teaching on social issues and a common work for justice, peace and the integrity of the creation. The events that marked the twentieth century were so often moments when Christians realised that they had to witness as one before the evils that they were confronting, whether genocide or weapons of mass destruction or cruel dictatorships.

However, as John Paul reflected in *Ut Unum Sint* on his own office and its role in the search for unity, he spoke with ever-growing sensitivity and openness. He asked for forgiveness if the exercise of the ministry of the Bishop of Rome had any hurtful memories. He went on to remind us that his ministry originated in the manifold mercy of God. It was a ministry with an authority completely at the service of God's merciful plan and had to be seen in this perspective.

By saying this the Pope was reminding us that the power of his office is not a power over others in the secular sense. It comes from an openness to God's grace that guides and helps us in our weakness. When John Paul went on to describe how, in the office of Bishop of Rome, he worked as a servant of unity, including teaching *ex cathedra*, he stressed that he did this in a collegiate way together with all the bishops. In this context Pope John Paul II then acknowledged that in the work for unity he was searching for a way of exercising the primacy that 'is nonetheless open to a new situation'.

Heartfelt plea

The Pope argued that for the first thousand years, a whole millennium, Christians were united. In times of dispute, the Bishop of Rome acted as moderator. His hope was that Christians in the third millennium could rediscover unity. How, he asked, can the ministry of the Bishop of Rome enable 'a new situation'? John Paul admitted that this was a huge task and made a heartfelt plea for help.

The closing paragraph of the main body of the letter challenged and called for action from all of us.

> When I say that for me, as Bishop of Rome, the ecumenical task is 'one of the pastoral priorities' of my pontificate, I think of the grave obstacle which the lack of unity represents for the proclamation of the gospel. A Christian community which believes in Christ and desires, with gospel fervour, the salvation of mankind can hardly be closed to the promptings of the Holy Spirit, who leads all Christians towards full and visible unity. Here an imperative of charity is in question, an imperative that admits of no exception. Ecumenism is not only an internal question of the Christian communities. It is a matter of the love which God has in Jesus Christ for all humanity; to stand in the way of this love is an offence against Him and against His plan to gather all people in Christ. As Pope Paul VI wrote to the Ecumenical Patriarch Athenagoras I: 'May the Holy Spirit guide us along the way of reconciliation, so that the unity of our Churches may become an ever more radiant sign of hope and consolation for all mankind.'[3]

The vision that emerged was one of the Bishop of Rome presiding in truth and love. Diversity would not impede unity and when authority was exercised as loving service, building communion and enabling collaboration, then the unity of the body was enhanced.

How far has the vision of *Ut Unum Sint* touched the life of the Church since its publication and enabled unity? How far is it still relevant under Pope Benedict XVI? Certainly the response of the Church of England and the agreed statement on authority that came from ARCIC II (the Anglican Roman Catholic International Commission) showed positive reactions. The vision of primacy as exercised in the first millennium of the Church's life is one that resonates with the Anglican Communion. The role of the Bishop of Rome as the one who signifies the unity and universality of the Church is accepted along with a special responsibility for maintaining truth and ordering things in love.

However, the issue that causes concern is the relationship between the Pope and the College of Bishops. Since Gregory VII in the eleventh century the papacy has become more monarchical and centralised in character. The reasons for that development have roots in a need to reform abuses in the life of the Church.

Yet the centralising tendency has grown so much that the Roman Curia is perceived as having ever increasing power. *Ut Unum Sint* favoured a collegial vision but the practice seems to be something else. This is a practical tension but it has obviously hugely important theological implications. The unique ministry of the Bishop of Rome cannot be gainsaid but the apostolic vision was always Peter together with the apostles.

Dominus Jesus

Concern about centralisation disabling the collegial expression of the Church was highlighted by the document *Dominus Jesus*, which was promulgated in August 2000. While the substance of the declaration concerned inter-faith issues, its references to matters of church unity seemed to undermine or even take little account of what had been achieved over the last 30 years. What was most unhelpful was the language and style, which was didactic and imperative and therefore sounded negative in regard to any position other than the Catholic.

The question of the appointment of bishops is another matter of concern if the role of the local Church is to be respected. Since Vatican II the ministry of the bishop has been set more firmly in its sacramental setting. The bishop is ordained to serve a local Church but how far is he in reality the authentic leader of that Church?

The process of selecting a bishop involved consultation but so often the gap between the wishes expressed at a local or even national level and the eventual appointment can be considerable. It can seem that a choice is made that fails to recognise the need of the local Church. Sometimes it works but some notable failures would indicate that all is not well. What is more important is the sense that the local Church, the Christian community in that place, is not heard.

This is perhaps the greatest problem – how we as a church listen. The new Pope and his bishops have that key role of teaching, handing on what is at the heart of our faith in Jesus Christ and how we live out that faith. However, the people need to receive what is being taught. A dialogue, a mutual sharing and understanding, is needed.

Jesus spoke with authority. He got to the heart of the matter and reminded us that it's what comes out of hearts that matters. He calls us friends and commands that we love one another. His community was a community of loving service with a commitment that included laying down one's life for one's friends. Graham Greene in one of his later works, *Monsignor Quixote*, celebrated the Church as a community of friendship bonded by Christ. I would hope that our journey and our ecumenical quest can be founded on love and a listening heart seeking truth, seeking the incarnate wisdom of God in Jesus.

I realise the journey is not easy. Division and defensiveness can come more easily than openness to healing. New divisions are emerging, fuelled by moral issues, but that same divided heart can be touched by the healing power of the Saviour whose glorification was on the cross. We need to dream dreams and then allow the vision to be realised; realised by the Spirit of love that can overcome all fear.

Notes

1. Enda McDonagh, *Vulnerable to the Holy* (The Columba Press, Dublin, 2005), p. 82.
2. Kevin Kelly, 'Eucharist and violence', *The Furrow* vol. 56 no. 1, pp. 33–4.
3. *Ut Unum Sint* (CTS, London, 1995), p. 109.

Chapter Eighteen

Changing Hierarchical Structures

Jeannine Gramick

Since the call of the Second Vatican Council to update the structures and practices of religious life, I have been concerned about, and involved in, church reform and renewal in one way or another. Growing to maturity in religious life in the late 1960s and early 1970s, when many of my companions were leaving the convent to marry or find careers outside church circles, I was often asked why I remained a nun. One of my reasons then, as now, concerns church politics. I have a deep desire to make the Church more human and pastoral, to help the institution become more of a conduit of God's love for all creation and less a channel of guilt for failing to follow regulations.

In addition to being the People of God, the Catholic Church can be viewed as a hierarchical institution. I do not believe the concept of hierarchy, which is essentially an ordering in authority, should be abolished. As a form of government, hierarchical structures enable large groups to function well. State and world governments, voluntary groups or clubs, as well as religious entities, operate with a semblance of hierarchy, with more or less rigidity. Congregational churches, for example, have a limited local hierarchy in the person of the minister or other church officers who carry out certain responsibilities. Even the family has a hierarchical structure: parents are entrusted with authority over their children.

Ultimately, however, authority rests with the individual, who, in turn, can choose to hand over his or her authority to a group to maintain good order. The individual delegates various duties to different persons to make appropriate decisions on behalf of the individual and the group as a whole. Without hierarchy, decision-making, especially in minute matters, would consume and waste valuable time.

Servant leadership

How can we as a church retain a hierarchy to maintain order in our worldwide community of more than one billion Catholics and still have that structure operate in human ways? The gospel model of exercising authority is servant leadership, not absolute monarchy or a totalitarian state. Those in hierarchical positions need to consult and collaborate; those not part of the hierarchy need to participate in multitudinous ways. Governance need not be tied to priestly ordination but should be exercised by anyone competent to serve and called forth by the community. Like the practice in the early centuries of the Christian community, the people should elect their leaders. Pope Leo the Great (440–61) understood human nature well when he wrote: 'It is essential to exclude all those unwanted and unasked for, if the people are not to be crossed and end by despising or hating their bishop. If they cannot have the candidate they desire, the people may all turn away from religion unduly.'

The organisation, Voice of the Faithful, that has emerged in the wake of the clerical sexual abuse scandal in the United States Church, has presented a plan of structural reform that includes the election of bishops by the faithful of the diocese, the selection of pastors by the faithful, pastoral and finance councils in the diocese and in every parish, and the right of the faithful to own church property. Other church groups have called for similar reforms, in which 'the members of the Church should have some share in the drawing up of decisions, in accordance with the rules given by the Second Vatican Ecumenical Council and the Holy See, for instance with regard to the setting up of councils at all levels' (*Justice in the World* 46).[1]

But it is not my intent in this article to elaborate on what humanised hierarchical structures would look like. I am more concerned about the process of transformation. How can this transformation be accomplished under the new Pope, Benedict XVI, when the Catholic Church has become so centralised during the pontificate of John Paul II? Many people attach their hopes for structural change to the papacy, but this way of thinking ignores the reality that the true locus of change resides in the individual.

The most recent example of global transformation, the Second Vatican Council, may appear to have been an example of change from the top down. But the 2000-plus Council Fathers relied on expert theologians and grass-roots movements of laity. Experimentation in liturgy, revisions in biblical interpretations, and engagement with modern sciences and the world all paved the way for change. Like bubbles in a kettle of boiling water, the heat of change came from the bottom up.

In religious communities, it is often said that the more one is tied into the structure, the more one can influence that structure to change. While that idea may be true in theory, practice has unfortunately shown the reverse seems to be more valid. Those at the lower levels of church hierarchy seem not to change, but to be changed by those at the higher ends of church authority. I have come to believe that, whatever one's position is in a hierarchy, one's degree of influence for change depends, not on where one stands in the chain of command, but where one decides to stand in the chain of resistance.

Temptations against resistance

I believe that structural change depends on the individual's conviction to speak and act in accord with good conscience, and on one's capacity to resist various temptations. The Caiaphas principle is a temptation named after the high priest who, during Christ's passion, said that it was better that one individual die than for the whole nation to perish (John 11:50). In church circles, some administrators will sacrifice an individual to an injustice for the common good of the institution. In my own experience, after twenty years of assigned lesbian/gay ministry by various leaders of my religious congregation, and after a Vatican order to cease that ministry, the Superior General and other community members urged compliance with the Vatican order for the greater good of the religious community.

What was sacrificed, however, was the greater good of worldwide solidarity with the lesbian/gay community and the prophetic nature of religious life. Many well-intentioned leaders fail to see that no group can become its best self unless it respects, safeguards and promotes the rights of all its members and the common good of humanity beyond its own organisation. The goal of serving others beyond their own boundaries, and not institutional self-preservation, is the reason religious communities were founded and they need to be constantly reminded of this fact.

A second temptation that impedes change of church structures is self-silencing even before an authority imposes any unwarranted command or request. Time and time again, I have witnessed pastors unwilling to sponsor an educational programme on homosexuality because they believe the local bishop might interfere. Instead of taking the risk to see what would happen, they succumb to projected fears and silence themselves.

Chances are that often no higher authority will intervene. In the event he does, the intervention could be an occasion for real dialogue with the possibility of policy change. Because of fear of potential consequences, individuals fail to act in ways they would otherwise consider appropriate or needed.

A third temptation in the chain of resistance is recourse to the Eichmann principle. Like Adolf Eichmann in his defence for Nazi war crimes, many people say, 'I was only following orders' or 'I'm just a cog in the machine'. Many, like Eichmann, claim one cannot disagree with an order from above. The problem with such reasoning is that it avoids the individual's responsibility to examine the moral claims made by higher authorities. When the Congregation for the Doctrine of the Faith (CDF) ordered me to cease my pastoral ministry with lesbian and gay Catholics, my congregational leaders said there were many European community members who could not understand how anyone could not follow an order signed by the Pope. This could have been a real opportunity to educate members in developing higher levels of moral responsibility.

Passive compliance

Another temptation to resistance is passive compliance to questionable commands. Individuals are passively compliant for various reasons: the ease of keeping the status quo, avoidance of economic or emotional hardship, feelings of powerlessness and futility, a spirituality of the redemptive value of sacrifice and personal suffering, a belief that obedience to hierarchical authority trumps personal conviction, to name but a few. I am not questioning the motives or sincerity of those who passively comply. Their obedience to the demands of higher authority may provide great spiritual comfort or material reward. But mere acceptance of unjust rules, without questioning them, only confirms and reinforces rigid power; it does not inspire the community to resist medieval tactics nor does it contribute to a change in the status quo.

A fifth enticement to inaction may be a seemingly realistic opinion that one's action will not effect change. Did the writings of Dietrich Bonhoeffer condemning the Nazi persecution of the Jews prevent their extermination in the gas chambers? Did the public stands of other pastors ameliorate the situation or did they cause their own arrest and imprisonment in concentration camps? Even if their actions do not appear to make a difference, they have inspired others to speak out in nonviolent resistance. There will always be martyrs to the cause of change. They take a stand to be true to their own convictions and maintain their own integrity. They open the eyes of others, stimulate discussion, and motivate the masses to question the status quo. Others will harvest the seeds of change they plant.

So what strategies for transformation can individuals use? Although there are probably many tactics, I will describe three: active compliance, creative circumvention and prophetic obedience.

Active compliance

When I use the term 'active compliance', I mean that one basically accepts the current structure and works respectfully with church representatives to help the institution operate in more meaningful and life-giving ways. Active compliance means actually working to change a law, a process, or a structure, but essentially abiding by the decision of the higher authority.

This strategy of active compliance was used by most communities of men and women religious as they were grappling with how to articulate changes in their constitutions. After years of experimentation and discussion, religious congregations presented their revised constitutions for approval to the Vatican's Congregation for Religious. There were often discussions with Vatican representatives about items the Vatican wanted or did not want in their constitutions. Religious communities tried to argue persuasively for acceptance of their point of view, but there was no move on the part of religious congregations towards changing structures by a move towards decentralisation; that is, no attempt to submit their constitutions for review to a body of peers, rather than to the Vatican. Religious communities abided by the decisions of the Vatican although the Vatican was aware that many communities were thinking differently.

In my own case with the Vatican, Sister Patricia Flynn, the Superior General of the School Sisters of Notre Dame (SSND), attempted to make the investigative process more equitable. In 1988, the Congregation for Religious informed SSND and the Society of the Divine Savior (SDS), the community of my colleague, Father Robert Nugent, that a Vatican Commission was being established to investigate our lesbian/gay ministry and that three members had been appointed to this commission.

Sister Flynn pointed out that, in United States culture, both the defence and the prosecution agree upon a jury that renders a decision. Because the Vatican Commission would be acting as a jury in that it would submit a decision to the CDF, Sister Flynn requested that SSND and SDS have input into the composition of this Commission.

The Congregation for Religious told Sister Flynn that one person would most likely resign from the Vatican Commission, that the Vatican would accept a list of names for replacement, but that the choice would be made by the Congregation. The Superiors General and Provincials of SSND and SDS sent a common letter containing two lists of acceptable replacements, with the request that the Vatican select one person from each list. After five years of silence, the Vatican informed SSND and SDS that a third person, not mentioned on either list, had been named to the Commission. When SSND objected to the appointment, the Vatican responded that it had made no commitment either to augment the membership of the Commission or to choose names only from those submitted.

Sister Flynn wrote to the Vatican that her understanding about the replacement differed from the Vatican's interpretation, but there was no follow-up to state that the process was flawed because it was not culturally sensitive and did not honour an implied acceptance for improvement. There was no declaration by the religious communities that they could not continue in this flawed process. There was compliance, but the communities' action called the Vatican's attention to the fact that the current structure was not satisfactory.

Creative circumvention

A second strategy for transforming hierarchical structures is creative circumvention. This strategy involves ignoring structures in various imaginative ways. Some may say the substitute action follows the letter, but not the spirit of a law, or that one finds a way around a brick wall, instead of going through it. Canon Law may be used to one's advantage to find 'wiggle room'. There is no outright challenge or public confrontation to ecclesiastical authority; the hierarchical command is simply sidestepped or ignored.

Creative circumvention may be easier in some way on one's psyche than active compliance because direct confrontation with intransigent authorities requires courage that mere disregard does not. I believe this strategy holds much promise for structural transformation because this is the evolutionary manner in which mores change. There is no flouting of customs or laws; people merely disregard them with little flourish or fanfare.

Many liturgical 'problems' are resolved by creative circumvention. For example, when the Vatican legislated that only priests could deliver homilies, the faithful responded by having women and non-ordained males deliver 'reflections' after Communion. Unfortunately, the bishops have allowed the Roman Curia to usurp control over liturgical matters that Vatican II had granted to national episcopal conferences. In this, as in many areas of church life, the laity and bishops have only themselves to blame for collaborating in a centralisation of curial power.

Long before the Vatican established its Commission in 1988 to investigate my ministry, it had established a file on my pastoral activities. The first Vatican intervention occurred in 1979, at the time when New Ways Ministry, the organisation Father Nugent and I co-founded for justice and reconciliation for lesbian and gay Catholics, was sponsoring a retreat for lesbian nuns. Being apprised of the event and determining that the nuns were using the word 'celibate' as a 'slogan', the Vatican informed the SSND Superior General that New Ways Ministry should cancel the retreat.

The week preceding the retreat, I received a phone call from Sister Ruth Marie May, my SSND provincial leader, who made it clear that she was not instructing me to act in any particular way, but was merely communicating the message she had received. The retreat was held. There was no challenge to the Vatican, no public controversy, but the unreasonable request was circumvented.

SSND creatively circumvented two additional Vatican attempts to suppress my ministry. Archbishop James Hickey, in whose diocese I lived and worked, had informed all the United States bishops and major superiors of the women's and men's religious congregations that he did not approve of my ministry. He also wrote to the Vatican to request that the Vatican pressure my religious leaders to remove me from lesbian/gay ministry. In 1981 and again in 1985, the Vatican asked my community leaders to investigate my ministry and to recommend appropriate sanctions, with the obvious implication that the ministry should be suppressed.

Each time SSND found my ministry in accordance with the pastoral outreach of the Church. In 1989, Sister Christine Mulcahy, my provincial at that time, tried to circumvent Cardinal Hickey's influence by requesting that the United States Conference of Catholic Bishops communicate the SSND affirmation of my ministry to anyone who raised questions or doubts about its validity.

Creative circumvention can have the advantage of moving the Church in a gospel direction and aiding the people the Church is intended to serve. It also makes use of the full range of the hierarchy, not just the top of it. It creates confidence in those at the immediate scene to exercise the God-given authority they possess. Although creative circumvention produces a satisfying outcome, it does not directly confront hierarchical jurisdiction. This is done through prophetic obedience.

Prophetic obedience

A prophet is one who can recognise the inadequacy of the present reality and envision an order different from the status quo. The prophet's insights arise from a close personal relationship with God and a commitment to God's people, particularly the poor, the marginalised, and the powerless. The Hebrew Scriptures offer us inspiring examples of prophets, such as Moses, Hosea and Jeremiah, who were called by God to confront established regimes.

For Christians, Jesus is the prophet par excellence who championed persons over institutions and who witnessed a love built on equality, not domination. For him, no religious or civil authority could trump the Reign of God and its obligation of love as it relates to the common good of humanity. His acts of socialising with sinners, Samaritans, pagans and women challenged the status quo. We too share in the prophetic character of Jesus' mission through prophetic obedience to the Reign of God. When prophetic obedience runs counter to the policies or directives of ecclesiastical authorities, it may look like ecclesiastical disobedience. Some may dismiss prophetic obedience as defiance. It is not. If the individual engages in prolonged moral discernment and makes a decision to disobey a religious command in good conscience, then it is not a frivolous act of flouting or rejecting authority; it is a call to obey a higher authority.

Prophetic obedience requires boldness and courage like that of Jesus of Nazareth who broke the law in performing good works on the Sabbath. Like Jesus, the person openly disregards a religious rule or an arrangement that is hurtful to people in favour of a life-giving alternative. Like Jesus, the person needs to be prepared to accept the sanctions that may ensue.

After the decades-long investigation of my ministry, I felt called to engage in an act of prophetic obedience. While my moment of stating what could be called ecclesiastical disobedience was filled with trepidation and uncertainty about my future, there eventually followed a deep sense of peace, relief and freedom that I was making the right choice in God's eyes. There was great pain in proclaiming this non-compliance to representatives of SSND, a community of women whom I loved and who loved me, and with whom I had shared life for forty years.

Despite solid support for my lesbian/gay ministry from different provincial and general administrations for almost thirty years, various internal and cultural conditions prompted SSND leadership to eventually cooperate with the Vatican. In 1999, the Vatican's Congregation for the Doctrine of the Faith, headed by the then Cardinal Joseph Ratzinger, now Pope Benedict XVI, issued a notification that I should cease all pastoral ministry to lesbian and gay people. The notification itself did not prohibit my speaking or writing about lesbian/gay issues.

Following the publication of the notification, I travelled across the United States, telling audiences about the investigation, revealing facts which showed that the process violated principles of fair judicial procedure outlined in the Catholic Church's 1971 document, *Justice in the World*. I suggested that the Catholic community write asking the Vatican to reconsider its decision. Tens of thousands of letters arrived in Rome and annoyed Cardinal Ratzinger and his congregation. At the instigation of the Vatican, SSND imposed a set of obediences that forbade me to speak or write about homosexuality or the investigation I had experienced, or to utter any criticism of the magisterium.

I gravely considered these obediences and felt deeply pained that the Vatican and my community leaders asked me to silence myself. I felt solidarity with those lesbian and gay people who have been asked by society and religious institutions to silence themselves for centuries. After finding my voice to tell my story, I chose not to collaborate in my own oppression by restricting a basic right to which all human beings are entitled. To me this was a matter of conscience.

After I declared I could not obey these directives, there were no repercussions from any hierarchical authority. I have since transferred from the School Sisters of Notre Dame to the Sisters of Loretto, a canonical congregation of women religious founded and based in the United States. Consequently, the obediences placed on me by SSND have been abrogated as I am now canonically under the jurisdiction of another congregation. However, the CDF directive to disengage from pastoral ministry to lesbian and gay people still stands.

Many people have questioned my decision, and hence the whole concept of prophetic obedience. How, some ask, can you set aside a vow of obedience? How can any person of faith not follow a command or exhortation from lawful church superiors? The simple answer is to meditate on the Holocaust and see the potential results of following a legitimate authority blindly. The more comprehensive answer is that the presumption of God's will lies with the pronouncements of duly constituted authority, but that there may be sufficiently serious reasons to put aside problematic commands in favour of following one's own convictions in an act of prophetic obedience.

Members of religious communities give special attention to the precepts of religious leaders and their community's documents as sources of knowing God's will, and try to live obediently in the light of these sources. They also take into account their life experiences and individual promptings from the Holy Spirit in making conscience decisions. They must obey the will of God as manifested in their consciences, just as any baptised Christian must follow his or her conscience, even when that conscience is not congruent with official church teaching. Vatican II's *Declaration on Religious Freedom* states that 'every one of us will render an account of oneself to God (Rom. 14:12), and for this reason [one] is bound to obey one's conscience' (11).

A choice to disobey a directive from religious authorities requires intense confidence in one's discernment because it does not feel comfortable to discount the accumulated wisdom of the community or to oppose spiritual leaders one respects. Even in trusting one's own discernment, one can fear potential negative ramifications. Like battered women, many Catholics have obeyed even when they disagreed with church authorities because they have been locked away in a closet of fear, unable to find a key that will open the door.

Catholics have not been trained to find the door of moral discernment nor encouraged to question, probe or analyse. They have been taught to memorise facts or teachings and to conform to the direction of authorities. In terms of Lawrence Kolberg's six stages of moral development, many Catholics are near the bottom rung of the ladder: a literal obedience to rules and authority.

I would like to mention two other examples of prophetic obedience. One occurred in 1984 after a signature ad appeared in the *New York Times* calling for a dialogue on the issue of abortion in the Catholic Church because there was a diversity of opinion among Catholics. Among the 97 signatories were 24 nuns from different communities of women. The Vatican's Congregation for Religious contacted the superiors general of the various communities and requested that they obtain a retraction from each of the nuns. If a retraction was not forthcoming, the superiors were to dismiss the nuns from their religious communities.

While each superior general was responsible for handling the Vatican's request with her particular community member, the nun signatories and their leaders met on several occasions to discuss ways of dealing with the dilemma. Basically, each superior general requested her sister(s) to explain why she had signed the ad. None of the nuns retracted her signature from the ad and none of the nuns was dismissed. The superiors general were prophetically obedient to a mutually respectful process. They did not obtain the retractions, nor did they dismiss their sisters. There were no repercussions from the Vatican for the respective religious congregations.

Another example of prophetic obedience occurred in 2001 when the Vatican requested Sister Christine Vladimiroff, the Prioress of the Benedictine Sisters of Erie, Pennsylvania, to silence Sister Joan Chittister, one of her community members, from speaking publicly at the Women's Ordination Worldwide Conference in Dublin, Ireland. After much prayer, discernment and consultation with her community and her Benedictine Federation, Sister Vladimiroff respectfully informed the Vatican that her sister's participation in the conference was not a source of scandal, as the Vatican alleged, but that the faithful could be scandalised when honest attempts to discuss important issues were forbidden. There were no repercussions from the Vatican for the Benedictine Sisters of Erie.

In the three examples above, it was individuals who expressed prophetic obedience, even though, in two cases, the individuals represented structural entities in the Church. How does individual ecclesiastical obedience get translated into structural change? How can individuals make a difference in transforming the configuration of a whole group? Quite simply, when a sufficient number of voices have been raised and a critical mass has been achieved to nonviolently resist higher authority, only then can real structural change occur.

The simple bell curve learned in introductory statistics courses explains how structural change occurs. The 1–2 per cent under one tail of the bell curve represents those innovators or leaders who begin the prophetic obedience. In time, more individuals recognise that certain church laws or policies are no longer useful. These individuals begin to follow the modernisers in ignoring the rules and practising prophetic obedience. Only when most of the Church in a particular culture comes to see the uselessness of certain practices, will the structures change. Even then, the 1–2 per cent under the other tail of the bell curve, the 'diehards', will not change.

A vivid and visual example of how ecclesiastical change comes about occurred at Bishop Frank Murphy's funeral in 1999. When the eulogist said, 'Frank Murphy belongs to that first, courageous, bold, and energetic generation' who lived the principles and vision of Vatican II, the Baltimore cathedral erupted with thunderous applause. The homilist gestured with his hands for the congregation to stop, but the people continued to clap and clap.

Then from the back of the cathedral, people began to rise to their feet. Still the booming acclamation continued. Again the homilist gestured for the ovation to cease so he could continue. But like a wave that gathered strength as it approached the middle, then front, of the cathedral, row upon row of people were rising to their feet and applauding with an energy they remembered from the late 1960s and 1970s. More than five minutes elapsed and still the congregation stood and applauded.

Finally, the cardinals, bishops and archbishops, seated around the main altar, rose to their feet. The congregation let out a rousing cheer, knowing they were paying tribute, not only to a beloved, collegial bishop, but also to the way the spirit of reform works in the Church. The People of God had enabled their hierarchy literally to change their positions.

As a result of the clerical sexual abuse scandal, the actions of individuals resulted in hierarchical change. In 2002, 58 per cent of the priests in the Boston archdiocese, where the scandals gained most notoriety, signed a petition calling for the resignation of their cardinal, Bernard Law. One of the priest signers told Angela Bonavoglia, in her book *Good Catholic Girls*,[2] why he signed the petition. He had been inspired by the prophetic obedience of the Erie Benedictines and their courage 'had an impact on me personally. A lot of us lived in fear – I can't speak because something will happen. If enough people speak, there's nothing that anyone can do.'

Prophetic obedience is the key to structural change. 'If enough people speak, there's nothing that anyone (in hierarchical authority) can do' except to acquiesce in the will of the people. No one in authority has power over a group unless the group cedes them the power. Through civil nonviolent resistance, which required patience, perseverance and deep spirituality on the part of the masses, India moved from British imperial control to self-government, South Africa ended apartheid, and the United States began to extend civil rights to all people of colour, and human rights for workers. Prophetic obedience is simply open or public, nonviolent resistance in the tradition of Mahatma Gandhi, Nelson Mandela, Martin Luther King, Dorothy Day and Jesus of Nazareth. Through prophetic obedience or ecclesiastical nonviolent resistance, I firmly believe the Catholic community will some day see the human face of the hierarchical Church.

Notes

1. World Synod of Catholic Bishops (1971).
2. New York: HarperCollins, 2005.

Chapter Nineteen

The Future of the Liturgy
Alan Griffiths

In the Catholic Church, as in other Christian bodies which practise liturgical worship, the last four centuries have witnessed a relative stability in their ritual traditions. Professional liturgists usually criticise this stability as ossification. Liturgy, it is said, became 'frozen' in the Roman Catholic Church by the post-Tridentine reforms of Missal and Breviary and other rituals. In the Church of England, the Book of Common Prayer was established by the end of the sixteenth century and remained so (with the exception of the Commonwealth period) until the ritualists began unpicking it in the later nineteenth century.

In the twentieth century, with the coming of the Liturgical Movement and its wide influence beyond the European Catholic Church, reforms and updating took place in the period after the Second World War. In the Catholic Church, these culminated with the reforms of the Second Vatican Council.

In our own day, however, another, much more widespread (at least in Europe and the American continents) process of liturgical change is very evident. This is the abandonment of liturgical practice in all the churches. People have simply stopped going to church regularly. The Christian bodies that seem to be prospering (at least in numerical terms) are those that claim spontaneity in their worship and reject 'liturgy'.

So what is the problem? And are there signs of hope for liturgy?

Decline – ritual in a strange land
In the forty years since the Council, liturgical formation and teaching has been a major feature of church life. Much of this was the explaining of the 'changes' that the Council brought us. But maybe it was just that – teaching 'about' the Liturgy. It is open to question whether we were really being trained to base our spiritual life on the Liturgy itself.

However, it is fair to ask whether such a spiritual formation is possible for us. Can we celebrate the Liturgy in such a way as to find in the rites themselves the basis of an authentic Christian spirituality? Does our world-view make this possible? In the first part of this essay I want to focus on some of the difficulties that flow from the world-view we inhabit. Four areas in particular seem to me significant.

From a holy to an indifferent cosmos

Ritual traditions, Christian liturgy included, were formed in cultures very different from our own. In particular, ancient religious practice suggests that ancient peoples perceived and engaged with the cosmos in ways that are no longer open to us. The heavens, earth and sea were a holy place. Ancient peoples preferred to pray out of doors, or at least where they could see and feel the open air. Open spaces and high places allowed one to be closer to the stars. Enclosed spaces such as forests had other numinous overtones.

For Judaism, Islam and Christianity, prayer was always 'oriented'. In Scripture, Daniel opened his windows to pray towards Jerusalem, the sacred place (Daniel 6:10). Christians faced east, to the place of the rising sun, to pray. In pagan classical culture the temple building was not itself a place of worship, but worship took place outside the temple. Such practice argues for a strong sense that prayer and worship were understood as cosmic events, direct engagements with the forces of earth and heaven, whether these were divinities in their own right as in non-biblical cultures, or creatures of the Most High, as in the biblical tradition. The 'Holy' was, literally, 'out there'. 'Heaven and earth are full of your glory' was a theological affirmation of the omnipresence of God.

Our world has demythologised that cosmos. We have lost the sense of the universe as a dynamic gift inviting reverent participation. We tend to see it as more an object. We find our 'place' in it through study and, increasingly, manipulation. Some recent writers have traced a meta-physical shift, beginning in the later Middle Ages, from understanding 'Being' as a process or totality of which we, like everything else, are an active part, to seeing it as a collection of individual 'objects' which may be scientifically examined.

We no longer conceive of the 'outside' as a place of the transcendent Holy. Modern 'spirituality' is much more 'inward' and sometimes little different from therapy. The 'outside' is seen as having no divine energy. The universe excites wonder (think of the pictures from the Hubble telescope), but this exists at the level of aesthetics or emotion – the modern equivalent of the Romantic experience of wilderness in the poetry of Wordsworth. The 'Holy' is more likely to be understood as 'within'. If rituals are employed, they seem to be understood as more about forming a meaningful context for what is still an inward activity than as sacramental acts which are themselves revelatory.

Public and private space

Our ancestors had a more 'public' understanding of divinity. Cities and communities 'did' their religion in the public place, as they did much of their human being. Households venerated their ancestors and household gods, but the public space was the primary divine space. This was acknowledged in the public rituals that enacted the civic reality and set it within the framework of something greater, a creation or foundation myth for example, on the continuing vitality of which everyone depended. Aidan Kavanagh[1] has demonstrated how this is as true of Christian cities as it had been of their 'pagan' predecessors.

The historian Miri Rubin[2] has shown how this public interweaving of religion and society found its medieval expression in the celebrations of Christian mysteries, in particular Corpus Christi. This twelfth- or thirteenth-century feast rapidly became popular as precisely this sort of public demonstration. It was the feast not only of the Mass, but of what the celebration of the Mass founded and held together, namely, the whole 'Body' of society united to Christ in a sense that St Paul (cf. 1 Corinthians 11 and 12), in his great writing on the Eucharist and the image of the body, would still have recognised. The Body of Christ – in every sense – manifested and enacted itself in public, in the squares and streets of the city.

As with its treatment of the cosmos, contemporary culture has largely deprived the 'public place' of human, shared meaning. It is a common-place to experience the public spaces of our cities as places of alienation or fear, where it is not safe to walk after dark and which are too often disfigured with graffiti and rubbish. We retreat from the public space. The square, and what goes on in it, has lost its sacramental quality. On the other hand, we exalt the private and the domestic, expressed in the obsession we in the (post-Protestant) English-speaking world have with 'the home', 'privacy', 'family values' and so on.

In Christian circles, liturgy has followed the 'domestic' trend. The Liturgy has increasingly been perceived as the self-expression of 'this gathered assembly'. We face the priest across the altar, forming a closed circle. A 'good celebration' is that in which a domestic atmosphere is developed between the priest and the congregation. The public space once celebrated by the Liturgy has been replaced by the sitting-room space of a domestic intimacy which covers our church floors with carpet and sees worship as simply the congregation enjoying itself, without reference to what lies beyond it.

The decay of a Christian symbolic world

The eucharistic debates that raged in the Latin-speaking Church in the eighth and eleventh century were between those who spoke of the Eucharist as a symbolic enactment and those who thought that 'symbol' was an insufficient term to comprehend the mystery of a 'real' presence. This may be seen to represent stages in a long-term decay of the idea of 'symbol' itself, which has reached its contemporary nadir in the use of the word in association with a diminutive: 'merely a symbol/merely symbolic'. This is a long way from its classical sense of 'sacrament', an action that enfolds both the seen and the unseen in a single piece, something that connects and unites, rather than expresses the distance between one and the other.

As time went on and active participation in the Mass became more and more a matter for the clerical party, contemplation took over. The fact is that for the greater part of our liturgical history, the 'faithful' never ate the eucharistic bread or drank of the eucharistic chalice. This has been of huge significance. 'Seeing' the consecrated bread was described in language redolent of actual reception. This decay of the liturgical action, the shrinkage of the sign, a process developing to its peak   in the Latin Middle Ages and the Baroque period, favoured a view of sacramental action that emphasised the 'real' at the expense of the sacramental/symbolic, the divine act at the expense of the human ritual enactment.

The value of the sign was set against the weight of the reality signified. The 'sign' was originally understood as the complex of actions and objects that together constituted the Liturgy. The 'sign' was enacted and this enactment 'did' what the sign 'signified'. There was an evident, as well as a causal, connection between sign and thing signified. In time, this 'sign' became devalued. This devaluation went hand in hand with a theory of sacrament that placed great emphasis on the degree of difference between sign and reality, and thought of sacraments, particularly the Eucharist, more as 'miracles'. The understanding of the sign as 'matter' to which a 'form' of words was applied to 'confect' the sacrament allowed the sign to become relatively unimportant.

Thus Baptism could be 'valid' even if only a sprinkling of water was employed. Just a few drops, and lo! you are reborn. The Eucharist became a miracle of an immeasurably transcendent divine presence in such a small white host, and so on. The 'sign' was important only in so far as it was in withdrawal; the language became increasingly reserved or 'pious'. All other aspects of the complexity which formed the sign were reduced in this conceptual framework to merely 'the ceremonies of Mass'. The idea of the sacraments as actions gave way to the conception of sacraments as things.

Sacrifice – a dead language?

The celebration of the Eucharist evolved in a society and culture where divine business was conducted through sacrifice. The passage of the victim to the gods was enacted through killing and the eating of the victim in a holy feast. Burning or other partial or total disposal of the thing sacrificed were also employed. Such ritual was the holy 'place', the meeting and exchange of heaven and earth.

Those who first attempted to account for the ministry and death of Jesus did so in terms of the ritual categories of sacrifice that they knew. Though we know how completely those categories were radicalised (as in the account of sacrifice given in the Letter to the Hebrews), the metaphor of sacrifice remained to mould the great Eucharistic Prayer traditions in East and West. The metaphor extended itself throughout the Liturgy. In particular, the Roman prayers 'over the offerings' show a way of looking at 'offering' as exchange, a sort of divine/human etiquette or play whose vitality stems from the fact that those who offer do so in the knowledge that such exchange develops the relationship between God and the Church, but that the relationship itself is not founded on their offering itself but on God's gracious initiative in the self-giving sacrifice of Christ. This insight is expressed beautifully in the words of the Roman Canon: 'offerimus tibi, de tuis donis ac datis'. We offer what God has first given us. That is the new pattern of sacrifice in Christ.

The medieval view of the eucharistic sacrifice as primarily propitiatory, against the context of an atonement theology which stressed the penal aspects of the cross at the expense of the resurrection, made it unacceptable to the Reformers, to whom the idea of offering to ensure God's favour was anathema. The Eucharist became simply a memorial meal, and as such, an optional observance dependent on the number wishing to share the bread and wine rather than on the objective necessity of 'doing this' for the sake of the public and universal good.

The reforms – education or mystagogy?

If the cultural and religious world that produced the historic traditions of Christian worship has gone, can those traditions themselves survive? On the face of it, the plausible answer might be No. I don't believe that is right. First, it is too easy to dismiss the tradition. Second, it serves as a mask for a real lack of understanding of what is going on in rituals. I believe that what we have in 'liturgy' is of immense value and subtlety, but I also think that its salvation (and ours) will not be achieved without hard work and, above all, an openness to new interpretations of old metaphors.

The Vatican Council drew heavily upon the European 'Liturgical Movement' for its account of what liturgy was, how it worked, and for its practical programme of renewal. The Movement had renewed the vision of liturgy as 'mystery' – a participation in the act of Christ the High Priest. This allowed a more dynamic understanding of the Liturgy as a complex of 'signs perceptible to the senses' that set it at the heart of the Church. Pope Pius XII's letter *Mediator Dei* allowed some of the Movement's insights to be seen as in some way 'accepted' by the broader tradition.

The Movement had called for a more open liturgy, with people participating 'actively' through innovations such as the 'offertory procession' and of course in the reception of Holy Communion. The Council revised the Liturgy to admit all this. Despite what is sometimes alleged, these 'changes' have been welcomed. However, the reform had its shortcomings.

Liturgical participation

The Second Vatican Council laid great emphasis on the need for participation in the Liturgy to become internalised, not to remain merely at the level of the ritual. More was required than the correct observance of rubrics. Such internal participation is required if the Liturgy is to be an action whose work is to convert and inform the heart – to worship God and to inform the life of faith and Christian practice. It is clear that no comparable level of success has been achieved in this field of 'internal participation', yet it was crucial to the Council's vision of the Church.

The Liturgical Movement made it a primary aim to stimulate such an internal participation. The promotion of this was a major crusade in the years between the First and Second World War. It was characterised above all by a desire to educate. Parishioners were encouraged to acquire 'missals' or other printed material which contained the text of the Mass together with interpretation or commentary. Inspiring though much of this was, the rigidity of the actual act of worship prevented it being experienced at first hand.

Much of the material written by significant figures of the Liturgical Movement gave people real insight into the richness of the liturgical tradition. It allowed people to 'follow' the Mass and devote mental space to reflections and ideas that were rooted in the prayers the priest was saying. This was a huge improvement on previous generations' dependence on devotional prayers with no ritual connection.

However, circumstances dictated that it was a literary or historical exercise rather than a liturgical experience. It is significant that while a great pastoral contribution was made by the Liturgical Movement in the making of 'missals' for the people, nevertheless the movement for participation had become simply a more intelligent facilitation of the spectator's role. It was as if the congregants were still the audience, remaining at one remove from the actors, the difference being that now, excellent introductory and interpretative materials were at hand to understand the play. Nobody, however, was able to engage in practice with the more fundamental notion that in the Liturgy everyone is in the cast.

In the matter of internal or 'experiential' participation, the renewal only had a limited success. Reform was happening at such a pace that any sense of how it might be internalised was lost. There was a thirst for internalised sharing in the Liturgy which was perceived to have been frustrated by the rites themselves. The 'changes' were being experienced too much at the level of simple ritualism in a culture that was all about relationships, not ritual, as a bearer of human meaning. Recent years have seen this trend give way to another. The complaint now is that our worship minimises mystery, deprives us of a sense of the holy, declines the pursuit of the beautiful. In short, it omits any account of the Transcendent altogether.

Time has done little to dampen these critiques. Indeed, they are heard with increasing stridency and have, unfortunately, become part of the bigger internal Catholic strife about how the Vatican II inheritance is to be interpreted. I wonder, though, whether both sets of complaint do not stem from the same origin.

Participation and renewal

The perception that somehow the call for renewal has either failed, or was misconceived in the first place, should be more correctly understood as a lack of experience of real participation in the Liturgy. We speak about 'internal' participation as if it were somehow bolted on to 'external' participation. This seems to me to be a very cerebral view. Instead of talking about internal and external participation, I should be inclined to substitute 'wholistic' or some equivalent term. It is not so much a question of internal and external, but of an indissoluble unity between the two. Internal can no more be separated from external participation than soul can be separated from body.

Such participation is essential if we are to give some account of worship that gives it a place in our lives prominent enough to make us approach it 'because we need to' rather than 'when I want to' and to go away from it as people who are being progressively changed by it, rather than as people who have been temporarily entertained by it. Wholistic participation is about both liturgy itself and our experience of it, and how that experience validates and interprets the rest of our lives as people trying to be followers of Christ. It is only when participation is wholly human – reflecting the body/spirit unity that we are – that some sort of true liturgical spirituality involving mystery, a sense of holiness and even aesthetic satisfaction, to say nothing of a sense of community, or human meaning, can emerge. It is only when participation is both enacted and experienced that liturgy can work on us as it should, that 'Go in peace to love and serve the Lord' actually means something: 'I have given you an example that you also should do as I have done to you.'

This is an urgent agenda, since the view now in some quarters seems to be that some sort of return to past liturgical 'styles' is all that is required to make the Liturgy 'work' again. It is a mistake to think that qualities of mystery, holiness or beauty are simply waiting around in lumber rooms or museums (or church furnishing catalogues) in the shape of vestments, altars and exposition thrones to be 'bolted on' to our practice. This is simply turning clocks back: we cannot reclaim older forms. To attempt to do so is simply to try yet another short-cut to liturgical spirituality, just another exercise in external participation. We can never experience older liturgical forms in the way our ancestors did. It is perilous to relocate the Holy in some imagined, idealised 'past time'.

So it seems to be an open question whether the postconciliar renewal has gone too far, or not far enough. The appearance of recent studies about such things as orientation ('facing' or 'with the priest's back to' the people), the calls in high quarters for a 'reform of the reform' or a 'new liturgical movement' would seem to suggest that there is an unease about what such renewal really is.

Liturgy is important

To accept the dogmatic authority of Vatican II is to accept its placement of the Liturgy at the heart of the Church. The Liturgy is the summit to which all the activity of the Church is directed, the source from which all its vitality flows. I would like to suggest three ways to account for that importance and to examine how they might point us in the direction of a real liturgical recovery, particularly in the area of making participation as well 'internalised' as it has been 'externalised' in the renewal of the rites we employ. My starting point is the character of liturgy as symbolic activity, considered in the deepest sense of 'symbol'.

Symbolic act – human identity in communion

Liturgy is important because it is symbol. Despite what was suggested earlier about the loss of symbolic sense, it is still true that to be human is to be a symbolic being. The human universe is a symbolic universe. It is not a closed system, but has for its health always to exist against a transcendent background. The religious imagination, at least in its Christian form, finds the final justification and explanation – the 'why' of things – not within the system but outside it. God is not part of the universe. To 'symbolise' means simply to communicate or connect, in Christian terms, with the transcendent Other. A symbol is simply connection, uniting, communion. Anthropologists note that there are two most basic symbols we use to express and enact our common humanity-in-transcendent-context. We touch one another in a variety of ways and we share things, most notably the food and drink that sustains us in life. Food and drink are not of themselves symbols. It is their role-in-being-shared that makes them so.

We think of symbols as nouns. A symbol is one thing that means, intends or indicates something else. But that is not the ancient meaning, which is to unite, to connect what should be whole. Our common usage makes a symbol merely a signpost, whose significance is purely static and abstract.

But if we tried to understand symbol as a verb, it might be possible to understand it as something more dynamic and less 'message oriented'.

Touching and sharing nourishment both have a direct bearing on the Christian sacraments. In Baptism, Confirmation, Ordination, even Penance (remotely) and in Marriage (intimately) we touch one another. In the Eucharist we share food and drink. For 'symbol' read 'sacrament'. Outside the restrictive medieval list of 'seven sacraments' there lies a much more generous abundance of symbols: rites such as the breaking of the eucharistic bread, the Maundy Thursday washing of feet, the sign of peace, the blessing with holy water at the church door, the lighting of candles and the offering of incense.

Such acts express our human communion, but they do not limit themselves to it. Their nature as activity, as something given, invokes a source for that communion which is greater than ourselves and which has the capacity to take ourselves out of ourselves. Human reality is experienced authentically only against a transcendent reality. Symbols are transcendent. Christian symbols point to the presence of the Trinity in our midst and simultaneously to the goal of a hope for an age to come in which what is spoken by those symbols is to be fully and completely realised. The highly formalised ritual expressions that we have developed for these things should not hide their human and transcendental significance from us. It was this insight that the Council was following when it called for the spirituality of a 'noble simplicity' in our ritual life. Noble simplicity means that the symbols must be free to speak.

Symbolic act – the communion of shared narratives

Liturgy is important because it is a narrative act. One of the accompanying features of symbolic act is, more often than not, narrative. Meals and intimacy generally are accompanied by the telling of stories. The principal Christian symbol has as its constitutive rubric 'Do this in memory of me.' The story of Jesus, taken in faith as the central narrative thread of all our stories both communal and personal, underlies all Christian symbolic activity. The story of Jesus connects with the present reality of Jesus, the life of the body of Christ, the 'form' which the Risen One is taking in the contemporary world. We understand the story of Jesus to be no less than co-extensive with what we call 'Sacred Scripture' – the sweep from 'In the beginning God created' to 'Behold, I make all things new.' We understand the story of Jesus somehow to recapitulate our own story, both the human story as a publicly shared narrative and our more individual human stories. The personal experience of believers is capable of being shared, and if it is so, then it is capable of being recapitulated in the Jesus story.

The link between the story of Jesus and our own history as individuals and as the Christian body is the symbolic complex that we know as the Liturgy. At the washing of the feet on Holy Thursday, for example, we rehearse (a too much underused term to describe the Liturgy) the example of service Jesus enjoins upon his people: 'I have given you an example, that you should copy what I have done to you.' We tell a part of his story and act it out, in full consciousness that this is not just a pageant but a call to live in imitation of Christ. In the Eucharist, the symbol of sharing food will make us repeatedly ask ourselves what are the consequences for us of sharing the Supper of the One who interpreted his death as something freely undertaken 'for you and for all, so that sins may be forgiven'. To share food is to connect, and what a connection!

The rehabilitation of sacrifice

We use the language of sacrifice to describe the eucharistic act. It seems to me essential that we re-learn this language. That language alone is daring enough to tell the story of Jesus in its fullness. The whole life, death and destiny of Jesus is described as a sacrifice, 'the forward movement of his self offering', as the ARCIC agreed statement on the Eucharist beautifully put it some years ago. The context of this takes us beyond the limited atonement theories of the medieval period and modern evangelicalism into the iconography of the everlasting High Priest of Hebrews, who is the same as the One who 'went about doing good' and had the extraordinary nerve to describe his own Passover as the meaning of the Last Supper ritual – a giving of body and blood that would be for all humankind and for all time a freeing from bondage and a bridge to life eternal. In Christian tradition, this has attracted the ancient stories of the suffering of the just in the Old Testament as ingredients for the full telling of the Jesus narrative. To offer the eucharistic sacrifice is to make real the Jesus narrative in the presence, real, true and substantial, of the person of Jesus under the appearances of bread and wine.

The language of sacrifice lets us into the realm of the 'victim' who, unlike us, will not himself victimise; the scapegoat who will not blame, the persecuted one to whom we must return as the only salvation for the rest of us who, by our own human muddle and tendency to make victims, are complicit in his death. So to 'offer' the Eucharist is to seek the dissolution of the cycles of violence and exploitation within which we human beings, even the very best of us, live, secure in the knowledge that such a dissolution is already accomplished in an act that is at once both sacrifice and the ending of all sacrifices.

The metaphor of sacrifice draws us into the story of Jesus and, as we share table fellowship with him, invites our deeper participation in his gospel values: 'Grant that we who are nourished by his body and blood, may be filled with his Holy Spirit and be found as one body and one spirit in Christ' (Eucharistic Prayer III). St Augustine famously invited his people to say 'Amen' at Communion, an 'Amen' not just as a passive 'I believe' in the real presence but as a dynamic self-alignment with the one present. It is no easy or comfortable matter to participate in the eucharistic sacrifice.

Conclusion – hope and hard work

I began this essay wondering whether liturgy had a future. Writing it has made me hopeful, but also conscious of an agenda that we have still hardly begun. I came across Archbishop Piero Marini's paper on the reform of the Papal Liturgy,[3] the first fruits of which were seen at the Installation Mass of Pope Benedict XVI. Some lines in the document caught my imagination. They show how a spirituality based in the experience of the Liturgy itself might begin.

Marini wrote of the actions of the Liturgy being the actions of Christ. This is exactly what is stated in the Vatican Council's *Constitution on the Liturgy*, but somehow this reiteration was so much simpler and fresher. Liturgy is not a heap of 'ceremonies' which for some arcane reason still exist and which somehow 'contain' a Christ-magic. Liturgy is simply how Christ works in the Body, the Church, to accomplish the work of giving the divine life to the world. The Liturgy is not something we can dispose of as we please. Like Scripture and tradition, it is a cornerstone of the Church.

That is a statement of hope for liturgy. But hard work is also required to find out how to help people to take that seriously and then to learn to live by it.

Notes

1. Aidan Kavanagh, *On Liturgical Theology* (New York: Pueblo Books/Collegeville, MN: Liturgical Press, 1992).
2. Miri Rubin, *Corpus Christi: The Eucharist in Late Medieval Culture* (Cambridge: Cambridge University Press, 1993).
3. Piero Marini, *Liturgy and Beauty: Experiences of Renewal in Certain Papal Liturgical Celebrations* (2004). http://www.vatican.va/news_services/liturgy/2004/documents/ns_lit_doc_20040202_liturgia-bellezza_en.html.

Chapter Twenty

Keeping It Honest: The Role of the Laity in a Clerical Church

Conor Gearty

I left Ireland for Cambridge in 1980. At the time I was convinced that the role of the laity in Ireland's clerical Church was emigration. Nothing in the next few years persuaded me otherwise. My second published article, on the Irish Supreme Court decision in which a narrow majority of the court rejected gay rights in what I thought were offensive and theologically inept terms (*Norris v Attorney General*), nearly never saw the light of day. The *Dublin University Law Journal* was concerned because of the insults it seemed I was flinging at the august Irish bench.

But these men were mere proxies for the Church that lay behind them. After that came the sad case of Ann Lovett, the young girl who died giving birth to her baby at the Grotto in Granard. No one was prepared to acknowledge that the baby was expected, and it died with her. I am from Granard, went to the same school as Ann Lovett; one of my sisters was still at the school when the deaths occurred. I looked on from the safety of my enlightened Cambridge world, and took what revenge I could on the institutions I held responsible for her lonely death by doing my best to support the pro-choice and pro-divorce sides in impoverished Ireland's cultural wars of the mid 1980s.

Then there was the Bishop Casey affair (what they would give for such a romantic scandal today?) and after it a succession of horrors in the form of church-protected systematic cruelty, sexual assault and sadistic criminality. When my family came to visit me in Cambridge, I led them on a mystery tour in search of the Catholic chaplaincy. It being increasingly clear as I wandered back and forth that I had not the foggiest clue where it was. I was proud of my ignorance. It showed I had travelled far from the little boy who had read the epistles every Sunday from the age of nine, who had served Mass with religious determination.

If I seemed free, then it was the kind of freedom an amputee enjoys when a rotten limb has been removed: relieved but not entirely whole. Without being even conscious of it, I began searching around for a replacement – and found myself looking in different parts of exactly the same Church from which I had so recently, so (it seemed at the time) joyously escaped. It was various individuals – clerical and lay – whose flourishing moral lives first entranced and then enticed me back to the fold: if they – manifestly liberal, engaging, public-spirited, outward-looking to a man and woman – could cope, how could I possibly claim that I could not?

The parish where I found myself in north London added something extra, a spiritual life that was profoundly democratic and diverse, not in its hierarchical structures, of course, but rather in the range of classes and ethnicities that were brought together under its benign authority. Before long I was a governor at the local Catholic girls' school, an occasional visitor to Archbishop's House, and a contributor to the *Tablet*. Not only had the limb returned, but it seemed, to me at any rate, to be in a relatively healthy state, focusing on the good bits of the Church into which I was born, and discounting the rotten fringes which I had earlier thought to be the core. My Catholicism had become à la carte, and I was a very choosy diner, not about what was on the menu but about which offerings I wished to consume.

Conscience's place

The role of the laity in a clerical church is a large subject, and begs questions – of faith, theology and Scripture – which I am not equipped to answer. The laity is not a homogeneous group but rather a collection of very different sorts of people, with a range of skills and talents to bring to their faith community. One unifying view of the function of the laity would be that its job is faithfully to follow the teachings of the Church. The point was very well expressed by Dr Tom D'Andrea from Wolfson College, Cambridge, at a colloquium on Catholics in public life held in January 2005 (see the *Tablet* website: http://www.thetablet.co.uk/lecturejan05b.shtml).

D'Andrea quoted the passage from John Henry Newman's celebrated *Letter to the Duke of Norfolk* (1875) about his willingness to drink to the Pope, but 'to Conscience first, and to the Pope afterwards' as evidence for the proposition (as D'Andrea put it) that 'conflicts between the individual Catholic conscience, properly understood, and the lawful exercise of magisterial authority are impossible at the level of abstract doctrine *or with respect to the magisterial condemnation of particular erroneous beliefs and practices*' (D'Andrea's emphasis).

This was the part of Newman on which he placed specific reliance:

> Conscience is not a judgment upon any speculative truth, any abstract doctrine, but bears immediately on conduct, on something

to be done or not to be done. 'Conscience,' says St. Thomas, 'is the practical judgement or dictate of reason, by which we judge what hic et nunc is to be done as being good, or to be avoided as evil.' Hence conscience cannot come into direct collision with the Church's or Pope's infallibility; which is engaged in general propositions, and in the condemnation of particular and given errors. (*Letter #5*, 255)

To D'Andrea it follows that once a bishop informs a member of the laity where his duty lies, obedience must follow:

Once informed, only a now culpably erroneous Catholic con-science could see the matter otherwise – this would be what Newman refers to in his Letter as conscience perversely mis-construed, conscience regarded as 'the right of thinking, speaking, writing, and acting, according to … [one's] judgment or their humour, without any thought of God at all … the right of self will'. (*Letter*, 250).

If a member of the laity ignores this authority 'persistently … after [being] reminded of its seriousness by an ecclesiastical authority, it becomes censurable behaviour and, as an item of belief, heresy'. The civil authorities have no stake in any of this:

The Church as any voluntary association is free to set its own rules for membership as long as these violate no established fundamen-tal civil rights. And individuals who do not like these rules have every freedom, have the human right honoured by the Church, to depart and to reject authoritative Church teaching in their action, thought, and speech.

The clarity of this vision of the proper role of the laity is one of its most appealing features. It has the complementary virtue of simplicity, and also fits well within a range of the historical narratives that are embedded in the Church's past. But I believe it is wrong-headed, and that it ought, in the interests of the entire Church, clerical and lay, to be unequivocally rejected.

The faith trap
My starting point is that we are all trapped by the moment of our birth. Contemporary Catholics cannot help but live in the present age. It is not our fault that we were not born into an era in which passive obedience is the norm. Such was the condition of much of the world once upon a time, with civil authority mimicking ecclesiastical power in its hold over the minds and bodies of its secular faithful.

In such eras, Tom D'Andrea's approach would have been common-place – and common sense. But times have changed. The absolutism of our earthly rulers is largely a thing of the past, either out or on the way out. The elimination of the despotic king by the middle classes has been followed by a further expansion of political power in the direction of universal suffrage.

Accompanying this has been a triumphant capitalism that has been rooted in the exercise of consumer choice. The modern world is about individual judgement: autonomy not acceptance is the oil in today's civil machine. Where none of this is yet the case, what we see is a pressure for change that is fast becoming overwhelming, as in parts of Africa, for example. Where it is only partly the case, as in China, the pressures for democratic reform are likewise becoming unstoppable. Even Russia's effort to unwind democracy is being challenged both from within (opposition to President Putin's growing authoritarianism) and from without (the peaceful renewals of the democratic spirit in Georgia and the Ukraine that have been occurring on its borders).

Catholics of the D'Andrea school may wish that none of this was the case, or they may be relaxed, enthusiastic even, about such democratic change. But in either case, their model of the laity requires an unattractive kind of schizophrenia, confident in the exercise of their political and market judgements when dealing with the outside world, but passive and accepting when receiving instructions from on high on exactly how to lead their spiritual lives.

Given the kind of world in which we live, for better or worse, this is simply asking too much of too many. This is especially the case when the Church claims sovereign authority in the definition of what is spiritual, determining for itself what lies within its sphere and allowing civil autonomy little more than the crumbs that are left over after the spiritual feast. It follows inevitably that those who are most at home in our progressive civil culture, and therefore most inured to the exercise of their own judgement on things material and spiritual, find the D'Andrea model extremely demanding and severe, too much so for many of them, who take his hint and exercise 'their human right honoured by the Church' to walk away.

For those laity who are uninterested in engaging in democratic society and who prefer to take instructions on how to lead their lives (from their king, their union, their party leader, or their stars), then the D'Andrea version of the Church fits comfortably with their personalities and no or little schizophrenia is involved. But are these really the kind of laity upon whom the Church wishes to rely? Can the Church afford to be blasé about losing those whose progressive instincts make them leaders of the civil world within which – for good or ill – the Church these days cannot help but be embedded?

Everything in context

There is another problem with the obedience model of the laity, once again rooted in the problem of living now and not in some distant age of deference. The authoritative pronouncements of the Church cannot help but be placed these days – even by the most faithful – in some kind of sociological context. Most people cannot avoid knowing that moral decisions made by a group of men in positions of authority over others are to some extent at least the product of the perspective these men have on life, rooted in their own upbringing and their own personal beliefs.

The decisions they make are also now unavoidably understood as in part resulting from an interplay of relations between various powerful individuals. God (including the Holy Spirit) may still be recognised by many as being involved, but it is not any longer as a ventriloquist with the church leaders as the benign dummy, the thoughtless passers-on of the good news; rather God today is seen more as a prompter of general lines which then get fleshed out in a way that the corporeal agents themselves wish and desire. The threshold event here was *Humanae Vitae*; the faithful turned to God for guidance and found a man instead. This breach in the wall of authoritative pronouncements has widened ever since.

The point can be amplified by reference to the recent remarks of Cardinal Murphy-O'Connor in which he reportedly expressed doubts about whether the Labour party any longer represented the working class, or at least the Catholic working class. These appear to have been unscripted and to have followed the launch of a church document intended to put certain issues at the forefront of the then imminent general election campaign.

The right Catholic reaction along D'Andrea lines would have been to unpick the statement in order to identify whether it was or was not authoritative in the Newmanesque sense of reflecting some church line in relation to which the conscience of the lay person could not be engaged. But most Catholics probably did not have the old-fashioned discipline to do this; to them it was in all likelihood just another remark by their church leader, among many such remarks on many issues, which they could take or leave as they fancied.

And this kind of reaction is also provoked by episcopal pronouncements which are closer to the core of church teaching, such as on abortion, homosexual practices, stem-cell research, euthanasia and the use of contraceptives: important interventions on the formation of opinion certainly, but not the formers, without more, of those opinions.

Just as the bishops are not God's dummies, so also is the laity no longer some kind of blind agent of the clergy, mouthing the judgements of their spiritual leaders with no intervening rational engagement allowed to get in the way.

Civil society

There is a mismatch, therefore, between the D'Andrea model of the role of the laity and the progressive influences at work in civil society. By 'progressive' here I mean those forces that are behind the increased democratisation of our world, both in terms of the involvement of more and more people in public decision-making on a representative basis and also in terms of the increased emphasis we now see on personal judgement and individual conscience in the private sphere.

In contrast, regressive elements in our civil society – those that hanker after authoritarian structures of government and that deny individual autonomy – fit comfortably with the passively faithful, instruction-receiving laity applauded by D'Andrea. Though D'Andrea himself is entirely convincing in his separation of Church and State, and in his paper at the *Tablet* conference showed himself to be a committed democrat, it is clear that some people who are attracted to his vision of the laity in the Church might also be attracted to a form of civil government that is more authoritarian than that provided by democratic structures. If it works for the Church why also not for the State, especially if the leaders of the latter are also loyal members of the former? This explains, I think, why fascist forms of government have a long history of support within the Church. This model is, I hope, on the wrong side of history.

So if the D'Andrea model is not the right approach, what is the proper role of the laity in a clerical Church? Put in a glib sentence, I think it is to keep the Church honest. I use the term honest here in a very broad sense.

Let us start with the proposition that there is a truth of which the Church is an expression and to which its presence in the world bears witness. The articulation of that truth depends for its effectiveness on its interaction with the consciousness of the particular age in which the Church at that moment or in this particular epoch finds itself.

The clerical part of the organisation is very good at detecting the truth and passing it on in ways with which its membership are familiar. But those ways might sometimes be out of date, passé in a newly arrived era, and therefore no longer effective as forms of communication. Every authoritarian organisation has real problems spotting the need for change, and the Church is no exception: the alleged new era will be described as no more than a temporary blip; the 'faithful' will be found at fault for not listening carefully enough; changes to current practice (themselves in all likelihood the result of some past updating or earlier tactical compromise with earthly reality) will be wrongly presented as the betrayal of a thousand years of tradition; and so on – well-trained minds can concoct an indefinite supply of reasons for inaction.

This is where the laity – faithful members of the Church but also full-time members of the secular moment – is indispensable to the health of the Church, to its capacity for effective communication. The laity forces the Church, often against its will, to tailor its truth to be heard, to confront honestly the world it finds itself in at that moment in time. This might involve insisting that account be taken of Marx's insights about exploitation, of Darwin's stunning revelations about evolution, or of Freud's opening up of the idea of the subconscious.

A foot in the real world

Left to themselves, clerical structures of governance might well prefer that none of this impacted on the purity of the Church's message, in just the same way that previous generations of church leaders thought Galileo's ideas to be a dangerous subversion of truth. The laity forces the Church to deal with whatever the 'real world' of the day demands. Perfectly loyal in its commitment to the Church, it throws itself across the chasm between the Church and the secular world, and invites church leaders to shed their fear and walk across.

An active and engaged laity protects the clerical branch from its own worst instincts, guards it against complacency, and protects it from inwardness by forcing it to communicate effectively with civil society outside, not the world as the Church wants it to be, or the world as it was yesterday or the day before, but the world as it actually is now.

Inevitably therefore in any healthy Church there is going to be tension between the otherworldly authoritarian tendencies of the clerical branch and the earthy contemporaneity of the secular wing. A case study in an area familiar to me is the way in which the Church has approached the subject of human rights. Though originating in a natural law perspective that is comfortably within the Catholic mainstream, the subject of human rights took a secular turn in the eighteenth century and has been on the progressive/democratic side of most issues ever since.

In the aftermath of the Second World War, the concept became one of the key organising principles of the new international order: the Universal Declaration of Human Rights; and afterwards the two international covenants signed in 1966 (on civil and political rights and economic, social and cultural rights respectively) amounted to a new kind of bible for those many ethically-minded people who were determined to try to live their lives well, but without the assistance of their traditional God.

Following the end of the cold war in 1989 and the consequent return of a more aggressive kind of capitalism than had been seen since the first quarter of the nineteenth century, the idea of human rights came to symbolise for many the possibility of a life lived free of political oppression and the tyranny of the market, a world in which all could be held in equal esteem and the dignity of every individual mattered. It is a seductive vision and belief in it explains why the idea of human rights has survived, prospered even, in these postmodern, anti-foundational times.

A friend of mine, Francesca Klug, coined a marvellous phrase to describe the human rights movement: it provided 'values for a Godless age'. But the absence of God is not a sine qua non; the subject does not need God but it thrives when God is around, adding ethical ballast and assisting in its growth.

At first glance here is a part of secular society which looks tailor-made for a strong alliance with the Church. There are plenty of arguments for such a concord in the record. Leo XIII was responsible for the superb encyclical *Rerum Novarum*, issued in 1891. This dealt with the rights of workers on the basis that 'Man precedes the state, and possesses, prior to the formation of any state, the right of providing for the sustenance of his body.' In *Divini Redemptoris,* Pius XI provided a list of human rights, which included life, bodily integrity, property and what we would call today economic rights.

In the fifty years or so since the end of the Second World War, the subject has become embedded in church teaching. In the words of *Pacem in Terris*:

> Any human society, if it is to be well-ordered and productive, must lay down as a foundation this principle, namely that every human being is a person, that is, his nature is endowed with intelligence and free will. By virtue of this, he has rights and duties of his own, flowing directly and simultaneously from his very nature, which are therefore universal, inviolable and inalienable.

Where's the applause?

So far so good. The Church is certainly right to be proud of its key role in initiating and sustaining one of the most important ethical features of contemporary secular society. It should be a popular and admired force within the human rights communities of today. Instead it is widely mistrusted, even seen sometimes as the enemy rather than the protagonist of human rights. How can this be?

This takes us back to the chasm that exists between clerical and secular visions of the world. Out of the democratic deficiencies of the Church in both its internal and external face flows a failure fully to protect and vindicate human dignity. Shorn of the dynamic quality that democracy has been able to give to the content of human rights, in the hands of the Church the subject has staggered into a dead end. Only those parts of the person that have already been seen in earlier generations are given recognition – so we have the right to life, the right to work, the right to found a family and so on.

But the richer aspects of human personality which the secular language of human rights has embraced – rooted in gender, in sexual identity, the right in certain circumstances to die – are resolutely ignored. So too is the desperate need to modify certain of its precepts (for example the chance of life that is required to be present in each sexual act) to secure basic rights in an imperfect world (in this example the right to life at a time of extensive HIV-infection). Despite its (to the secular eye) selectivity on human rights, the Church is not so much hypocritical on the issue as – through an institutional malfunction – institutionally blinkered in its approach to the subject.

The human rights movement is in many ways a visibility project: each generation seeks to see and therefore to respect more of the person before them, more of their attributes, more of their needs and the demands of their identity. With this greater sight comes a more civilised society, with more of us able to lead richer lives more of the time, unafflicted by unnecessary suffering and free from pointless cruelty. Frozen in time and with no effective mechanism for change, the Church sees only part of the person and – partly through fear and ignorance, partly through institutional paralysis – condemns the rest.

The challenge for the future is for the laity to perform its historical role and to expand the vision of the Church. Just as earlier generations of political activists persuaded the state that slaves mattered, that children mattered, that women mattered, so now must the laity persuade the Church to open its eyes. This can only happen, in my view, if the structures of the Church are made more open, and if – in the particular field we are now discussing – the content of human rights flows out of dialogue rather than being filled by declamation. Not democracy perhaps, but something resembling a democratic process is required.

Of course, the secular world has much to learn from the Church's perspective on human dignity. There will be an extraordinary series of challenges and therefore opportunities for powerful input in the future, on sexual orientation rights, on transsexual rights, on gene technology, on euthanasia, and much more. All of us – whether religiously inclined or secular – are in need of ethical guidance, and know we are. But to engage effectively, the Church has to be willing to contemplate a dialogue between adults, a conversation not a sermon. This openness has to involve a reaching down through the Church and a reaching out to other centres of ethical excellence, whether they be secular or faith-based. Helping this to happen is, in my view, the true role of the laity in a clerical Church, one upon which the very future of that Church depends.

Chapter Twenty-One

Do We Need a Vatican III?

Kevin Kelly

The older I get and the more I listen to the gospel texts, the clearer it becomes to me that why the religious authorities of his day rejected Jesus was because he opposed their subordination of the human person to their interpretation of the law, especially the pivotal sabbath law. 'The sabbath was made for humankind and not humankind for the sabbath.' The God Jesus reveals respects all human persons.

Human persons are created in the image of God. It is forbidden to create any false images of God precisely because God has provided us with the only true image of God – the human person.

Whenever the Jesus of the gospels encounters discrimination against any groups of people on the grounds that they are 'unclean' in the eyes of God, he utterly rejects such a position. To the disgust and scandal of the self-proclaimed righteous, he eats and drinks with publicans and sinners. His words 'I have not come to call the just but sinners' are directed against those who base their righteousness not on any gratuitous gift of God but on their self-proclaimed exclusive dignity before God due to their strict observance of the law.

It is this attitude which draws from Jesus some of his most outspoken condemnations, addressing the scribes and Pharisees in such terms as whited sepulchres and a brood of vipers. It is this same attitude which stimulates Jesus to produce some of his most powerful stories, such as the Prodigal Son or the Good Samaritan.

Even Jesus' anger with the scribes and Pharisees fits into the same picture. It is driven by a passionate desire to eradicate what is blocking their vision and heal them from their destructive blindness. His anger is like the cutting knife of a surgeon, causing pain and discomfort, but directed only towards restoring health. In Matthew's gospel, at the end of his sevenfold indictment of the scribes and Pharisees, branding them as hypocrites and blind guides, Jesus is almost in tears as he exclaims: 'Jerusalem, Jerusalem, you that kill the prophets and stone those who are sent to you! How often have I longed to gather your children, as a hen gathers her chicks under her wings and you refused!' (see Matthew 23:13–38).

In the eyes of Jesus, the witness being given by the scribes and Pharisees gives a false picture of the God whose true witness Jesus himself is. The Word did not become flesh in Jesus to enslave us to yet more moral rules but to reveal to us that the source of our true dignity lies in the very being of God. As human persons we are called to love each other as the Son loves us, and as the Father loves the Son. Empowered by the Spirit we are invited to share in the very life and love of God if we are to be true to who we are.

This mind-blowing truth is highlighted by Vatican II: 'It is only in the mystery of the word incarnate that light is shed on the mystery of humankind. It is Christ who fully discloses humankind to itself and unfolds its noble calling by revealing the mystery of the Father and the Father's love' (*The Church in the Modern World, Gaudium et Spes* 22).

In the decades prior to Vatican II, many Catholics were feeling more and more that their personal growth as free, thinking and responsible subjects was inhibited by an increasing number of depersonalising factors in the life of the Church. The simple words of Pope John XXIII that the Council would open the windows and let in much-needed fresh air spoke volumes to them.

What excited Catholics at the time of Vatican II was its insistence that human persons are far more important in the eyes of God than are man-made laws and human institutions. The Council Fathers seemed to be echoing in today's world the explosive words of Jesus: 'The sabbath was made for humankind and not humankind for the sabbath' (Mark 2:27).

This person-centred 'good news' of Jesus is writ large across the annals of Vatican II. It crops up in all sorts of places and in all kinds of guises. The opening chapter of the Pastoral Constitution, *The Church in the Modern World*, is entitled 'The Dignity of the Human Person'. Its first sentence states: 'Believers and unbelievers are almost at one in considering that everything on earth is to be referred to humanity as its centre and culmination.'

Later the bishops go on to speak of 'the exceptional dignity which belongs to the human person' and even appeal to Jesus' words about the sabbath as they highlight the social dimension of the human person: 'The social order and its progress ought, then, continually to favour the good of people since the order of things should be subordinated to the order of persons, and not the other way round, as the Lord indicated in saying the sabbath was made for us and not we for the sabbath.'

The *Declaration on Religious Liberty*, whose text was a battleground for opposing factions in the Council, actually bears the title, *The Dignity of the Human Person* (*Dignitatis Humanae*). Its opening words are reminiscent of the passage quoted above:

The dignity of the human person is a concern of which people of our time are becoming increasingly more aware. In growing numbers they demand that they should enjoy the use of their own responsible judgment and freedom, and decide on their actions on grounds of duty and conscience, without external pressure or coercion.

Four decades on

Forty years after Vatican II the bishops of Quebec were still exploring the riches of this person-centred teaching in their thought-provoking document, *Annoncer l'evangile dans la culture actuelle au Quebec*.[1] They bring it into conversation with the signs of the times at the turn of the millennium. In today's culture appreciation of the human person as subject is central. This means recognising that at the heart of our being human persons lies the fact that we are subjects, called to accept responsibility for our own lives. We cannot hand over this responsibility to any institution, not even to the Church. This has profound implications for the way we understand our membership within the Church and for how we relate to tradition and church teaching.

> Today, personal opinion rates first among the things that count: 'I think that' becomes more important than 'the tradition states that' or 'the magisterium teaches that'. Personal convictions rooted in the experience of the individual are important. A thing is true to the degree that it can be verified by experience. The theological committee of our assembly rightly remarked that our contemporaries are more sensitive to experience than to notional or abstract language. It is not so much that they are incapable of formulating their experience in concepts, but rather that experience carries more weight and authority than ideas put forward on a theoretical basis. A person's word becomes more authoritative when it is authentic, sincere, and backed up by experience.[2]

This echoes the words of Paul VI in his 1975 post-Synod Apostolic Exhortation, *Evangelisation in the Modern World*: 'People today listen more willingly to witnesses than to teachers, and if they do listen to teachers, it is because they are witnesses.' This way of seeing things affects our understanding of tradition. No longer something set in stone, it is seen as a living memory which challenges our limited perspective but which we ourselves need to critique. This reminds me of the wise medieval saying: 'We see further than our forebears; we are like dwarfs sitting on the shoulders of giants.'

The Quebec bishops write:

For our contemporaries, truth may come from tradition, but it is also the fruit of their own work of exploration. It is received, but it is also discovered. It may remain beyond us, but it comes to us by way of the subject's own activity on a personal journey. Tradition and teaching are not imposed as a kind of final or definitive word, but function as memory, reference points and markers or as a word which questions and confronts one's own discoveries, a word which evokes a response from the subject. Statements from tradition are critiqued before being taken up by the subject.

Two-way process

As the Quebec bishops point out, this has far-reaching implications for the whole field of communications within the Church. Communication is not a one-way process. It is not simply a matter of a speaker and a listener. Active listening involves assimilation and interpretation. What is communicated is enriched in the listening process and the actual speaker becomes a receiver by being helped to understand the message through the reflective response of the listener.

This is particularly important when it comes to the way the Church arrives at its teaching and laws and how these are communicated to the people at large. Teaching is seen less as an expert holding forth and more as a conversation between people who have their own insights to contribute. An appropriate image is the seminar group in which the leader enables all to pool whatever relevant learning they have so that the full riches of the group are shared in the pursuit of truth.

The Quebec bishops use a slightly different image:

> It is not sufficient to insist that the Church is not a democracy, even if that statement is correct. Integration into the Church in a democratic society leads to a new relation to authority and a different manner of proclaiming the gospel. What is required is a certain degree of participation and a careful listening to all the voices that want to be heard. Nothing can be imposed simply by authority.

Some may shy away from such an approach to the teaching process in the Church on the grounds that it would mean the end of all clarity and certainty and would be a recipe for confusion. However, for a pilgrim people a certain level of confusion is to be expected and has to be lived with.

Karl Rahner expresses this very positively:

> If the Church appears to be confused today, it is because society is

confused. Both go together. Sometimes I ask myself if, from the point of view of faith, this is all so bad. Why should we Christians and the Church in an age of confusion have answers for everything instead of putting up with the confusion along with our contemporaries?[3]

We cannot opt out of the mess of life, but have to trust God in the midst of the storm.

'The sabbath was made for humankind and not humankind for the sabbath.' Are there 'sabbaths' in the Church today to which we can be tempted to subordinate the good of human persons? Part of the contribution of Vatican II was to alert us to these modern-day sabbaths and put us on our guard lest in church life we dehumanise persons by making them subservient to these sabbaths.

All such sabbaths see things out of perspective. They lose sight of the primacy of the dignity of the human person as made in God's image. Hence, even biblical texts can become a sabbath in this sense. Texts which forbid things clearly beneficial to the good of human persons are accepted as binding in conscience. The same is true with regard to tradition, teaching, laws and liturgical rules in the Church.

In terms of reading the Bible, this approach is described as fundamentalist. In its extreme form, it turns the written text into an idol. No room for interpretation. The text is sacrosanct and must be followed. Few would go that far. However, many follow a more moderate fundamentalist approach today. Once a text is understood in the light of the culture in which it was written and what it meant to the people of that time, they insist on applying its teaching immediately to the present day. God's word does not change, they say. God's law for people's lives remains the same yesterday, today and for ever.

I may be wrong, but I get the impression that fundamentalist thinking of this kind lies at the root of the present division in the Anglican Communion over homosexual activity. The fundamentalist position maintains that homosexual acts are clearly forbidden in the Bible. Hence, though homosexual persons should not be condemned for being who they are, no homosexual expressions of love can be condoned.

Not so, argues the opposite view. Today we have a better understanding of God's gift of sexuality. Homosexuality, as an innate condition of a significant minority in society, is no longer seen as deviance but rather as diversity within the full spectrum of human sexuality. To deny homosexual men or women the life-fulfilling opportunity to express sexually their lifelong love and fidelity for each other is to deny them something fundamental to their lives as human persons.

With the Pharisees

This final assertion seems to get to the root of the issue. If loving and faithful homosexual relationships and their sexual expression can truly be shown to be, in their own way, authentic personal expressions of human love and fidelity – and many hold that is the case – they would seem to be fully in accord with God's will for the people concerned. If that is so, how can we proclaim the Gospel as good news for human persons and in the very next breath condemn such homosexual acts as contrary to God's will since they are forbidden in the Bible?

This shows up the fault-line in this kind of fundamentalist approach. It seems to line up with the Pharisees against Jesus. It rejects Jesus' core principle of interpretation, 'The sabbath was made for humankind and not humankind for the sabbath.' This primacy of the human person principle implies that any interpretation of biblical texts which demands that the manifest good of human persons be made subservient to an alleged faithfulness to the text is not interpreting the text according to the mind of God revealed to us in Jesus, the Word made flesh.

Some might argue that the Catholic Church still has a 'get-out' clause. It claims it has God-given authority to interpret both the natural law and the Bible. So, for instance, this would seem to give it the authority to settle the issue by declaring that homosexual activity is both unnatural and forbidden in the Bible. It can then insist that Catholics are obliged to accept and follow this teaching.

Such a crude view of the Church's teaching authority is fairly common both within the Church and beyond. Yet it is utterly false and has no basis in Catholic theology and church teaching. Church authorities do not have the freedom to teach whatever they like.

A responsible use of teaching authority demands widespread consultation, especially amongst those best informed and most experienced in the matter in question. It would be highly irresponsible to short-circuit the essential consultation needed and instead appeal to the inspiration of the Holy Spirit.

The Jesuit philosopher and moral theologian, Gerard J. Hughes, made that point very strongly some years ago:

> In practice the appeal to tradition and to teaching authority tends to short-circuit the need for proper inquiry and for argument which will withstand criticism in open debate. These are the normal human means to the attainment of truth, which we ignore at our peril. I suspect that the ultimate cause of disagreement in moral theology today stems from a notion of revelation and the guidance of the Spirit in the Church which is largely independent

of human cooperation, and a contrasting notion in which such guidance is to be expected only when we have in fact done what is humanly possible. I think one of the most valuable aspects of the natural law tradition in moral theology is that it comes down firmly in favour of this latter view ... We cannot confidently lay claim to the guidance of the Spirit, whether as individuals or as a Church, unless we take the normal human means to try to arrive at the truth.[4]

Going back to the basic principle of interpretation, 'The sabbath was made for humankind and not humankind for the sabbath', that principle should apply across the board in the life and ministry of the Church. In other words, anything in church life and ministry which is detrimental to the good of the human persons concerned cannot be an authentic discernment of the will of God.

I may be wrong, but it seems to me that there are quite a few aspects of the Church's life and ministry which are in conflict with this fundamental principle. I suspect that others may wish to add to the list I give below. Of course, in a short piece like this it is impossible to look at each issue in any detail. All I can do is limit myself to some brief comments on each.

Lay participation

Words like co-responsibility, collaborative ministry, consultation, shared decision-making, have become common parlance in the wake of Vatican II. However, they tend to be more honoured in word than in actual practice. Ladislas Orsy SJ, a canon lawyer of international repute, made the following comment about the way the laity are excluded:

> You could put it this way: They can say something, they even have a right to, but there is no way of making sure that they will be listened to. The new code uses fine expressions that can be interpreted in various ways. The practice, however, after the publication of the new code, is not to admit the laity into any kind of decision-making processes, and consequently not to use the *sacra potestas* (sacred power) that is given to the People of God at large by the Holy Spirit and that every single Christian shares. In fact, recent canonical literature has developed the custom of speaking about the 'sacred power' as if it belonged to the episcopal body exclusively. This is poor theology. The bishops' ministerial power is holy, but it does not equal the immensely rich and sacred gifts given to the whole Church.[5]

Some years ago Yves Congar showed that the term *magisterium* has suffered a similar impoverishment to that of *sacra potestas* in the Church in recent centuries – and with similar consequences for wider participation in the magisterium.[6]

In his 1988 Cardinal Heenan Memorial Lecture delivered a few days before his death, Paul Sieghart concluded a very positive overview of the Catholic Church's involvement in promoting human rights by complaining that the Church 'has not yet even begun to practise what it has so forcefully preached for 25 years and more in the matter of human rights'.[7] This is part of the same wider picture.

There has been some progress in lay participation, it cannot be denied, but there is still a long way to go.

General absolution

A good friend of mine, the late Father Hugh Lavery, a much-revered theological thinker and speaker, used to say that the prime form of the sacrament of reconciliation was its communal rather than its individual form. This is because, as human persons, we are essentially relational, interdependent and social beings. Human sin of its very nature has a communal dimension to it.

Solidarity in sin is a condition which affects each of us. Reconciliation is not just about individuals making their peace privately with God. It is also about eradicating the structures of sin which are the root cause of so much evil and injustice in our world. As the recent 'Make Poverty History' campaign makes clear, this reconciling work lies beyond the capacity of isolated individuals. In more traditional terminology, our purpose of amendment, to be effective, will often need to be communal if it is be truly personal.

Intercommunion

Our current normative practice of excluding other Christians from receiving the Eucharist (with some apparently grudging exceptions) seems to many to fly in the face of our deepest human instincts. For many years I have felt that in time to come we will look back on our current practice and wonder how we could possibly have behaved in such an inhuman fashion.

To invite someone to share our table and encourage him or her to share fully in all the companionship and table-talk and then deny that person any share in the meal itself would seem to be an extraordinary thing to do. All the more so when we are not actually the host at the table. And especially so when the host is notorious for welcoming everyone at his table and has actually caused scandal by the kind of company he keeps.

To accept an 'open table' approach to the Eucharist would mean moving from an attitude of toleration to one of appreciating the gift of difference. If the Church claims to be a sacrament of the unity of the human family, the Eucharist should not be a meal at which the presence of outsiders is tolerated within certain strict limits, but a meal at which their presence is treasured and accepted as a gift. Communion will be more truly communion. A Benedictine friend of mine makes the point.

> Perhaps the power and fire the Eucharist contains as the breaking of the Lord's body has to be thrown open to the world and all Christians so that no one is excluded who does not choose to be ... For Christians it would be the bread of pilgrims searching for unity rather than a celebration by the few of a unity they believe they already possess. Perhaps the destruction of the temple of One Bread, One Body is needed if the real Body of the Lord is to be given shape in the world today.

Divorced and remarried

Accepting the primacy of the person principle might radically alter our approach to many people who have suffered the painful trauma of marriage breakdown and found healing and new life in a second marriage. It could mean welcoming them as fully participant members of the family and dispelling their understandable, though mistaken, feelings of being second-class Christians due to some kind of unforgivable sin. In an unpublished paper, a theologian-friend puts this point very forcefully: 'The idea that a past broken relationship (e.g. divorce-remarriage) should bar a person from the very sacrament whose purpose is to heal wounds and rebuild life seems as perverse and blind as the criticism of Jesus by the Pharisees for a miracle of healing performed on the sabbath.'

Birth control

Giving primacy to the human person might have a liberating impact on couples facing decisions about birth regulation. No longer would they be given the impression that the natural processes of their bodies are sacred and absolutely inviolable and take precedence over their own personal needs, as well as those of any existing or future children. Hence, they would feel able to look together at all the factors involved which affect them deeply at the personal level.

For instance, how will any method chosen affect their love as life-giving towards each other, helping them to feel truly loved and respected by each other? How reliable is it? Is it a method in which they carry a shared responsibility or does it put all the responsibility on either husband or wife? Does it involve a health hazard or even a bodily mutilation for either of them? Is it permanent or can they change their decision later?

Of course, all the above assumes that a couple are in a relationship of mutuality and equality. Sadly, that is not always the case. There are additional factors to be considered in some HIV/AIDS scenarios where the relationship might be very oppressive to the woman.

If it is the husband who is HIV-positive and he demands intercourse as his right from his wife, sexual ethics must make it crystal clear that this is not his right. He has no right to endanger the health of his wife in this way. She has every right to refuse him, unless he is prepared to take adequate precautions. Obviously, in such a situation, it may be very difficult, even dangerous, for a wife to refuse her husband. To do so could put her at risk in a different way, as a result of her husband's violence towards her.

The Church's earlier understanding of marriage implicitly legitimated this kind of behaviour and attitude on the part of a husband. Today we recognise that this violates the Church's own criterion of the dignity of the human person. Hence, every effort needs to be made to disabuse both husbands and wives of this earlier understanding and so reduce the harm it is still causing, especially to women, within marriage.

Moreover, the criterion of the dignity of the human person means that, if a wife feels she has to agree to sex in the kind of scenario envisaged above, any church official who told her that it would be better if her husband did not use a condom would be perpetrating a serious injustice against her.

Once again, the dignity of the human person is paramount. This exposes the inhumanity of turning 'no condoms' into a moral absolute. In some instances, condom-use is actually saving life rather than preventing birth.

Virtue of *epikeia*

Some years ago the National Conference of Priests asked me to submit a short pre-conference reflection paper on the gap between certain church laws or moral rules and what many priests believed to be demanded by the true good of persons in their pastoral care. In it I draw attention to an attitude of mind (actually called a 'virtue' by Aquinas) which enables a person to discern between the general good envisaged by a particular law (or even a moral principle) and the demands of the particularities of a specific situation and their bearing on the good of the persons involved.[8]

Epikeia, the technical name for this virtue, is sometimes denigrated as providing a soft option in any difficult situation. In reality, the very opposite can be true. The sabbath healings by Jesus were no soft option. They actually lie at the root of his eventual judicial murder. Many find *epikeia* attractive precisely because it rings so true to the basic attitude of Jesus himself.

Wider remit

I am conscious that the particular issues I have raised are all to do with the Church's own life and ministry. There is a much wider agenda which must be equally the concern of the Church. However, it is important that the Church's life and ministry bears witness to the gospel values it is trying to share with others.

Timothy Radcliffe, another contributor to this book, got it right in his words to the 2002 National Conference of Priests:

> When Jesus ate and drank with tax collectors and prostitutes, it was not a duty. It was utter delight in their company, in their very being. When he touched the untouchable, it was not a clinical gesture, but the hug of joy. It belongs to our priesthood that we rejoice in the very existence of people, with all their fumbling attempts to live and love, whether they are married or divorced or single, whether they are straight or gay, whether their lives are lived in accordance with Church teaching or not. The Church should be a community in which people discover God's delight in them ...

Because I say so

Accepting the primacy of the human person principle would pull the carpet from under all those non-person considerations which, in their claims to absoluteness, too often operate as conversation-stoppers in any debate. As the Quebec bishops put it so succinctly, 'Nothing can be imposed simply by authority.' In other words, any specific exercise of authority needs to be justified not simply on the grounds that any human society needs authority, but on much more specific grounds relating to this specific exercise of authority. 'Because I say so' might be the last court of appeal for a frantic parent. It is certainly not good enough for a community claiming to follow one who defined authority precisely in terms of service.

I am not advocating that every exercise of authority should be rejected and disobeyed unless it can be proved to be manifestly for the good of all the persons concerned. Far from it. What I am suggesting is closer to the view of Aquinas. He presents obedience as the virtue of cooperation for the common good. Cooperation does not mean unquestioning obedience. Rather it may well demand questioning obedience – and occasionally even faithful disobedience.

Once again, Vatican II's approach to the human person can provide an important safeguard here. Each person may be unique, but we are not simply isolated individuals. We are essentially relational and interdependent as persons. Even the word 'conscience' has a communal and social dimension to it. It literally means 'knowing with'.

Discerning the truth is not an individualistic process. It involves attentive listening as well as honest speaking. It means tuning in to the story of our shared pilgrimage as well as listening to our fellow pilgrims today.

Cardinal Hume brought out this communal and social dimension of the human person very beautifully in a lecture he gave in 1998: 'It has been well said that "I" needs "we" to be really "I". We are persons in relationships; we are better persons as those loving relationships grow. We share a common humanity. We share too a common home, and respect the natural world and other creatures.'9

Vatican III?

As I reach the end of this essay, I have become more aware of a deeper reason why I am instinctively opposed to any suggestion of the need for a Vatican III at the outset of the papacy of Benedict XVI. I believe that the Church is not yet ready for the glorious grace and life-giving inspiration that Vatican III could be. If we as Church really succeed in living out Vatican II in the way we have been considering, the whole Church will be in listening mode, ready for Vatican III, open to hearing God's Spirit from whatever quarter that Spirit speaks to us.

Listening implies openness to learn from and be enriched by others. Listening can be a painful process too. For the Church to be prepared for that, a major sea change is still needed in the so-called magisterium as well as in the members of the Church at large. For the former, that means much more profound listening both before any teaching activity and after – a good conversation needs to keep on going. For the rest of the Church, much greater confidence in the value of their own experience is needed as well as the willingness to share this with others. Otherwise, they will continue to be excluded from the conversation. A laity-excluding council would not be worthy of the name Vatican III.

Dialogue

Listening and speaking lies at the heart of genuine dialogue. Cardinal

Walter Kasper speaks of the ecumenical importance of dialogue:

> The truth is always bigger than our formulas. None of us has the truth, but the truth has us. Through dialogue, with its exchange of gifts, we don't reach a new truth, but we come to a fuller understanding of the truth, which we believe we have in Jesus Christ. This is the dynamic dimension in ecumenical dialogue, and it helps us to discover our full 'catholicity'.[10]

For Jacques Dupuis, even in inter-faith dialogue, 'The same God is present and acting in both dialogue partners.' It involves 'getting inside the skin of the other, walking in the other's shoes, seeing the world as the other sees it, asking the other's questions'. Dialogue is something sacred. To quote Dupuis again, 'The same God speaks in the heart of both partners, the same Spirit is at work in both.'[11]

It is remarkable that Pope Benedict XVI, a man who chooses his words carefully, used the word 'dialogue' four times in his brief homily to the cardinals in their first Mass together after his election. After speaking of 'theological dialogue' and pledging himself 'to do all in his power to promote the fundamental cause of ecumenism', he turns his attention to 'everyone, even to those who follow other religions or who are simply seeking an answer to the fundamental questions of life and have not yet found it'. He promises to 'build an open and sincere dialogue with them in a search for the true good of mankind and of society'. He also commits himself to continue 'the promising dialogue with various civilisations', accepting that 'mutual understanding' is essential. And he ends by signing up to 'maintaining a dialogue' with young people.

Dialogue is clearly high on the agenda of Benedict XVI. Perhaps the Church and the world will be ready for Vatican III when he has succeeded in creating the conditions and climate needed for genuine and open dialogue.

For those fearful of dialogue, a story from the National Pastoral Congress whose anniversary is this year, 2005, might help us end on a hopeful note. In a sermon prior to the Congress, when people challenged him with 'aren't you afraid of calling together 3000 Catholics to a three-day meeting with such an open agenda?', Archbishop Derek Worlock said his reply was always: 'Don't you believe in the Holy Spirit?'

Pope Benedict has followed his call to dialogue with a similar call not to be afraid. His inauguration homily ends with the words: 'Do not be afraid of Christ! He takes nothing away, and He gives you everything. When we give ourselves to Him, we receive a hundredfold in return. Yes, open, open wide the doors to Christ – and you will find true life. Amen.'

Notes

1. Montreal: Fides, 1999.
2. Quoted in *The Ecumenist*, Winter 2000.
3. Karl Rahner in *Dialogue: Conversations and Interviews, 1965–1982* (New York: Crossroad, 1986), p. 154.
4. 'Natural law ethics and moral theology', *The Month* (1987), pp. 102–3.
5. *America* (7/10/1995), p. 12
6. Cf. my *New Directions in Moral Theology* (London: Geoffrey Chapman, 1992), pp. 140–1.
7. Cf. *The Month* (February 1989), p. 51.
8. 'Pastoral Care and Church Law: Mind the Gap', ch. 4 in my *From a Parish Base* (London: Darton, Longman & Todd, 1999), pp. 69–74.
9. *Briefing* (18/6/98), p. 9.
10. See www.uscatholic.org/2002.htm.
11. Jacques Dupuis, 'The Church's evangelising mission in the context of religious pluralism', *The Pastoral Review* (Jan/Feb 2005), pp. 21–31 at 30.

POSTSCRIPT

A Day of Blessing

Jim Cotter

In solidarity with men and women who have worked these past years towards the liberation of those who have been bound by sexual guilt and fear and shame ...

In solidarity with those who have struggled through narrow gates into wide open spaces of freedom, which for the ancient Hebrew mind was a real sample of 'salvation' ...

In solidarity with all those whose days have, wonder unforeseen, included days of blessing:

A day of blessing,
a day to focus all your nights and days,
as intense as sunlight focused through a glass,
as ordinary as sunlight's daily warmth.

A day of blessing,
that declares that your love for each other is good,
that publishes it, through us your witnesses, to the world.

A day of blessing,
that brings into the light of day
what has so banefully and for so long been buried and obscure.

A day of blessing
that banishes fear
and celebrates with open joy.

A day of each a blessing to the other,
of declaring each to other
that the love you share is very good
and binds you close.

A day of blessing
of all the hidden creativity between you

and within each of you,
as yet unknown,
to flower in the maturing of love's surprise.

A day of blessing,
in and through all these things,
by the Divine Creator-Lover,
a blessing full of wonder and of laughter.

A voice from heaven was heard,
These are my beloved in whom I take great delight.

© Jim Cotter, 1999, 2005,
adapted from a piece originally written for the blessing
of a life-intended love between two Catholic men.